Ayn Rand's
Marginalia

Ayn Rand's Marginalia

Her Critical Comments on the Writings of Over 20 Authors

Edited by Robert Mayhew

Second Renaissance Books
ideas for the rational mind

New Milford, Connecticut 06776

Published by Second Renaissance Books, Inc.

First printing, November 1995
3 5 7 9 10 8 6 4 2

LIBRARY OF CONGRESS CATALOGING-IN-PUBLICATION DATA:

Rand, Ayn
Ayn Rand's marginalia: her critical comments on the writings of
over 20 authors / edited by Robert Mayhew.
p. cm.
Includes index.
ISBN 1-56114-250-6
1. Rand, Ayn—Books and reading. 2. Marginalia
I. Mayhew, Robert. II. Title.
PS3553.A547Z475 1996
813'.52—dc20   95-25776
                                                   CIP

Printed in the United States of America

For a free copy of our catalogue of books and tapes—including the largest selection
of Ayn Rand's writings and lectures available—please contact:

Second Renaissance Books
143 West Street
New Milford, CT 06776
(860) 355-7164

CONTENTS

PART THREE:
POLITICS AND CULTURE

Acknowledgments

I wish to thank Leonard Peikoff for allowing me to undertake this project and for giving me access to Ayn Rand's marginalia. Thanks also to Mike Berliner and his staff at the Ayn Rand Institute for their help (which took many forms), and to Estelle Mayhew, Harry Binswanger, Peter Schwartz and Marlene Trollope for their many helpful comments.

I would also like to thank the following for permission to reprint copyrighted material:

The Estate of Ayn Rand, for *Letters of Ayn Rand* edited by Michael S. Berliner, (New York: Dutton, 1995). Copyright 1995.

Columbia University Press, for *Aristotle* by John Herman Randall, Jr., (New York: Columbia University Press, 1960).

Scribner, an imprint of Simon and Schuster, Inc., for *The Unity of Philosophical Experience* by Etienne Gilson, (New York: Charles Scribner's Sons, 1937). Copyright renewed 1965 by Etienne Gilson.

Abingdon Press, for *How to Think Creatively* by Eliot D. Hutchinson, (New York: Abingdon-Cokesbury Press, 1959). Copyright renewed 1976 by Eliot D. Hutchinson.

John Hospers, for his three unpublished essays "Egoism," "Liberty" and "Some Aspects of My Conception of Freedom."

Prentice Hall, for *An Introduction to Philosophical Analysis* by John Hospers, (New York: Prentice Hall, Inc., 1953). Copyright renewed 1981.

Harper Collins Publishers Limited, for *The Abolition of Man, or Reflections on Education with Special Reference to the Teaching of English in the Upper Forms of Schools* by C.S. Lewis, (New York: Macmillan, 1947).

The Estate of Helmut Schoeck, for *Envy: A Theory of Social Behavior* by Helmut Schoeck, trans. from the German by M. Glenny and B. Ross (New York: Harcourt, Brace & World, Inc., 1969).

Contemporary Books, Inc., Chicago, for *Human Action* by Ludwig von Mises, (New Haven, Conn.: Yale University Press, 1949).

Robert Sennholz, for *Bureaucracy* by Ludwig von Mises, (New Haven, Conn.: Yale University Press, 1944).

The University of Chicago Press and the Estate of F.A. Hayek, for *The Road to Serfdom* by Friedrich A. Hayek, (Chicago: University of Chicago Press, 1944).

University Press of America, for *The Great Idea* by Henry Hazlitt, (New York: Appleton-Century-Crofts, Inc., 1954). Later republished as *Time Will Run Back*.

Dutton Signet, a division of Penguin Books USA, Inc., for *This Little Band of Prophets: The British Fabians* by Anne Fremantle, (New York: New American Library, 1960). Copyright 1959, renewed 1987 by Anne Fremantle.

Charles E. Tuttle Co., Inc., Tokyo, Japan, for *Brainwashing in Red China: The Calculated Destruction of Men's Mind* by Edward Hunter, (Tokyo: Charles E. Tuttle, Co., 1952).

The Estate of Fulton J. Sheen, for *Communism and the Conscience of the West* by Fulton J. Sheen, (New York: Bobbs-Merrill, 1948).

Cambridge University Press and Sir Alan Neale, for *The Antitrust Laws of the United States of America: A Study of Competition Enforced by Law* by A.D. Neale, (Cambridge University Press, 1960).

Publisher's Weekly, for "The Reader is Your Market: Ways to Break the Roadblocks to Bookbuying" by Elmo Roper, *Publisher's Weekly*, June 16, 1958.

INTRODUCTION

Ayn Rand made extensive comments in the margins of many of the books and periodicals she read. This work is a collection of these notes, or marginalia. In *"Philosophy: Who Needs It"* Ayn Rand writes:

> To take ideas seriously means that you intend to live by, to *practice*, any idea you accept as true. Philosophy provides man with a comprehensive view of life. In order to evaluate it properly, ask yourself what a given theory, if accepted, would do to a human life, starting with your own.
>
> Most people would be astonished by this method. They think that abstract thinking must be "impersonal"—which means that ideas must hold no personal meaning, value or importance to the thinker. . . . But if you are the kind of person who knows that reality is not your enemy, that truth and knowledge are of crucial, personal, *selfish* importance to you and to your own life—then the more passionately personal the thinking, the clearer and truer.

In the marginalia we can observe the distinctive seriousness—the insistence on applying abstractions to concrete reality—with which she approached ideas. For example, consider her concern for the practical effects of ideas. In his book on Kant, Friedrich Paulsen writes:

> Although in the details of [Kant's] philosophy there may be much that is not agreeable to us, it is its enduring merit to have drawn for the first time, with a firm hand and clear outline, the dividing line between knowledge and faith. This gives to knowledge what belongs to it—the entire world of phenomena for free investigation; it conserves, on the other hand, to faith its eternal right to the interpretation of life and of the world from the standpoint of value.

Ayn Rand reads this and disagrees—but not simply by presenting an epistemological objection to any acceptance of faith. Rather, she names the real-life consequences of allowing faith to be the arbiter of values: "And it leads to the 20th Century, to Hitler and Stalin, as its necessary, <u>logical</u> climax!"

Similarly, when C.S. Lewis claims: "Each new power won *by* man is a power *over* man as well. Each advance leaves him weaker as well as stronger"—she responds: "So when you cure men of TB, syphilis, scurvy, small pox and rabies—you make them <u>weaker</u>!!!" (Note the exclamation points, which abound in the marginalia. Here is an individual whose thinking is "passionately personal.")

As Ayn Rand observes, a corollary of taking ideas seriously is the commitment to precision in language. She writes: "You must attach clear, specific meanings to words, i.e., be able to identify their referents in reality. This is the precondition, without which neither critical judgment nor thinking of any kind is possible."

This is what underlies her superlative ability to "translate" some innocuous—or incomprehensible—passage into its actual meaning. For example, in *Human Action*, von Mises writes:

> In studying interpersonal exchange one cannot avoid dealing with autistic exchange. But then it is no longer possible to define neatly the boundaries between the kind of action which is the proper field of economic science in the narrower sense, and other action. Economics widens its horizon and turns into a general science of all and every human action, into praxeology. The question emerges of how to distinguish precisely, within the broader field of general praxeology, a narrower orbit of specifically economic problems.

To which Ayn Rand replies in the margins:

> Translation: in dealing with interpersonal exchange, one cannot avoid dealing with individual motivation. Then one invades the field of philosophy by inventing a new science [i.e. praxeology] whose boundaries one cannot define.

Or consider Jerome Rothstein, who, in *Communication, Organization, and Science*, writes:

> Engineering is a system whose input is the world as the engineer finds it and whose output is the world as the engineer wants it. This statement seems like an exaggeration and an oversimplification. But if one broadens the definition of engineering so that it is synonymous with all branches of applied science (a cattle raiser is a zoological engineer, a truck farmer a botanical engineer, etc.) . . . then the engineers include a large part of the human race and the statement is less open to criticism.

She responds: "Beef stroganoff is made up of wood and gasoline. This statement seems inaccurate, but if one broadens the definition of wood to include all solid matter, and the definition of gasoline to include all liquids, the statement is less open to criticisms."

Her attention is especially drawn to innaccurate definitions. For example, in *Human Action* von Mises states: "[L]aw is the complex of rules determining the orbit in which individuals are free to act." On which she comments: "Good Lord! Look at what the premise of 'definitions by negatives' will do!

'Everything which is not permitted by law is forbidden'? (See 'Anthem.')" And in *The Road to Serfdom*, Hayek says: "The essential features of... individualism . . . are the respect for the individual man *qua* man, that is, the recognition of his own views and tastes as supreme in his own sphere, however narrowly that may be circumscribed." She responds:

> Rotten definition! A collectivist could subscribe to it. You can circumscribe "a man's own sphere" to mere breathing—and not too much of that. Who decides on what a man's "own sphere" is? If a defender of individualism can offer no better definition than this—it's proof of why the cause of individualism has failed. It had no real base, no moral base. This is why my book is needed.

As a thinker, Ayn Rand took a fresh, independent approach to complex philosophical issues, and offered solutions that got to the *root* of the matter. And that root is always *reality*. It was Ayn Rand's distinctive approach to ask: What facts of reality give rise to a particular concept? Consider her brilliant analysis of the contemporary analytic notion of "logical possibility"—a notion which, as she demonstrates, is possible only if one detaches logic from existence.

In *An Introduction to Philosophical Analysis*, John Hospers writes: "It seems to be empirically impossible for living things to exist without oxygen, nitrogen, carbon and hydrogen. But it is logically possible that life in some form could exist without one or more of these." Ayn Rand responds:

> Translated, this means: since no attribute of an entity is essential, how do we know whether that entity will still preserve its identity without any or all of them? The gimmick is so blatantly contained in: what do we mean by the concept "life"? But they answer that we are free to mean anything we wish. And more: it is here made obvious that the logical vs. empirical distinction rests on taking the "single-attribute," primitive level of abstractions (the level corresponding to the first, visual abstractions of a child, one step above the level of perceptions) as the base, root, source, absolute and irreducible primary of logic (!!!). Thus, logic is the discipline that belongs to the epistemology of those of "arrested mental development"—and to nobody and nothing above that level (!!!). Else why are "square circle" or "male aunt" logically impossible, but "life without oxygen" is not? Merely because "square," "circle," "male" and "aunt" use simple, almost single-attribute concepts, which do not require a long chain of prior, precise, specific concepts with unequivocal, absolute definitions? Logic, therefore, stops and breaks with reality at the point where a retarded mind (or an anti-effort mind) begins to waver, cloud and vacillate.

This is what Ayn Rand had in mind when she said we must attach clear meanings to words—i.e., "identify their referents in reality." This is also what it means to take ideas seriously, for only when we anchor our ideas in reality can they guide human life.

*   *   *

The material I chose to include in this collection comes from over 20 books and several boxes of newspaper/magazine clippings. With few exceptions, her marginalia date from the period after the publication of *Atlas Shrugged* (1957), when Ayn Rand turned with increased interest to writing non-fiction. (Several of these books were reviewed in *The Objectivist Newsletter* or were discussed in various articles by her.)

I should explain my criteria in selecting the marginalia. My starting assumption was that if Ayn Rand wrote it, it was worth including, unless I had a good reason not to. Here, then, are my major grounds for omitting a marginal comment:

(1) **Obviousness**. (There were surprisingly few of these.) For example, if Ayn Rand were to write "Oh, God" next to some claim that capitalism is bad, this would represent nothing new or unanticipated. In some cases, however, I included even this kind of comment, if it helped provide a more revealing picture of the author.

(2) **Repetitiveness**. If the same essential point was made time after time, I did not include each instance. For example, Ayn Rand comments nearly thirty times on von Mises' view that morality is subjective and that the ends of human action are "ultimate givens."

(3) **Incommensurateness**. If, for example, Ayn Rand drew a line alongside three paragraphs, and simply wrote "unclear" or "equivocations," I omitted the passage on the grounds that it was too little commentary for so much text. (However, even in a few of these cases, I decided the text with comment was just too interesting to pass up.)

(4) **Ambiguity**. Since her marginal comments were written all over the page, and occasionally on separate pages of notes, it was sometimes unclear exactly what she was commenting on. If no intelligent estimate was possible, and if her note could not stand on its own, I excluded it. (Fortunately, this was never the case with significant, lengthy comments.)

I have presented as much of the original text as was needed to make it (and the comment on it) self-contained and intelligible, but without making it too lengthy. Ayn Rand's comments appear in a separate column to the right of each passage, as close as possible to specific sections she is annotating. Generally, if a comment begins at the top, it is meant to refer to the whole passage.

Given the extemporaneous and private nature of the marginal comments, it is remarkable how little line-editing was necessary. I saw to it that none of the (very few) changes I made transformed the meaning of her statements in any way. My aim was merely to improve the grammar through an occasional change of the tense of a verb, or the addition of the word "the" or "a," etc.

Note that pointed brackets < > represent a word(s) from Ayn Rand's comments that I am almost, but not absolutely, certain is correct. (Ayn Rand's handwriting was often hard to decipher; I thank Harry Binswanger and Estelle Mayhew for their help in figuring out some of the more difficult words.) Square brackets [ ], except where they occur within parentheses, represent my editorial insertions. Note that all underlining, double-underlining and circling of words (indicated by the graphic device of screening) are Ayn Rand's. The page number(s) of the book is cited in parentheses, at the end of each passage.

* * *

I feel compelled to say something about the predominantly negative nature of her marginalia. Ayn Rand definitely had many positive comments. For example, in Barry Goldwater's *The Conscience of a Conservative* (especially in the chapter on how to deal with communist countries), she writes in the margins: "Good," "wonderful," "excellent," etc. But these are clearly in the minority. Let me explain why I think this is so.

When confronted with an idea with which you agree, you may be delighted, but not really have much to communicate (especially if writing comments in the margins) other than such concurring sentiments as "great," "true," etc. After all, the *author* has already stated the point, and you are simply acknowledging the truth of his observation. But when you encounter something you find unclear or with which you disagree—especially in the field of ideas—a whole range of critical thoughts should immediately come to mind, to name what you see but the author does not. You should retain this context when considering the "negative" aspect of Ayn Rand's comments.

And of course you need most of all to keep in mind the nature of her targets: as angry and condemnatory as she can be, I do not recall a single case where what she said was unfair. In fact, I was often filled with admiration for her patience, and for the strength of her stomach, in being able to go through some truly horrible book that she had decided was worth reading. (I, for one, could *never* have completed C.S. Lewis' *The Abolition of Man*.)

* * *

Ayn Rand wrote these comments for her own eyes only, and never imagined that they would be published. They should be read accordingly—i.e., the marginalia are in no way to be taken as her final, considered viewpoint. Nevertheless, they provide fascinating and important insights into Ayn Rand.

What primarily set Ayn Rand apart from other people was her method of thinking. When we see her sort through a jumble of words (whose meaning the author himself would often not grasp), go to the basic premises and then translate the passage into plain English—with both the fluff and the garbage stripped away—we are seeing her matchless ability to think in principles, in fundamentals, in essentials. So although the marginalia do tell us something new about the content of her thought (especially her views of other thinkers), the far greater value is the glimpse of Ayn Rand's matchless mind in action.

ROBERT MAYHEW
Department of Philosophy
Seton Hall University
September, 1995

Part I
Philosophy

first as in a whole, there must be a perfect syllogism of the extremes. I call that term middle which is itself in another and contains another in itself; in position also it comes in the middle.[14]

In the illustration, the "middle" is "animals." Proof consists in finding such a "middle." The middle, *to meson*, is the "reason why," *to dioti*, the connecting link, between the conclusion and the premises. The aim of science is to find such links, such middles: to trace such an intelligible structure between things.

The precise wording of the basic Barbara syllogism in the *Prior Analytics* is:

> If A is predicated of (or "belongs to") all B,
> and B is predicated of (or "belongs to") all C,
> then A is necessarily predicated of (or "belongs to") all C.

That is, Aristotle's conception of the syllogism in the *Prior Analytics,* as Jan Łukasiewicz has shown in his brilliant book, *Aristotle's Syllogistic from the Standpoint of Modern Formal Logic,*[15] is that of a purely formal instrument, or, as we should say, of a purely formal calculus. It is consistently formal, where the later tradition became confused and introduced various material elements. There are in the *Prior Analytics* no psychological terms, no laws or forms of "thinking." There are no singular terms, for the same term must be used both as a subject and a predicate, and a singular term cannot be used as a predicate. There are no concrete terms in the statement of the syllogism, only letters, variables. Aristotle's introduction of variables into formal logic was as epoch-making as their later introduction into arithmetic. In the one case, "formal" logic was created, in the other, algebra.

Aristotle presents the syllogism as an implication, not as an inference. It takes the form: If A and B, then "necessarily" C; not the form: A and B are, "therefore" C is. The "necessarily,"

[14] *Prior Analytics* I, ch. 4: 25b 32–36.
[15] Jan Łukasiewicz, *Aristotle's Syllogistic from the Standpoint of Modern Formal Logic* (Oxford, 1951; 2d ed. enlarged, Oxford, 1957).

Is this what *they* call "variables" or is it another modern package-deal + dishonest equivocation? (An abstraction is a "variable"?!)

Ayn Rand's marginalia from John Herman Randall's *Aristotle*

Ayn Rand's very positive review of Randall's Aristotle first appeared in The Objectivist Newsletter, vol. 2, no. 5 (May 1963), and has been reprinted in The Voice of Reason. She wrote that although Randall's book was flawed, "if read critically, [it] is of great value to the study of Aristotle. It is a concise and comprehensive presentation which many people need and look for, but cannot find today....Above all, this book is important culturally, as a step in the right direction, as a recognition of the fact that the great physician needed by our dying science of philosophy is Aristotle...."

Besides substantial marginal comments, Ayn Rand wrote thirteen separate pages of notes (dated April 9, 1963) in preparation for her review. Some of these notes are incorporated into this presentation.

Chapter 1: The Aristotelian Approach to Understanding

To understand the world of Greece meant [for Aristotle], first, an understanding of human life as something lived in human groups set in a physical environment. . . . Groups of men in their natural setting—what the Greeks called "cities," *poleis*—formed the most insistent fact in the Greek world. (4)

(But "groups" are man-made.)

For Aristotle, [the question "How is knowledge possible?"] would be a wholly unintelligible question. Knowing is for him an obvious fact. What does it mean? How are we to construe and understand that fact? The real question, as he sees it, is, "In what kind of a world is knowing possible?" What does the fact of knowing imply about our world? (6)

This is the prior certainty of consciousness![1]

Keynote of R[andall]'s error: ascribing "the primacy of consciousness" idea to Aristotle.

Aristotle . . . approaches every subject matter from the standpoint of living, of life as the fore-ground of nature; from the standpoint of know-ing, of the way in which the mind grasps it, of the intellectual instruments it employs; and from the standpoint of talking, of the ways in which know-ing proceeds, by means of language, making dis-tinctions, arriving at an understanding, at a state-ment of what it can be said to be. (8)

(Dangerous as hell! It is not the same thing as arriving at the knowledge of what it is—as expressed in language, i.e., in the terms of a human consciousness, a human means of knowing, with "language" as the form of grasping facts.)

Chapter 2: Aristotle's Life and Corpus

[Aristotle] became a "Platonist": that is, he shared the mystic faith that is "Platonism," the

He treats mysticism as a virtue!

devotion to "the Ideal," the aspiration after what is deathless and eternal—he shared and expressed these idealistic and religious interests. Aristotle was not an unimaginative fellow who was too stodgy to feel the appeal of "Platonism." (13)

Randall's "apology" for Aristotle to the Platonist mystics.

Aristotle's own thinking is not closed, like theirs [i.e., the Hellenistic systematic philosophers], but open. For Aristotle knowledge is not a neat "system," but a living growth, like a tree—it goes on and on, it is biological.(30)

Danger!

?

[L]ogic, "Analytics," is for Aristotle not a science but a _dynamis_, a "power"; a _technê_, an "art"; an _organon, a "tool."_ Aristotle's analysis is never an end in itself, but is always for the sake of "knowing," of science. It may be suspected that Aristotle would have had little sympathy with modern mathematical logic, which aims at beauty rather than use. . . . (30)

(Correct!)

?!?

In modern terms, he can be viewed as a behaviorist, an operationalist, and a contextualist, with a thoroughgoing philosophy of process. (31)

Good God! Are they all as concrete-bound as that?

Here chaos breaks loose over the issue of Aristotle as a "modern."

Chapter 3: Science as Right Talking: The Analysis of Discourse

We possess science when we can prove and demonstrate statements about [things], by relating those statements to other statements of which they are the necessary consequences.(34)

Danger!

"Science" is thus for Aristotle a knowledge of the whys, the _dioti's_, the "reasons for" the true statements. It is knowledge of the dependence of true statements on more fundamental truths, on "first things," _ta prôta_, or "causes," _aitia_. . . . (34)

Deduction from axioms or induction from definitions?

We add two apples to two apples, and find we get four apples; we add two marbles to two other marbles, and we get four marbles. In this way we come to learn that two and two are four: we "see" it in a kind of intellectual vision, we "recognize" its truth. But two and two are not four _because of_

Total disaster!

the apples, or *because* of the marbles: the apples are clearly irrelevant to the truth of the arithmetical proposition. (45)

<u>"We see, we recognize, that it is so." We grasp its truth by *nous*, by intellectual intuition, by insight.</u> (45)

Disaster in re: A's view of "insight"—of "<u>nous</u>" as some sort of "intellectual intuition."

If, then, we are not content to rest with the "fact that" men are mortal, that they will eventually die, which we have all learned from experience; if we demand "science," a "reason why" men are mortal, we can put it, <u>Men are mortal, because men are animals, *empsycha*, and all animals or animate things are mortal</u>. Men, that is, belong to that kind of being that has that kind of property, and hence they all exhibit that property also: it is essential to being a man that men are mortal. (47)

Is <u>this</u> Aristotle or Randall?

Dubious view of syllogism.

There are no concrete terms in the statement of the syllogism, only letters, <u>variables</u>. Aristotle's introduction of the variables into formal logic was as epoch-making as their later introduction into arithmetic. In the one case, "formal" logic was created, in the other, <u>algebra</u>. (48)

Is <u>this</u> what they call "variables" or is it another modern package-deal and disastrous equivocation? (An <u>abstraction</u> is a "<u>variable</u>"?!)

Aristotle defines a proposition, a *protasis*, as "a statement affirming or denying something of something." Its elements he calls "terms," *horoi*, the "limits" or "boundaries," the "termini" of the statement. <u>He avoids all psychological or metaphysical overtones</u>, all words like "notion," "concept," in the Greek equivalents. (49)

How in hell do you discuss language without "psychological or metaphysical overtones"?

Aristotle is no advocate of a logic without ontological implications—quite the contrary! This is the instrument of proof, of demonstration, of science. In what kind of world can you use it successfully? What kind of structure of things can be so expressed? (49)

(In reverse.)

The syllogism will operate in a world exhibiting "kinds," *genê*, a world in which are to be found real species and genera, a world in which individual things are what they are because they are of a certain kind, <u>because they belong to a certain species</u>. (49)

<u>This</u> is the root of all misinterpretations of Aristotle!

<u>This</u> is the total inversion (the primacy of consciousness): the universe consists of species and

genera <u>because</u> logic demands it—<u>not</u> logic establishes these categories <u>because</u> such is the nature of the universe.

For what a property is, and the reason why it is a property of that kind of thing, are identical. The "nature" of a property and the "cause" of a property are the same, and are expressed in the definition of that kind of thing. (50)

???

(What a package-deal!)

[Quote from John Dewey, "Logic," Encyclopedia of the Social Sciences, IX, 599:] Aristotle was above all a naturalist. He asserted that the universal is united with the particular existences, binding them together into a permanent whole (the species), and keeping within definite and fixed limits the changes which occur in each particular existence. The species is the true whole of which the particular individuals are the parts, and the essence is the characteristic form. Species fall within a graded order of genera as particular individuals fall within the species. Thinking is the correlate of these relations in nature. It unites and differentiates in judgment as species are united and separated in reality. (51)

?!?

Oh boy!

This is true—but the rest does not follow from it.

To take <u>Dewey</u> as an interpreter of Aristotle!!

The second step in inquiry is to examine previous "opinions" or hypotheses as to the best way to understand the subject matter in question, the *archai* proposed by Aristotle's predecessors among the Greeks. . . . He accepts proposed *archai* or hypotheses, as he accepts everything else, as material to be worked over, to bring out the best in them. (52)

Good God! Aristotle did <u>not</u> confuse the natural with the man-made—only his Ethics and Politics may be so interpreted, but even then I doubt it.

[Quote from Metaphysics Alpha Minor, ch. 1:] While no one person can grasp the truth adequately, we cannot all fail in the attempt. Each thinker makes some statement about nature, and as an individual contributes little or nothing to the inquiry. But the combination of all the conjectures results in something big (*ti megethos*). . . . It is only fair to be grateful not only to those whose views we can share, but also to those who have gone pretty far wrong in their guesses. They too have contributed something: by their prelimi-

This is a courteous remark in re: the pursuit of knowledge—<u>not</u> an epistemological principle.

nary work they helped to form our scientific way of thinking (*hexis*). (53)

[O]ur modern scientific enterprise was born in the rejection of such "empiricism" for some form of "rationalism"—in the rejection of <u>trust in sheer observation for faith in mathematical demonstration</u>. (56)

<u>This</u> is what I call a totally meaningless phrase.

Chapter 4: Aristotle's Functional Concepts: Living and Desiring

<u>Life is the end of living bodies, since they exist for the sake of living.</u> (70)

(Good)

[*Quote from* De Anima *III 9:*] It is not the power of reasoning or what is called *nous* that is the mover. For the theoretical *nous* thinks nothing that is practical and says nothing about what is to be avoided or pursued, whereas motion always implies that we are avoiding or pursuing something. . . . (73-74)

Here's the explicit difference between Aristotle and me: the theoretical "nous" unconcerned with practical problems.

[*Quote from* Nicomachean Ethics *VI 7:*] Wisdom must be a combination of Nous and Science: it must be a consummated knowledge of those things that are most exalted. For it is absurd to think that political or practical intelligence is the loftiest kind of knowledge, <u>since man is not the best thing in the world.</u> . . .

? !

It is also clear that theoretical wisdom cannot be the same thing as political intelligence; for if we are to call knowledge of our interests wisdom, there will be a number of different kinds of wisdom, one for each species: there cannot be a single such wisdom dealing with the good of all living things, any more than there is one art of medicine for all existing things. It may be argued that man is superior to the other animals, but this makes no difference: since there exist other things far more divine in their nature than man, for instance, to mention the most visible, the things of which the celestial system is composed. (79-80)

Mixture of the abstract and the concrete; the basic principles of medicine <u>are</u> one for all living things (the preservation of the life of the organism)—and the same is true of <u>ethics</u>.

Chapter 5: The Power of Selective Response: Sensing and Knowing

<u>In Aristotle and the whole Aristotelian tradition, the line is drawn between sensing and "nousing,"</u>

This is important.

between sensing the particular and knowing the
universal, not between "body" and "mind." Des-
cartes was thus introducing a genuine and fundamental revolution into the analysis of human nature and human knowledge, when he took sensing
and all the other "passions" of the soul out of the
physical world, now reduced to extension alone,
and put them into "mind," *penser,* a revolution
from which we have hardly recovered yet. (88)

Aristotle takes "nousing" as, like sensing, a being
acted upon. (89)

> The root of the disaster in
> epistemology.

That we can know things as they are, that such
knowledge is possible, is the fact that Aristotle is
trying to explain, and not, like Kant and his followers, trying to deny and explain away. (91)

> Good![2]

That knowledge is not the passive reception of
the structure of things, that it is an active process
of interpretation and construction, is the biggest
difference between our voluntaristic and biological conceptions of knowledge and that of Aristotle. (92)

> True!
>
> False!
> (in their sense of it.)

Nous must be "unmixed" with any other structure
than that of the object of thought. It must be unmixed with any structure of its own, as we have
seen; it must be unmixed with any structure of
what it thinks, save that structure it is thinking;
and it must be unmixed with any structure of the
body, in the way the sense organs are so mixed.
. . . Likewise it must be "unaffected" by what acts
upon it, and by the body, in a way that sense is
not. (92-93)

> What a way of groping for the
> concept of "objectivity"!
> This is a clue to what men have
> not discovered to this day.

This dependence of all knowing on observation
constitutes what can be called Aristotle's "empiricism." It is what distinguished medieval "Aristotelianism" from medieval forms of Platonism:
the position that intellect cannot know "immaterial substances," completely "intelligible objects"
or "pure forms," but only the intelligible aspect
of sensible objects, the intelligible forms of what
can be observed in sense experience. (95)

> Important!

As "rational," man can understand the universe;
as "animal," he is limited to that aspect of the

> This is very interesting—an
> example of the same primitive

universe which such an animal can experience through his senses. On the one hand, man can know of the world only what he can learn from "experience" with it: he is limited by the extent of his rational observation. In Aristotle, this was a protest against those "Platonists" who boasted of a direct and internal vision of truth. On the other hand, the world *is* intelligible to a rational animal with the power of *nous*, for there is nothing in it that cannot enter into man's experience of it. "Experience" is the means whereby the intelligible aspect of the world and things is conveyed to the intellect, *nous*. Whatever exists has a "form" or "essence" by which it can be understood. Whatever occurs has a set of "reasons why" by which it can be rationally grasped. . . . To find them is the aim of human knowledge: to advance from observation, from sense, to reasons why. (97-98)

epistemology that "explained by means of gods and demons," here being applied to man's consciousness—to the "mystery" of <u>concepts</u>.

(Men anthropomorphized inanimate nature—and reified the functions of their own consciousness.)

[B]esides the power of knowing and becoming all universals, *nous* as *pathêtikos*, "passive intellect," there must be "another distinction in the *psychê*," *nous* such that it makes all things, a kind of quality (*hexis*) like light. And it is this *nous* that is . . . separable (*chôristos*) and unaffected (*apathês*) and unmixed (*amigês*). It does not become, but is a deathless and eternal activity, and knows "no intermittence," and without it the *nous* that becomes all things would not think at all. And it is such *nous* that makes us know, just as light makes us see. . . . (99-100)

("Nous" as <u>focus</u>, as free will— "unaffected and unmixed," i.e., a primary: Never mind the "eternal," etc.)

The great Arabic commentator Averroes, living in Spain in the twelfth century, held that man does not really think himself at all. The "passive intellect" is also the same for all men, one and single. Only "intellect" ever thinks—in us! The "rational intellect," *nous*, both active and passive, is not the form of the human body, it is not a human function at all. It is the lowest of the "intelligences" informing the heavenly spheres: its proper "sphere" is the entire human race. (100)

Good God!

(This is an excellent presentation of the steps by which Aristotle is turned into a mystic.)

Of course, what Aristotle *ought* to have meant by "the *nous* that makes all things," the active intellect, in terms of his own thought, is clear enough. To his question, What makes us know? What ac-

(This is where the nonsense comes in: "language" and "discourse" or "communication" are <u>not</u> the same concepts. The

tualizes universals? the answer is, it is *logos, discourse, language and communication*. The "active intellect" is actually *logos*. Moderns like Mead and Dewey seem not only to be right— they are also thoroughly Aristotelian. But it is striking that, important as Aristotle makes *logos*, what things can be said to be, he never treats *logos* itself in biological and functional terms, as an activity of organisms with the power of *nous*: he never treats *logos* as a "part" of the *psychê*, as one of the functions making up "life." Such a treatment is not in the *De Anima* at all, but it ought to be. [*Randall adds in a footnote:*] The author has sometimes thought he might write out this section himself on papyrus and bury it in Egypt, where a future archaeologist might discover it. (102)

If we grant "knowing" to be a fact—if we hold that intelligence is not merely an organ of adjustment and adaptation, but a means of arriving at what may fairly be called "truth"—then mind does not seem to rise above the limitations and conditions of its bodily instruments, and to be, as Aristotle puts it, "unmixed and separable," and in its vision "deathless and eternal." This is Plato's insight. It is not so much a theory about the ontological status of *nous*, as an appreciation of what *nous* can do. (103)

The human mind *is* "unmixed with," "unaffected by," "separable from" its bodily conditions: it does seem to be in some sense "free" to seize on truth. Yet—we could not think at all if the world were not thinkable. . . . (104)

Thinking and knowing is the "thought" embodied there in the world, "potentially," Aristotle would say, being actually thought by us mortals. (104)

[Aristotle] treats knowing as a function of the human organism responding to its environment, as a way of dealing with its world, a way of func-

---

second are the consequences of the first.)

Oh, no!

(No, brother—I will. Or have.)

(Here's the revolt against identity: "if it's consciousness, then it's impossible"— therefore, mystical.)

This is the essence of all the philosophical confusions.

What do they imagine as an alternative?

("If the world were not thinkable" means: "If we were not conscious.")

(Why does a "thought" have to be "embodied" in the world? This is Locke's "photographs" in reverse.)

(Fine—except that the interaction between "mind" and "environment" is not what the

tioning in its context. <u>He treats it as a natural process: there is no gulf between "mind" and the rest of nature</u>. Mind is an intelligible interaction between a knowing organism and a knowable world. There is no problem of "How knowledge is possible, and why it isn't." <u>For Aristotle, "knowing" is not a problem to be solved, but a natural process to be described and analyzed</u>. (105)

pragmatist made of it. And the "<u>active</u> intellect" is a fact—in <u>Objectivist</u> terms.)

[A]ny construing of the fact of "knowledge," whether Kantian, Hegelian, Deweyan, Positivistic, or any other, seems to be consistent and fruitful, and to avoid the impasses of barren self-contradiction, and insoluble and meaningless problems, only when it proceeds from the Aristotelian approach, and pushes Aristotle's own analysis farther, as in the light of our scientific knowledge they must be pushed farther today—<u>only, that is, in the measure that it is conducted upon an Aristotelian basis</u>.

Indeed, in some respects Aristotle's <u>functional and contextual behaviorism</u> seems to be superior to our own <u>biological and mechanistic behaviorism</u>, because it views human experience, not as the interaction between a "merely" biological organism and a wholly illogical world, but as a co-operation between an intelligent biological organism and an intelligible world. (106)

In these two last paragraphs, Randall is truly superficial and "<u>modern</u>." What would be left of Kant, Hegel, Dewey and the Positivists if one removed their "non-Aristotelian elements"? The reference to philosophy being "pushed" by science is meaningless, "lip-service" nonsense. And to call Aristotle's philosophy "behaviorism" can be justified only on some such ground as: "Well, he deals with human <u>behavior</u>, doesn't he?"[3]

Chapter 6: First Philosophy: The Ultimate Distinctions

This science [i.e., metaphysics] emerges as the Aristotelian counterpart of mathematics in our own body of sciences. It can be said that mathematics and mathematical logic are the "metaphysics," in the Aristotelian sense of being the "First Philosophy," growing out of our own physical science, our mechanics and physics. That is, they set forth the formal structure or order in terms of which we find natural processes intelligible, they constitute our instrument of distinguishing, measuring, and relating. (109-110)

This is an interesting "metaphor" or view of mathematics.

(Randall cannot get away from the "primacy of consciousness" premise: observe the enormously dangerous difference between the issue of <u>knowing</u> what things <u>are</u>—and "making things <u>intelligible</u>.")

To this generalized question [i.e., What is it merely "to be"?], Aristotle finds we can give two kinds of answers:

(1) "To be" anything means "to be something that can be stated in discourse." . . . In this sense, anything that is, any *ousia*, is anything that can be talked about, any *subject of discourse*.

Danger!

(2) "To be" anything, in the world of natural processes, means "to be something that comes into being and passes away." . . . In this sense, anything that is, any *ousia*, is anything that is what it is as a result of a process, a *kinêsis* . . . , as the outcome of a process, as the operation or functioning of powers, and ultimately as sheer functioning, activity. (111-112)

Double-danger!

?!!

He is turning Aristotle into Heraclitus! (And taking "the law of identity" away from Aristotle.)[4]

[O]*usia* or *substantia* is defined precisely as that which undergoes change in change, what is at the end of any process different from what it was at the outset. And in the most important and fundamental kind of change of all, *genesis kai phthora*, "generation" and "corruption," a new *ousia* or substance is present at the end that was not there at all in the beginning, or a substance has disappeared completely. (112-113)

Here, he is taking the concept of "potentiality" away from Aristotle.

Note bene: For Aristotle all existence is "determinate" and "individual," and is hence plural: existence forms a many of things and processes, *ousiai* and *kinêseis*. This he takes for granted from common usage: "to be" means "to be something," an *ousia*. (113)

This is correct—and it contradicts Randall's Heraclitian interpretation of "sheer activity."

[*Quote from* Metaphysics *Gamma, ch. 4:*] If it be said that "man" has an infinite number of meanings, obviously there can be no discourse; for not to have one meaning is to have no meaning, and if words have no meaning there is an end of discourse with others, and even, strictly speaking, with oneself; because it is impossible to think of anything if we do not think of one thing. (116)

Excellent.

(Ask LP [Leonard Peikoff]: is it the discussion of the Law of Contradiction in the context of "discourse," that has made them think it is confined to discourse and does not apply to reality [or to "ontology"]?)
—absolutely false
(LP): Aristotle regarded it as a law of reality, of "being qua being."

But the "essence" of a thing, . . . since it is not common to anything else, and since in a sense it

Here is the source of the confusion about "universals"

is identical with the thing itself, can be said to be the *ousia* of that thing. The *ousia* of an individual thing is peculiar to it and belongs to nothing else. ... The "essence" of each thing is that which it is said to be in itself (*kath' hauto*) and in accordance with its own nature (*kata physin*). Hence the essence is one and the same thing with the particular thing. [*At this point Randall quotes from* Metaphysics Zeta, ch. 13:] [F]or it is when we know its essence that we have knowledge of a thing. ... It follows that each individual thing is one and the same with its essence, and not merely incidentally, because to have knowledge of the individual is to have knowledge of its essence; so that it is evident that both must be identical. (119)

and "particulars."

Here is where my theory of "essences" as epistemological and contextual, is crucially important.

[E]xisting things, *ousiai*, are clearly more than their definitions alone, they are more than what they can be truly said to be. Such concrete things can never be exhausted by what we can say about them. We can never exhaustively "define" any particular and individual *ousia*, we can never say everything that is true about it. (121)

Disaster!
This is the result of the reification of universals.

We can state in words the 'essence' of things, but we cannot state in words their 'existence.' (122)

Total disaster!
!!?!

These concrete things, that cannot be stated about anything else, that are always subjects of discourse, always what we are talking about, but never predicates, never what we are saying, are things or existences, *ousiai*, in "the first and best sense." They are primary things, primary *ousiai*, "primary substances," the ultimate subject matter of discourse. ... Thus when we say 1) "This table is thus and so," we are using "table" to designate a subject, a primary *ousia*, a primary substance. When we say 2) "This is a table," we are using "table" to designate a predicate, secondary *ousia*, a secondary substance or essence. (122)

This is an interesting passage: its actual meaning is that "existence" is a primary (but I don't think that Randall understands this). And it is this that has made philosophers say that they can "dispense" with "existence," since it is not a part of "discourse."

Whatever is can be expressed in words and discourse. There is nothing that cannot be talked about, nothing wholly inaccessible to discourse, nothing "ineffable." But discourse is not its own subject matter—unless the talking is about itself. Discourse is "about" something that is not itself discourse; <u>though what it is about—its subject matter—has a discursive or logical character</u>, and that character, that intelligible structure, is just what discourse can express and state. <u>Whatever is can be known. There is nothing that is unknowable</u>. (122-123)

(?)

<u>Excellent</u>—except for one modern (?) touch

Check with LP [Leonard Peikoff] (Conflict is in Aristotle—LP.)

For although for Aristotle nature, apart from human arts, exhibits no discoverable purposes, it *does* exhibit natural ends or *telê*. Nature is the scene of productive enterprises, that are not to be understood as mere mixings and unmixings of elements. Events do not merely "happen." . . . Nature is indisputably teleological; its processes are full of ends, *telê*, that are achieved, of conclusions that are reached over and over. <u>Only in human life are these ends and conclusions consciously intended, only in men are purposes found. For Aristotle, even God has no purpose, only man</u>! (125)[5]

<u>This</u> is the trouble: it is still primitive anthropomorphism. Or: the lack of a full understanding of <u>identity</u>.

Aristotle's viewpoint and approach are, we often say, biological, rather than "merely" mechanical. They spring out of the experience of the biologist that Aristotle was. He takes biological examples, living processes, as revealing most fully and clearly what natural processes are like. He analyzes the behaviour of eggs, not of billiard balls. He seems to have spent much time with the chickens, while the seventeenth-century founders of modern dynamics seem to have spent their lives, like Pascal, at the billiard and the gaming tables. (126)

<u>Good passage on "eggs vs billiard balls."</u>

Aristotle's Unmoved Mover is an ideal. It is what Arthur O. Lovejoy calls "<u>Self-Sufficing Perfection</u>," the Platonic "Idea of the Good," and contrasts sharply with the Demiurge of [Plato's] *Timaeus*, which he calls "<u>Self-Transcending Fecundity</u>," a creator of being and good. (139)

(This seems to be a clue to the anthropomorphising of a <u>human</u>, moral issue: the self-sufficient versus the "serving," egoism vs altruism.)

The Unmoved Mover may well be called a Platonic myth, like the "Active Intellect" of the *De Anima*. If so, the "mythical" element is not the manifold specific "unmoved movers" to be found in every process, for they are literal enough. <u>It is rather the generalization and the unification into</u>

<u>This</u> is an example of the switch from metaphysics to epistemology which <u>I</u> find unbearable in philosophy.

a single Cosmic Unmoved Mover. But then, the unification of the Divine by means of myth is common enough in philosophical theology. (141)

Aristotle argues that the perfected functioning of the highest activity in the world is the only justi-fication, the only "reason why" for the world's existence. (141)

<u>That's</u> Aristotle's trouble.

Where is *nous* actualized? Where does *nous* think itself? in things? in separate ideal exist-ence? To be consistent, Aristotle must answer, No, in the minds of men. So interpreted, Aristotle's natural theology would be sound, probably the only sound natural theology in the Western tradition. For it would be maintaining that the only "reason" for the existence of the world as a whole . . . , the only fact that justifies nature to man, is that the world exists to make life possible, and at its fullest, to make possible the best life, which for Aristotle is the life of sheer knowing, "*Nous* nousing *nous*."(144)

This is beautiful psychologically, as a mythical expression of a moral intention, as a "fictionalized" way of saying that the ideal man's life is an end in itself—but, oh God! what a disaster philosophically!

The psychological pride of the Unmoved Mover.

Chapter 7: The Heavens

It was also this cosmology of Aristotle's that be-came the acceptable formulation of the closed world of ancient and medieval thinking, whose destruction was necessarily involved in the birth of modern science and philosophy. (145)

The God-damn fools!

Man, even in his most exalted function, has found his own natural status in the Whole: by nature he desires to know, he is the living being that knows. (150)

The "even" in this passage is a curious confession about the nature of mysticism.

[*Quote from* De Caelo *I, ch. 2:*] it is clear that there is to be found a kind of bodily substance besides the four in our sublunary world, more divine than and prior to these. . . . Thus the rea-soning from all our premises goes to make us be-lieve that there is another kind of body separate from those around us here, and a nobler nature as it is removed from the sublunary world. (154)

("Little stuff"?)

The ancients also have handed down the name; for believing that the first body was something different from earth, air, fire, and water, they

(A hint of "little stuff"?)

called the uppermost place "aither" or "ever running." (155)

Yet even in the *De Caelo*, for all its youthful brashness and self-confidence, Aristotle is hardly the dogmatist of the Schoolmen's closed system. He is with great assurance offering "explanations" for the observed facts that are far too facile. But Galileo ... was not wholly without self-confidence himself. ... (161)

Is this a flaw? (Brashness, dogmatism and self-confidence are not the same thing. Here is the modern mentality at work.)

Chapter 8: The Understanding of Natural Processes

Thus for Aristotle physics is not applied mathematics; rather mathematics is "separated" or abstract physics. ... This Aristotelian philosophy of mathematics prevailed throughout the classical tradition, down through Newton. It avoids a host of difficulties that have created great philosophical perplexity: those of Kant, for example, to say nothing of those implicit in our own view of mathematics as a pure postulate system. (164)

The "perplexities" and "problems" are all matters of "the stolen concept."

[*Randall quotes nearly half of* Metaphysics Theta, *ch. 3. What follows are the first few lines, which present a view of potentiality that Aristotle will go on to refute:*] There are some, for example the Megarians, who say that a thing has a power only when it is functioning, and that when it is not functioning it has no power. (171) [*Aristotle goes on to present three objections to this view.*]

[*Ayn Rand drew a line beside the entire passage quoted by Randall and wrote beside it:*]
(Very good.)
[*In her notes she wrote:*]
Good quote from A. on motion and "potentiality."[6]

[M]ovement and process is what he is trying to understand in terms of "nature" (*physis*). Nature indicates and delimits a certain subject matter of inquiry, "natural bodies" (*ta physika*) or the things that exist by nature (*ta physei*). In just the same way, "life" (*psychê*) indicates and delimits a certain subject matter, "animate" or "organic things" (*ta empsycha*), which form a large and distinctive class among *ta physika*. Thus "nature" (*physis*) is, like "life" (*psychê*), an *archê*: it is that in terms of which a specific subject matter or field of inquiry is set off and distinguished, and then analyzed and understood. (172)

(Slightly dangerous: it seems to imply categories other than "nature"—unless, of course, Aristotle meant it as distinguished from the "eternal" or the "divine.")

This specific way of acting which natural bodies,

(No. This is sloppy modernism.

ta physei, display, is called their "nature" or *physis*. It might equally be called, as it came to be in early modern times, the "law" of their operating. (174)

The "law" of whose "operating"? What Aristotle is here clearly struggling to establish is identity.)

[A]n individual acorn can do an indefinite number of things. It can serve as a missile in a boy's slingshot; or it can become a squirrel's breakfast. But only certain of these powers are "essential" to its being an acorn: those, namely, involved in the power to grow into an oak tree. (176)

Is the error here an undefined, undifferentiated concept of "powers"? So that the "power to be eaten by a squirrel" is regarded as a separate capacity? Is that Aristotle's view of "contingency"? Such an error is the mixing of a thing's attributes with all the limitless specific uses that can be made of it.

[*Quote from* Physics *II, ch. 1:*] As for trying to show that there is such a thing as nature, that would be ridiculous; it is clear that there are many such natural beings. To demonstrate what is clear by what is obscure is the act of a man who cannot distinguish what is self-evident from what is not. That such a state is possible is plain: one blind from birth can indeed argue about colors, and such men must needs talk about words, since they have no knowledge. (177)

Good quote from A. against "talking about words."

!!!

[*Quote from* Physics *II, ch. 5:*] We must first admit that of all beings there is none whose nature permits it to act on another or be acted on by another in any chance way whatsoever, nor is there any coming into being of any kind of being from any other kind. (178-179)

Here is causality as "the law of identity applied to action."

Chance is the name given to all events caused by factors that are not relevant to the ends of natural processes, by all the non-teleological factors, the brute events interfering with the natural working out of a process, or achieving a quite different end incidentally, causing the acorn to become a squirrel's breakfast, impinging in the process "by violence" from without. Chance is any event having no end, no For What. (183)

(This is correct epistemologically, not metaphysically, since the squirrel eating the acorn is a "natural" process.)

Chance hence presupposes an order of natural teleology, and is posterior to that order. It is said to be "against nature," or "contrary to nature," like the birth of distorted monsters. . . . Chance is

(This is the disaster—the implication that only "the essential" is natural, that that which we do not know at any

what in individual cases is never equal—the particular, the contingent, the variable, the unpre-
dictable about specific events—what is logically
incidental. . . . (183-184)

given time is unknowable [like
the birth of a monster].)

Aristotle is keenly aware that science deals with
regularities, "always or for the most part," in a
much more complex world, which also reveals
precariousness, contingency as well as stability,
order, and regularity. That is why outside mathematics he says things happen in certain ways,
"always or for the most part," except in the heavens, where there is no observable chance or contingency. This is Aristotle's way of recognizing
the facts the modern scientist expresses by saying
that his laws are statistical averages. We often
think this is a recent modern discovery, because
it was forgotten in the seventeenth century. (184)

(Here is where my "translation"
of Aristotle's "metaphysics" into
"epistemology" is desperately
needed.)

God, no!

If there is to be a saw, then teeth of hard iron, or
some similar material, are necessary. If there is to
be an oak tree, then there must be a proper acorn,
and conditions necessary for its growth. This is
what Aristotle calls "hypothetical" necessity.
Such natural necessity is teleological. If they are
to be attained, the ends of processes impose their
necessary conditions. Such natural necessity is
always relative: certain conditions are "necessary
for" the achievement of the end. . . . [But] [t]he
attainment of ends is not necessary by any kind
of simple necessity. (184-185)

(?!)

(This is a deadly mixture of the
"metaphysical" and the "man-
made.")

Aristotle does not view the causal relation temporally: for him it is not a matter of "necessary connection," but of "necessary conditions." And
such necessary conditions can only be discovered
experimentally, by manipulation, not by mere
observation of sequences. Aristotle is much
closer to the present-day notion of a manipulative
and experimental science, and of a corresponding
and appropriate conception of causation and of
natural necessity, than is Hume. (185)

Oh, no!
"Experimental manipulation" is
only one of the means, not the
end, of science. The end (that
which can be taken as
knowledge) is the discovery
of identity.

There is also for Aristotle a certain brute "necessity" in matter, in materials needed in any process. This may result in the birth of monsters that
are "contrary to nature"—that is, contrary to the
nature or teleological pattern of that kind of

(This is the concept of nature
which Aristotle did not, but
should have pursued.)

thing. (186)

Why is it not enough to say, he asks, that nature acts always by necessity, and that the ends that are achieved by natural processes are purely "incidental." ... (186)

(Here is where the confusion starts. It is enough—but not in their sense of the concept of nature.)

Wherever ends are achieved with regularity, we discover a fixed order of means, that has to be followed one after the other, a functional or teleological order, and the following of this order of means is a necessary condition of the achievement of the end. (187)

(But this is "nature acting by necessity.")

[*Quote from* Physics II, ch. 8:] If a house were a thing generated by nature—if it grew—it would be produced in the same way in which art now produces it. If natural things were not produced by nature alone, but by art also, they would be produced by art in the same way that they are produced by nature. Each stage leads to the next. (187)

(?!!)

(The "metaphysical" and the "man-made.")

In general, art "imitates" nature, even when it goes beyond the ends that nature unaided can attain—when it builds a ship or writes a poem. Hence if art is for an end, so is the nature it imitates. (188)

Oh God!

[*At the end of page 188, Ayn Rand listed Aristotle's errors in the topic covered in this chapter.*]
(Aristotle's great virtue is also his trouble, particularly here: it is his "bio-centricism.")
(A. has not answered the atomists.)
(Aristotle is like primitive anthropomorphism elevated into a philosophical system—but it is an epistemological anthropomorphism.)

Chapter 9: The Analysis of Motion

Aristotle's formal definition of place (*topos*) runs: "Hence the immediate unmoved limit of the surrounding body is place" [Physics IV, 4]. . . . Place is hence relative to a whole system of bodies. [*He now quotes* Physics IV, ch. 5:] "If a body has outside itself a body which contains it, it is in place; if it has not, it has no place. . . . Hence the whole universe is nowhere. For a thing which is somewhere is first of all a thing in itself, and it then presupposes something else next to it which contains it. But next to the universe, there

Good quotes from A. on the question of "place." (Place as "a relation between bodies in a common system." R.)

is nothing outside the whole, rather, everything
that is, is in the heavens; for it is clear that the
heavens are the whole. Now, place is not the
heavens, it is the extremity of the heavens which
is in contact with the moving body as an unmoved limit. Hence earth is in water, water is in
air, air is in ether, ether is in the heavens, but the   (?)
heavens are not in anything else." [A few lines
later Randall writes:] [I]t is a relativistic view, like
our own: "place" or "space" is a system of reference, not an independent existence. There is no
empty "space" which existed before bodies came
into existence, and which continues to exist as
the absolute container of all bodies. There is
nothing like Newton's "absolute space," which he
could identify, following Henry More, with the
mind of God. Aristotle examines and rejects the
notion of such a "space"—the "chaos" of Hesiod,
the *chôra* of the *Timaeus*—in favor of the alternative notion of "place"—a relation between
bodies in a common system. (197)

[T]he Pythagoreans take the void as limiting   (Existentialism)
things, including numbers. (198)

Chapter 10: The Emergence of Novelty: The Analysis of Genesis

[G]enesis is not to be understood as a mere combination of existing elements with their properties. In terms of our own, though not of
Aristotle's, chemistry, when hydrogen and oxygen unite to form H_2O, in the new combination
the elements interact and are modified. The
chemical combination H_2O manifests new properties not to be found in either of the elements
taken by themselves, like "wetness," or "liquid-
ity." Aristotle characteristically puts it, the elements continue to exist in the new whole "potentially"—that is, they can always be analyzed out
again, with nothing left over. But when they are
operating in combination in the whole, they display novel characteristics and powers. That is, a
new "form," a new "nature," comes into being. . . .
(210-211)

(This is somewhat equivocal or
"concrete-bound": what is it
that "interacts"? Since the
elements still exist, it is not a
genesis out of nothing.)

Bad misinterpretations on the
issue of "new genesis," equating
it with chemistry.

[I]t is reasonable enough that coming-to-be
should never fail. For coming-to-be is a passing-
away of "what is not," and passing-away is a

(This is disgraceful for Aristotle.
It's the "reification of the zero.")

coming-to-be of "what is not." (212)

Chapter 11: Aristotle's Functionalism Illustrated in Biological Theory[7]

No kind of thing, no species, is subordinate to the purposes and interests of any other kind. In biological theory, the end served by the structure of any specific kind of living thing is the good—ultimately, the "survival"—of that kind of thing. (229)[8]

(Ask Randall how he reconciles that with socialism?)

[Quote from De Partibus Animalium I, ch. 5:] Just as the sawing is not there for the sake of the saw, but the saw for the sake of the sawing, because sawing is the using of the instrument, so in some way the body is for the sake of life (hê psychê), and the parts of the body for the sake of those functions for which they are naturally suited. (234)

As a metaphor, this is excellent—but the literal equation of the material with the man-made, is deadly.

[Quote from De Partibus Animalium IV, ch. 10:] Since man stands upright, he has no need of legs in front; instead of them nature has given him arms and hands. Anaxagoras indeed asserts that it is his possession of hands that makes man the most intelligent of the animals. . . . [Randall comments:] It is very difficult for us not to approach a passage like this with our ingrained evolutionary attitude, and not to sympathize with Anaxagoras. (237)

This nonsense is as old as that!

?!! Why would "evolution" lead to the development of hands and not of the brain, if survival is the standard?

Aristotle's illustrations make clear the difference between this kind of necessity and hypothetical necessity. The latter always characterizes a relation of means to ends, of conditions "necessary for" some outcome: it signifies a teleological or functional relation. This other kind of necessity indicates the absence of function, and looks to the origin rather than the function of parts. Hence it may be called "material necessity." (238)

(The concept of "hypothetical necessity" presupposes the "absolute" necessity of identity: if certain things are "necessary" for certain results, it is because the identity (the nature) of the actors involved is an absolute.)

Chapter 12: The Practical Sciences: Knowing How to Choose Relative Goods[9]

His ethics and politics are actually his supreme achievement. (243)

Good God, no![10]

[Quote from Nicomachean Ethics VII, ch. 1:] It is proper to state the accepted views on the subject,

(Aristotle, the teleologist, as a determinist?)

and after thoroughly discussing them, to establish the truth of all, or at least the most important of the popular opinions. (246)

Intelligence is capable of perfecting animal life into the "life of reason" or *nous*. The natural materials of living—impulses, desires, the accepted customs and ideals—the family, slavery, the city-state and its political organization—can all be made excellent by intelligence. (247)

> Superficiality and traditionalism. <u>Where</u> did all this come from?

The very core of the Aristotelian attitude toward the conduct of man's life is this insistence that we must start with what we find at hand, and perfect the tendencies that are actually there. (247)

> Boy, what an error!

<u>[T]hese excellences [i.e., the moral virtues] described by Aristotle are obviously not the socialized ideals and values possible and necessary in our own world today.</u> It is hardly enough to say, let us abolish <u>our form of slavery</u>—perhaps, as Aristotle suggests, through automation—and then let all men live like Athenian citizens, then let us set up a whole society of "high-minded men." This is to confuse Aristotle's conclusions, inescapably rooted in the facts of his own Greek culture, and necessarily alien to our quite different way of life, with his starting point, his *archai*, with his method and his concepts. (249)

> ???!
>
> What sloppiness!
>
> Is "social metaphysics" Aristotle's "<u>archai</u>"??!

<u>What is distinctive about man is the possession of *logos*, discourse and reason: it is man's talking and thinking that set him apart from the other animals. And hence man's specific function is the operation of all his powers and capacities in accordance with *logos*; that is, it is to act intelligently.</u> (253)

> Observe the switch of one word which destroys everything: "<u>logos</u>" is reason, not "<u>intelligence</u>."
> "<u>To act rationally</u>" is not the same thing as "<u>to act intelligently</u>." "Intelligence" is a vague and relative term: "reason" is a specific faculty, on any level of "intelligence."

Hence "society," the *polis*, exists "by nature," *physei*; and man is "by nature" a social animal, *a zôon politikon*, an animal who lives in a *polis*. <u>That man who is "by nature" solitary and unsocial, who is *apolis*, is either a beast or a god.</u> The "reason why" man lives in a *polis*, *to dioti*, is that alone of all animals man possesses *logos*, the

> BS!
> <u>Speech</u> is not merely <u>social</u>; speech is a tool of reason even

power of speech. It is significant that the same *logos* that makes man a "rational animal" in its sense of "reason," also, in its sense of discourse and language, makes him a "political" or social animal. For speech serves to indicate the advantageous and the harmful, and hence also the right and the wrong. Through speech it is man alone who has a sense of good and bad, of right and wrong. And it is partnership in these things that makes every human association, from the family to the *polis*. (254)

on a desert island.

Yes—partnership of values. But—(which comes first: the partnership or the values?)

Hence the *polis*, or "society," is "prior in nature" to each of us. For all things are to be defined by their powers and functions. And the individual man displays and exercises his powers and functions only in the *polis*. That is, society is "prior" in understanding any particular man. (254)

Double BS! Who is "society?"

The best *polis* is the one that best fosters all human excellences, all conduct in accord with moral excellence and intelligence. (255)

By physical force?

Aristotle . . . stands for the omnicompetence of the state. There is nothing that political government must refrain from doing, if it makes for human welfare. Aristotle thus quite literally is stating the theory of the "welfare state." (255)

Unspeakable BS! Aristotle is wrong in politics, but even in Aristotle's own terms, the fostering of "excellence and intelligence" and the need-worship of a "welfare state" are not the same concepts.[11]

[N]either Aristotle nor Hobbes recognizes anything in the nature of an independent "spiritual" power standing outside the control of the state, like the Church, or like the University, which might well join the churches today as an independent spiritual power, to safeguard us from the perils of creeping totalitarianism. Aristotle thus states the theory of the rights and duties of the citizen of some particular state. No proclamation of the rights and duties of man, quite in independence of his *polis*, was made in Greece till the appearance of the Stoics, though the Cynics had come close to it. (256)

What incredible evasion and superficiality! What can be "independent" when and if the state is declared to be omnipotent, all-good and an end in itself?

[*Quote from George H. Sabine,* History of Political Theory:] At some date not far removed from the opening of the Lyceum, however, [Aristotle] conceived a science or art of politics on a much larger scale. The new science was to be general; that is, it should deal with actual as well as ideal forms of government and it should teach the art of governing and organizing states of any sort in any desired manner. The new general science of politics, therefore, was not only empirical and descriptive, but even in some respects independent of any ethical purpose, since a statesman might need to be expert in governing even a bad state. . . .

!!!?!
Why do the miserable little New Dealers (Sabine's book is of 1937) have to distort Aristotle, the father of the U.S.A., into a totalitarian statist?

The complete art of the statesman must take governments as they are and do the best it can with the means it has. It might even divorce itself from moral considerations altogether and tell the tyrant how to succeed in tyranny, as Aristotle actually does later.

What is "statesmanship" in a bad state? Governing for governing's sake?

[Randall comments:] The more completely Aristotle approached the attitude of the *physikos*, the natural philosopher of politics, the nearer he came to the similar attitude of Machiavelli. (258-259)

Good God Almighty.[12]

(That's the clue of what the statists regard as "natural" and "practical.")

[*Quote from* Politics *IV, ch. 1:*] For it is proper to consider not only the ideally best constitution, but also what is the one possible of achievement; and likewise, what is the one easiest to work, and most suitable to cities generally. . . .

(By what standard?)

The proper course is to bring forward an organization which men can be easily persuaded, and will be readily able, to graft onto the one they already have. For it is no less a task to reform an old constitution than to frame a new one from the beginning. . . . (260)

?!!

What errors!!

[*Quote from* Politics *IV, ch. 3:*] If the mind is to be reckoned as more essentially a part of a living being than the body, parts of a similar order to mind must equally be reckoned as more essentially parts of the city than those which serve its bodily needs. (261)

There's the pre-industrial error! (Besides, metaphors are not arguments.)

[*Quote from* Politics *IV, ch. 3:*] And such is also the union of natural ruler and natural subject for the sake of security; for he that can foresee with his mind is naturally ruler and naturally master, and he that can carry out these things with his body is a subject and naturally a slave. (262)

!!??!
Good God!

Dreadful quote from A[ristotle].

Both democracy and oligarchy . . . tend to degenerate into the worst of all forms of government, tyranny, which is also the least likely to be successful or to endure. Hence the statesman governing either a democracy or an oligarchy finds his chief task to keep it from following out the logic and the natural process of degeneration of its particular form. (263)

Here's the source of the "middle-of-the-road."

[*Quote from* Politics *IV, ch. 9:*] Those who belong to either extreme—the over-handsome, the over-strong, the over-noble, the over-wealthy; or at the opposite end the over-poor, the over-weak, the utterly ignoble—find it hard to follow the lead of reason. (264)

<u>What</u> is the "<u>over</u>" in regard to values?!

[*Quote from* Politics *IV, ch. 9:*] It is clear from our argument, first, that the best form of political society is one where power is vested in the middle class, and, second, that good government is attainable in those cities where there is a large middle class—large enough, if possible, to be stronger than both of the other classes, but at any rate large enough to be stronger than either of them singly; for in that case its addition to either will suffice to turn the scale, and will prevent either of the opposing extremes from becoming dominant. It is therefore the greatest blessings for a city that its members should possess a moderate and adequate property. (264)

This is true—but not for A.'s reasons.

[I]n Aristotle's analysis excellences (*aretai*) or "virtues" are twofold. For there are two levels of human behavior, two "parts" of the *psychê*, or "soul": there is the part that "has *logos*," intelligence itself, the part that knows and chooses; and there is the part that, though it does not "have *logos*" and is therefore "non-rational," is not "irrational," but can still "participate in *logos*" and obey it, the human impulses and desires which can either resist and fight *logos* or intelligence, in those who lack *sôphrosynê*, or self-control, or else be guided by it, in those who exhibit such *sôphrosynê*, the "continent." (267)

A.'s fatal error on emotions as independent of reason (but able to obey reason).

It is significant that what is the right action in specific situations <u>is not arrived at for Aristotle by *nous*, by moral intuition, by insight or hunch,</u>

<u>A's worst error: nous as intuition, reasoning as some other sort of power (which</u>

by "conscience," but by *logos*, reasoning, and *phronêsis*, foresight or "prudence." (268)

There are for Aristotle no general rules, no universal moral laws, no "principles" in ethics, save the one and single *archê*, always to act intelligently in any individual situation, and thus to realize human welfare, *eudaimonia*. The function of the intelligent or "prudent" man, *ho phronimos*, and hence of the good or the "moral" man, is never to create the havoc that comes from acting on universal moral or political "principles," never to be so stupid as to "follow the right, *ruat caelum*," but rather, to make the very best he can out of every situation. (268-269)

Boy, is <u>this</u> wrong!—both of A. and of Randall. <u>What</u> is "acting intelligently"? <u>Whose</u> "eudaimonia"?

Eloquent nonsense, both by Aristotle and by Randall.

Chapter 13: The Productive Sciences: Knowing How to Make Things

Perhaps Plato, with a premonition of aesthetic discussion and its terrors, judged it wiser not to talk about art, but to illustrate it. He does say, in the *Ion* and elsewhere, that <u>poetry is a kind of divine inspiration, or madness, hardly to be given a rational explanation</u>, thus anticipating the Romantic philosophy of the artist as inspired prophet and divine creator. (273)

Plato did not "anticipate" it—he <u>started</u> it. (This is like Toohey's "anticipation" of a public trend—in the movie of "The Fountainhead.")

[F]or Aristotle there is no distinction at all between what have come to be called in modern times the so-called "fine arts" and the "practical arts." Such a distinction would have been quite unintelligible to a Greek thinker. For Aristotle and the Greeks, the "artist" is a maker, a craftsman, like the shipbuilder or the physician. The different and separate arts are distinguished only by the fact that they make different kinds of thing: the shipbuilder makes ships, the physician makes health, the poet makes plays. Good ships, good health, and good plays are all a delight to behold, because each does something well: the ship sails and parts the waves, the tragic poem arouses pity and fear, and thus purifies the soul. The effect in each case is "an innocent joy and pleasure." (278-279)

(All this is <u>primitive</u> thinking— and disastrously bad psychology, on the part of Aristotle.)

<u>That which is not in excess is good</u>; and also that which many aim at and compete for, and that which is praised. Generally speaking, all that is

"A little bit of lying"? or "of pregnancy"?

deliberately chosen is good. (282)

Just plain nonsense on the part of A.

[*Quote from* Rhetoric *I, ch. 7:*] That which men of practical intelligence (*hoi phronimoi*), either all, or more, or the best of them, would judge, or have judged, to be a greater good, must necessarily be such, either absolutely or in so far as they have judged as men of practical intelligence (*phronêsis*). The same may be said in regard to everything else; for nature, quantity, and quality of things are such as would be defined by science (*epistêmê*) and practical intelligence (*phronêsis*). (282)

Primitive thinking—and, in fact, B.S.

[*Quote from* Rhetoric *I, ch. 10:*] Now wish (*boulêsis*) is a desire for the good, for no one wishes for anything unless he thinks it good. . . . (284)

Good God!

Tragedy . . . must be "universal," not in dealing with universal types, as the neo-Classicists of the seventeenth and eighteenth centuries misinterpreted Aristotle, but in being "intelligible," in making us understand, in exhibiting men, as it were, *sub specie aeternitatis*. (290-291)

No! In presenting principles of human conduct.

[*In her notes, Ayn Rand presented the following summary of the last part of Chapter 13, section 3 ("How to Write a Tragic Poem"):*]
Good ideas by A. on literature: poetry as more important than history—men "as they ought to be"—plot as the most important element of a play—"characters exist 'for the sake of action,' not vice versa." (R.)

Chapter 14: The Heritage of Aristotle

But a logic that had literally no relevance to ontology, to what there is, would be about as "meaningless" an enterprise as the wit of man could devise. (296)

Good line of R.'s.

Knowledge is a matter of language and saying, of words and sentences, of verbalized distinctions and of precise statements. It is not a mere opening of the eyes, a looking and seeing—though it must start from and be about what we can see. This is why it is so difficult to translate what Aristotle is saying into any other tongue, and also why what his Greek says seems usually so clear.

No!

Good, but—?

This emphasis on language makes Aristotle seem exceedingly relevant today, when we likewise start out from a critique of other men's language. But Aristotle's view of language is naturalistic, like that of Dewey and Mead, and not the supernaturalistic view that language is something imposed on nature from above—from the Oxford English dictionary, perhaps. (298-299)

Good!

Clearly Aristotle did not say everything; though without what he first said, all words would be meaningless, and when it is forgotten they usually are. (300)

Good!

[L]ogos is an art, a *technê*: it rearranges and manipulates, in constructing its products, sentences and questions and the rest; though what it makes it makes out of discovered materials. (300)

"Logos" is not just language—it is reason, (and language is its necessary tool). Their problem is the nature and validation of "concepts." (But if they could see that, their "problem" would cease to exist.) Is my epistemology needed!

[O]n all these fundamental matters it is the Aristotelianism of Aristotle that will tell us where to set out. And with Aristotle as a guide—perhaps the Aristotle who did not forget Plato but also remembered the world—did Plato ever forget it?—we may hope to arrive at last where he so often arrives himself in the end, at the Platonic *nous* which he shared to the full—the imaginative vision of truth. (300)

Why do they all bow to mysticism, such as an "imaginative vision of the truth"? Fear of the religionists—or plain whim-worship—or both?
("They are not placating the other side—they are the other side."—LP) [Leonard Peikoff]

Wilhelm Windelband, *A History of Philosophy, vol. 1: Greek, Roman, and Medieval,* James H. Tufts, trans. (New York: Harper & Brothers, 1958)

This book was favorably reviewed by Leonard Peikoff in The Objectivist Newsletter, vol. 3, no. 9 (September 1964).

Part I: The Philosophy of the Greeks.

Chapter III: The Systematic Period.

11. The System of Idealism: Plato.

[T]he ground of the world of phenomena must be sought in the telic relation of this world to the Ideas. This relation Plato expressed by the idea of a *"world-forming God"* (demiurge) who formed or shaped out that which is not Being, *i.e., space,* "with regard to the Ideas." . . . Divine activity according to ends and natural necessity are set over against each other as explaining principles, on the one hand for the perfect, and on the other hand for the imperfect in the world of phenomena. (130)

If one substitutes "desires" for "ends" (i.e., "activity according to desires"), the motive becomes clear.

12. The Aristotelian Logic.

If now Aristotle asked how one can prove anything scientifically, i.e., in a manner universally valid and relating to true knowledge, he found that this could consist only in the *deduction of the particular from the general.* To prove scientifically means to state the grounds for the validity of what is asserted, and these are to be found only in the more general under which the particular is subsumed. (134)

No. It consists of reduction to philosophical axioms and to the self-evident perceptual data.

In all these investigations and the contrasts that appear in them, the chief question for Aristotle is that with regard to judgments; but in connection with this he treats also *concepts.* As a judgment is proved or deduced, by being concluded from more general judgments, by means of the middle term, so a *concept is deduced or derived* by being formed from a more general concept (the next higher class or *genus*) by adding a particular characteristic mark or *difference.* This deduction of the concept is *definition.* (137)

Oh, no!
The exact opposite is true.

No!

13. The System of Development: Aristotle.

Discussing the Prime Mover: The highest Being
or Essence, thus determined according to its relations, is also characterised by Aristotle as regards its content. Such an activity, related to no
possibility, resting purely within itself (*actus
purus*), is thought, and thought alone; not, of
course, that mental process which applies itself to
individual things and their changing phenomena,
but the *pure thought*, which is employed with it-
self and its eternal nature; that thought which pre-   This is a glorious metaphor.
supposes nothing else as an object, but has itself
for its constant, unchanging content, the thought
of thought,—*self-consciousness*.

    In these conceptions, so determined, dwells   And that's the disaster. (W.W. is
a significance of mighty import for the world's   wrong here, in the case of
history. On the one hand, monotheism was here-   Aristotle.)
with conceptionally formulated and scientifically
grounded; on the other hand, it passed over from
the pantheistic form, which it had with
Xenophanes, and even still with Plato, into the
theistic form, since God is conceived of as a self-
conscious being different from the world. But
besides this *transcendence*, the doctrine that *God
is the absolute mind or spirit (Geist)* involves at
the same time the metaphysical advance that the
immaterial, the incorporeal pure Being, is made
equivalent to the spiritual. *Spiritual monotheism*
is the ripe fruit of Grecian science. (145-146)

Etienne Gilson, *The Unity of Philosophical Experience* (New York: Charles Scribner's Sons, 1937)

> What follows are not marginal comments, but notes from Ayn Rand's journal, dated June 19, 1945. Where these comments are not fully intelligible on their own, the passage she was commenting on is provided. Otherwise, they are presented as they were found in her journal.

[Ayn Rand began with the following remarks. Though she did not indicate what passage she was commenting on, these are likely general comments on Chapter 1 ("Logicism and Philosophy"), which ends with the idea that reason and logic, though important for philosophy, are by themselves "lifeless and barren."]

All the errors which [Isabel Paterson] ascribes to the destruction of Christian philosophy were committed—and with the same consequences—long before that destruction. Christian philosophy was open to and had the same faults. The basic error—the denial of reason and man's dignity—was there.

Chapter 2: Theologism and Philosophy

Using reason against reason in behalf of religion is by itself a legitimate, and eventually a noble, attitude; yet, if we adopt it, we must be ready to face its necessary consequences. (33-34)

If the fool understands the consequences—how can he call such an attitude "legitimate" and "noble"?

If, as seems to be true, mystical life is one of the permanent needs of human nature, it should not only be respected, but protected against the too frequent assaults of superficial minds. (35)

If "need" is an argument in favor of the truth of anything—this is pragmatism. (And, incidentally, who decides on what is a superficial mind?)

[The following are some of the basic tenets of the Islamic Asharites, a sect of Muslim theologians founded by Al Ashari (873-935) who, among other things, denied causality. Their goal was to defend religion against philosophy.] The first proposition was that all things are composed of atoms. . . . Not only are their atoms invisible, but they have no magnitude [and thus] have neither shape nor size of their own. . . . Moreover they are not eternal, but created by God when it pleases Him. (42)

The religious doctrine of the Islamic Asharites is pure "dialectic materialism," only it's not materialistic—it's a dialectic "spiritualism": God creates things constantly, everything changes, nothing is real or absolute. God moves your hand —you do not move it, which is a total denial of free will.

[Discussing St. Bonaventura, Gilson writes:] [M]an alone has been created with a knowing mind and a loving heart, in order that, by knowing and loving all things in God, he might refer them to their origin, which is at the same time their end. . . . [T]he ultimate meaning of our arts and tech-

St. Bonaventura preached that the end and meaning of Man is to "symbolize" God on a lower plane; God is the end and goal of Man. This is making Man a means to an end.

niques, of our various sciences and of philosophy itself, is to symbolize on a lower plane the perfection of the divine art and of the divine knowledge. (49-50)

[Bonaventura held] that God has created all things present and future at the very instant of creation. (53)

St. Bonaventura preached complete <u>determinism</u>—God created everything in the beginning as it was to be forever—the first seed of anything contained all that was to follow.

<u>Page 54</u>: The whole aim of Medieval philosophy seems to have been to reconcile reason and God. If God meant Truth—they put every obstacle in their way to the knowledge of Truth, by allowing the concept of God to [supercede and thus] destroy reason, which is man's only means to the discovery and knowledge of truth.

<u>Page 57</u>: It seems as if all these philosophers simply gape at the phenomenon of consciousness and reason—and instead of studying it, understanding it and accepting it for what it is, they have to ascribe it to a mystical, mysterious miracle of God, never to be understood by us. They are doing—in relation to man's spirit—the same thing savages did in relation to nature: they have to invent demons instead of accepting facts. (This is one of the reasons why physical science progressed, but ethics never got anywhere. Man is the hardest thing for man to understand. Rationality has triumphed everywhere—except in relation to man. That still seems to be the field of hocus-pocus.)

Chapter 4: The Breakdown of Medieval Philosophy

<u>Page 97</u>: The skepticism of the end of the Middle Ages—the idea that "philosophy can prove nothing"—was brought about by the desire to save theology from philosophy. This is one example of the "Rand Law"—of how and why, once you put something, <u>anything</u>, above reason, you destroy all reason eventually. There can be no compromise on this question. <u>There can be no "mixed economy" of the spirit</u>. Once you have accepted the possibility of a compromise between two diametrically opposed, mutually-destructive conceptions—such as Reason and Faith—you have destroyed the validity of all clear, positive, absolute concepts, the validity of the mere definition of being, of existence as an entity which is what it is, you have destroyed both reality and consciousness. And the destruction will show up, sooner or later, to destroy you. The recognition of an <u>entity</u> is <u>the first absolute</u>. (The difficulty here, of course, is in defining the entity—to establish what it is and to cut it from what it is not.)

Chapter 11: The Breakdown of Modern Philosophy

Whatever else it may be, Communism is emphatically *not* a scepticism. I wish I could make

Here is a crucial quote to show the worthlessness of the whole

clear that I am not here alluding to the spirit of <u>heroism</u> and self-sacrifice by which the <u>noblest</u> among its representatives were and <u>still are</u> animated. (289)

Catholic ethics (if Gilson is its valid representative—and he must be, being a thinker and a Thomist). Here is the basic error that made all the rest impotent. And this was written in 1936-37! ("Still are"!?!)

Friedrich Paulsen, *Immanuel Kant: His Life and Doctrine*, translated from the Revised German Edition (1902) by J.E. Creighton and Albert Lefevre (New York: Fredrick Ungar Publishing Co., 1963)

Ayn Rand discussed this book in her article "From the Horse's Mouth," The Ayn Rand Letter, vol. 4, no. 1 (October 1975), which has been reprinted in Philosophy: Who Needs It. *At the beginning of the essay she wrote: "Paulsen is a devoted Kantian; but, judging by his style of writing, he is an honest commentator—in the sense that he does not try to disguise what he is saying...." At the end of the piece, she noted: "If Paulsen is a representative of the nineteenth century, the twentieth never had a chance."*

[W]e may distinguish two fundamental forms of philosophy: I shall name them with Kant the *dogmatic* and the *critical*. The essence of dogmatic philosophy consists in the fact that it undertakes to found faith upon knowledge; it seeks to demonstrate what is to be believed. (2)

> Boy, what a set-up!
>
> Good God Almighty! What an inversion!

Now, the real purpose of the critical philosophy, the philosophy of Kant, is to overcome the opposition which has extended through the entire history of human thought. Kant undertakes with positive dogmatism to restore the agreement between faith and knowledge. In the last resort, however, he establishes this agreement by means of a philosophy of morals, not by means of a philosophy of nature. In this way, he is able to grant to negative dogmatism its right to a free, unprejudiced investigation of the entire world of phenomena. (4)

> This is the key to Kant's success.

[T]he critical philosophy solves the old problem of the relation of knowledge to faith. Kant is convinced that by properly fixing the limits of each he has succeeded in furnishing a basis for an honorable and enduring peace between them. Indeed, the significance and vitality of his philosophy will rest principally upon this. Although in the details of this philosophy there may be much that is not agreeable to us, it is its enduring merit to have drawn for the first time, with a firm hand and clear outline, the dividing line between knowledge and faith. This gives to knowledge what belongs to it,—the entire world of phenomena for free investigation; it conserves, on the other hand, to faith its eternal right to the interpretation of life and of the world from the stand-

> And it leads to the 20th Century, to Hitler and Stalin, as its necessary, logical climax!

point of value. (6)

To this [i.e., Paulsen's own] interpretation of the Kantian philosophy there are opposed two other views. Criticism is combated by two forms of dogmatism. Though opposed to each other, they agree in their unfavorable opinion of Kant. Negative dogmatism accuses him of treachery to knowledge; positive dogmatism, of yielding the rights of faith. (7)

> What a sewer of contradictions!
>
> (But it's true that Kant is a lousy middle-of-the-roader who made mysticism respectable.)

[*Paulsen briefly discusses the Catholic condemnation of Kant.*] There can be no doubt that this condemnatory judgment regarding Kant is a direct consequence of the Catholic principle. The autonomy of reason and the infallibility of the dogma are evidently irreconcilably opposed. . . . *Philosophia celestis* [i.e., heavenly philosophy] has only one opposite, the *philosophia terrena* [i.e., earthly philosophy], unless one should oppose to it a *philosophia infernalis* [i.e., "infernal" philosophy], which, moreover, also stands in the same relation. Both are sisters born of arrogance and disobedience.

What attitude would Kant have taken towards such criticism? I think he would have accepted unconditionally the characterization *philosophia terrena*. (9)

> Of course—because that is what he wanted to destroy: reason and this earth.

[*Paulsen writes that although Catholic philosophy claims to be a perennial philosophy, it is, despite its revival, dead.*] Moreover, there still remains the question of whether continuance of existence is in general something of which a philosophy can boast. Perhaps fruitfulness is a better characteristic, and this the Kantian philosophy shows; it still gives rise to new systems of thought. Thomism, on the contrary, though of course a great achievement for its own time, yields to-day nothing except unfruitful repetitions. It does not set free the spirit, it enslaves it, which of course is just its intention. (11)

> The evil purpose comes through.
>
> The bastard!

From his youth [Kant's] bodily strength had been frail. He was small of stature and had a hollow chest cramping his lungs and heart. . . . He was not disinclined to society, and possessed a gift of lively and pleasing conversation, and moved eas-

> Like Toohey.
> [*See The Fountainhead*]

ily and lightly in the forms of polite society. He did not choose his society especially from the academic circle, but loved to mingle with people of the world, with office-holders, merchants, book-dealers, etc. (44)

It cannot be doubted also that Kant's sympathies were not with a monarchial and absolute form of government, but with a democracy, such as had just been established in North America. . . . (47)

> Good God, no!

In an oft-quoted passage from a letter to Mendelssohn, of April 8, 1766, Kant makes the following remark regarding himself: ". . . .The loss of self-respect, which arises from a sincere mind, would be the greatest evil that could ever happen to me, but it is quite certain that it never will happen." He adds: "It is, indeed, true that I think many things with the clearest conviction and to my great satisfaction, which I may never have the courage to say; but I will never say anything which I do not think." (53)

> ??!

> "The truth, but not the whole truth."

[Kant] governs his life according to principles, in moral as well as in economic and dietetic respects. He is the complete opposite of Rousseau. . . . Reason is everything, nature nothing, nothing but the substratum for the activity of reason. Kant himself evidently sat as a model for his moral philosophy: the man of rational will, who acts according to principles, is the perfect man. . . . Perhaps we may say that there is an inner relationship between Kant's ethics and the Prussian nature. The conception of life as service, a disposition to order everything according to a rule, a certain disbelief in human nature, and a kind of lack of the natural fulness of life, are traits common to both. It is a highly estimable type of human character which here meets us, but not a lovable one. (54)

> ??!

> That's not reason!

> !!!

> And not "estimable" either!

Kant has been often compared with Socrates. . . . There is a real kinship of character and thought between the two men. . . . The personal mission was dominant; external position and influence were of little importance. This was true even of authorship: Socrates never attempted it, and Kant was nearly sixty years old before he attained in-

> BS!

fluence as an author. And this came almost without his seeking; it is seldom that a book has been written with so little thought of the reader as the *Critique of Pure Reason*. (55)

True, but not in the sense he means.

The internal form of instruction corresponded with the external. It was not dogmatic and scholastic, but zetetic and critical: it did not seek to lay down and inculcate ready-made philosophical doctrine, but to afford direction to investigation and independent thought. . . . The presupposition of this procedure is that philosophy is not a completed system. That was the conviction on which the traditional scholastic instruction proceeded. . . . Kant from the very beginning opposed this conception with the new view, which he announces [in his *Logik*] as follows: "Philosophy cannot be learned, as mathematics, physics, and history can be learned; but one can learn only to philosophize. One reason why philosophy cannot be learned is that it does not yet exist as a complete and universally recognized science. Every philosophical thinker builds his system upon the ruins of another. . . ." [*Paulsen adds:*] A philosophy which is 'learned' would cease to be a philosophy, and would be merely 'historical' knowledge, not philosophy.

Good God!

!!

It is the age of the illumination which speaks to us in these words. To lead students from a state of pupilage to independent thought was the task that the universities began to set before themselves. (61)

No! This is scepticism as anti-concept for "independent thought."

[Kant's] thinking was scholastic: it was not intuitively contemplative, but logically constructive. The energy of logical thought predominates over the tendency to resign one's self to the perception of things. . . . Kant brings to his view of things a dominating and imperious *a priori* understanding. This understanding does not wait upon things: things must conform to its concepts. It makes logical dichotomic or trichotomic division, into which things are compelled to fit without much thought whether the classification is adapted to them or not, or allows the true relations of their members to appear. Thus it may happen that thoughts are obscured and darkened. Or, on the other hand, thoughts may be built up

Fine summary.

merely for the sake of rounding out the treatment,
and thus <u>many parts of a system which appear
most stately and magnificent may be like the ar-
tificially inserted branches of the fir trees sold at
the Christmas fair.</u> (67)

Very well I remember that on first reading the
Critiques I often came to a stand, disheartened
and discouraged. <u>My experience was not unusual. I venture to say that there are not a few
persons who, when they first attempt to read the
Critique of Pure Reason, doubt the possibility of
understanding it, and then go on to doubt their
own capacity for understanding philosophical
books in general.</u> (73)

Here it is!

If an ordered world could, or rather must, have
arisen from the movements of given elements
according to merely natural laws, it is hereby
proved that the very "nature of things depends
upon and is determined by a significant rational
arrangement." (77)

Cheap BS!

It is Hume's problem, and also the problem of the
critical philosophy which is here formulated. <u>The
relation of cause and effect is not a logical rela-
tion</u>; the effect cannot be derived from the cause
by means of a logical process. (83-84)

Good God!
This makes <u>induction</u> non-
logical.

[Kant] defines philosophy as the "science of the
relation of all cognition to the essential aims of
human reason. . . ." In this sense, the philosopher
is "not a theorist who occupies himself with conceptions, but a <u>law-giver, legislating for human
reason</u>"; his completed manifestation is the ideal
of the sage. (111-112)

BS

Oh boy! Here's pure power-
lust.

A few years after the appearance of the *Critique
of Pure Reason*, K.L. Reinhold made the following remark in his *Letters upon the Kantian Philosophy*: "The *Critique of Pure Reason* has been
proclaimed by the dogmatists as the attempt of <u>a
sceptic who undermines the certainty of all
knowledge</u>;—by the sceptics, as <u>a piece of arro-
gant presumption that undertakes to erect a new
form of dogmatism upon the ruins of the previous
systems</u>;—by the supernaturalists, as <u>a subtly
plotted artifice to displace the historical founda-</u>

tions of religion, and to establish naturalism without polemic; —by the materialists, as an idealistic contradiction of the reality of matter;—by the spiritualists, as an unjustifiable limitation of all reality to the corporeal world, concealed under the name of the domain of experience; —by the eclectics, as the establishment of <u>a new sect, that for self-sufficiency and intolerance never had its equal</u>, and that threatened to force the slavish yoke of a system upon the neck of German philosophy, which had shortly before become free;—by the popular philosophers, finally, it has been sometimes called <u>a laughable endeavor, in the midst of our illumined and cultured period, to displace healthy human understanding by means of scholastic terminologies and subtleties derived from the philosophical world</u>. At other times, however, they have regarded it as <u>a peculiar stumbling-block, which had made impassable the path to popular philosophy, lately become smooth through so many easily intelligible writings;</u> and as <u>a rock upon which not only the understanding of hopeful youths, but also the philosophical reputation of celebrated men, had been already shattered.</u>"

All of this is true!

In a measure, this characterization of the reception which the critical philosophy experienced on its first appearance is applicable also to that which it still meets with even at present. (114-115)

And it's not enough!

[In Kant's theoretical philosophy, the antithesis to Metaphysical idealism is] the atheistic materialism which regards the corporeal world as the absolute reality, and <u>mechanism as its absolute law</u>. (116)

<u>This</u> package-deal is the destroyer of reason.

The first reviews of [the *Critique of Pure Reason*] by Garve-Feder and Mendelssohn [referred to Kant as] <u>the complete iconoclast</u>. (116-117)

True!

How is it thinkable that that which pure thought establishes as truth which is evident to it, is binding also for objective reality that exists independently of the understanding? Whence the objective (not merely logical) validity of such propositions of the pure understanding?

What do they think "pure" thought is?!

This is just the Kantian problem. That logical propositions possess logical validity—validity in the conceptual world—is evident, and it is likewise evident that experiential propositions possess objective validity. But the great problem is how propositions that are not based on experience, but on pure thought, can, nevertheless, possess validity for the objects of the world. Or is Hume right in saying that all such propositions are impossible? (140)

> This is the essential BS.

He finds the clue to the solution [to the above problem] in mathematics, the guiding star of all rationalistic epistemology. Geometrical propositions are, without doubt, pure truths of the understanding, not empirical generalizations. At the same time they possess objective validity. What the mathematician discovers by means of construction and calculation holds good for the corporeal world, and is verified by measurement. How does this anticipation of reality on the part of the understanding come about? How is the objective validity of mathematical judgments to be construed? Kant answers that it is because the space in which geometry projects its *a priori* constructions, that is to say, the space in our representation, is precisely the same space as that in which bodies are. <u>Space is not an empirical datum, but an original construction, a mere form of our perception and therewith of our perceptual world</u>. Bodies in space are nothing but objectified perceptions, and therefore they are subjected to the laws of perception; consequently, everything that geometry establishes for space and spatial representations in general holds good also for filled space or the corporeal world. Now the same principle, Kant discovers, is true of the laws of the understanding in general. (141)

> <u>This</u> is the vicious inversion, and the primacy of consciousness. Material reality is "constructed" by man's mind, but another, mystical (or noumenal) dimension is not!

> BS

True concepts as such have reality; every thinkable essence has at least an implicit claim to reality, a kind of half-reality. This is implied in its inner 'possibility.' When this claim is realized we have reality in the full sense. Wolff expresses this in the proposition: "Existence is the fulfilment of possibility. . . ." (143)

> What BS!

Jerome Rothstein, *Communication, Organization, and Science,* with a Foreword by C.A. Muses (Indian Hills, CO: Falcon's Wing Press, 1958)

Foreword, by C.A. Muses

Indeed only the arbitrary skepticism of a reductivist viewpoint—a skepticism as logically unwarranted as credulity—would attempt to assert otherwise, in the vain hope that <u>unsupported denials</u> should be any more scientific than unsupported affirmations. (lvi)

The denial of an unsupported affirmation <u>need not</u> (and cannot) be supported. ("Zero" premise.)

Thus the first dimension of time may be likewise partially represented as a fourth dimension of space, whereby the juice enters the orange without passing through the skin by the simple expedient of its having *previously* entered through the stem before the rind sealed itself off at the stem in ripening. The interoperation of negative and positive time axes explains such phenomena. (lviii)

"Thus the miracle of a man entering a room without crossing the walls. P.S.: There were no walls." ("Shyster" premise.)

The quantized appearance of energy is necessitated by the wave-nature of time. <u>The waves of time breaking on the beach of occurrence, so to speak,</u> in releasing their energy create the effect of discrete particles or quanta of energy, while actually the source of the continuity of the phenomena lies in the wave itself. (lxii)

And <u>that's</u> a mathematician speaking! With all the precision of their proper science, <u>this</u> is the kind of sloppiness they permit themselves in philosophy. Even the lousiest poet knows that a metaphor is only a metaphor.

Until we cease desiring love affairs with paradoxes we shall never know the grace of truth, which follows only upon the unremittingly vigilant determination to omit nothing that exists from the framework of our conceptions, no matter how awkward that may be for our preconceptions. (lxiii)

True—but does <u>he</u> observe this rule in <u>his</u> kind of epistemology?

There is a further ambiguity as to units, and we write algebraically $1^3 = 1^2 = 1$, although geometrically it is not correct to state that a unit cube equals a unit square or a unit length. (lxvii)

And why doesn't the gentlemen remember just <u>this</u>? This is an example of mathematical-philosophical equivocation: 1^3 taken as a measure <u>does</u> mean <u>1</u> cubic measure.

<u>Even the phobia against considering the scientific importance of feelings is itself a feeling.</u> Far from

<u>There</u> is the formal "whim-worshipper."

being irrelevant to logic, feelings are the prime basis in all human activity—including science—for selection among alternatives of otherwise equally acceptable premises. And premises underly all logical demonstration. (lxxii)

And <u>what</u> equivocation!

Thus, in the empirical realm of human observation a two-valued logic is far less realistic than a three-valued system containing a 'Yes,' a 'No,' and an immense 'Maybe' reaching over a vast number of data, each tagged with a thus-far-ascertained probability. On the other hand, a two-valued logic becomes far more appropriate for data within a strictly limited and specifically defined universe of discourse, or, more generally put, for data on which full information is available or accessible; in other words, for informationally closed systems. It is worth noting in this connection that pure noise also exists only for informationally closed systems, and may be alternatively defined as irrelevancies with respect to those systems. Otherwise, there is no such thing as "pure" noise in an informational sense. Radio static may tell us about the ionosphere or even the stars, as in radio astronomy. . . . And thus the noise metamorphoses into information. (lxxv-lxxvi)

Oh God!

("Concrete-bound" premise and worse: setting up a straw man made of one concrete under a certain abstraction, in order to destroy the abstraction.)

[T]he U.S.A. and the U.S.S.R., for all their vaunted opposition, appear rather, by a common denominator of de-individualization, to be approaching each other psychologically; and hence in terms of their effects upon their component "cogs"—the forgotten individualities of the peoples. (lxxvii-lxxviii)

Equivocation and "package-dealing": the U.S.S.R. <u>is</u> in theory what it is in present practice—the U.S.A. at present is "de-individualized" only to the extent to which it is abandoning its own theory and adopting that of the U.S.S.R., namely collectivism.

[Ayn Rand's final comments on the Foreword:]
My guess as to the point at which the author will collapse into mysticism: statement on p. lxxxiii to the effect that there is "reason" in the process of writing poetry for "an electronic computer." The fact is that there <u>is</u>, and more: that such a process <u>is</u> performed by <u>an electronic computer</u> or its equivalent—by the subconscious, automatic functions of the brain. The conscious mind is the selector and the feeder of the material, the subconscious "files" are the "univac."

Preface

I think a scientist should be an out-and-out opportunist philosophically, using whatever tools or viewpoint he finds helpful. The theorist does this with mathematics; the experimentalist, with techniques. A theorist probing as deeply as he can should not hesitate to do the same with any other conceptual tool. (lxxxviii-lxxxviii)

("Subjectivism" and "floating abstractions.")

While I am willing to admit idealizations and abstractions, even to go along with the usual practice of making them the bricks from which theories are built, it does not follow that I believe they are the "realities" behind appearances. Idealizations of any kind are man-made constructs, and we must be very cautious in identifying them with things outside our heads. Because of the fuzziness of our pictures of the world imposed by observational limitations and the finiteness of our experience, there will always be an infinity of theories compatible with known data, and probably an infinity of kinds of idealized brick out of which to build them. (lxxxix)

("Pre-abstraction and pre-language stage")

(No concept of objectivity)

Some measure of objectivity can arise only if this information and the pictures based on it are interpersonal, i.e., communicable. (xc)

(The "collective" in place of the "objective.")

Purposeful behavior and theory of games emerge in a purely physical context. I feel it is not too much to believe that these powerful extensions of the entropy concept make biology understandable in principle on physico-chemical grounds. (xci-xcii)

(Here is the result of assuming the possibility of a "disordered" universe: a physical object obeying a law of nature is taken to be "purposeful." This is the return to the demonology of savages.)

My own philosophical viewpoint, if I have one consistent enough to merit the title, has been strongly influenced by the writings of Einstein and Bohr, also by Mach, Poincaré, Russell, Weyl, von Neumann, Pauli, Dirac, and Bridgman; very much by the laboratory; by a considerable exposure both to technology and to administrative and organizational problems; by democratic and ethico-religious values; by aesthetic considerations; and by wide and unsystematic reading about things as diverse as astrophysics and an-

(This sort of thing should, among rational men, disqualify any writer then and there. I must ask Mr. Muses what he would say to me if I wrote the following in a preface to a book on physics by me: "My own scientific viewpoint has been strongly influenced by Norman Vincent Peal, Walter Winchell, Pres. Eisenhower, Billy Graham,

thropology, religion and rheology, semantics and seismology, <u>zoot suits and zoology.</u> (xciii-xciv)

Korzybski and Elsa Maxwell, by a considerable exposure to television, automobiles and the organizational problems of ladies' clubs; by socialistic and fortune-telling values; by vaudeville-show considerations; and by a wide skimming through such publications as the Wall Street Journal, the Sears-Roebuck catalogue, the Ladies' Home Companion, racing forms and comic strips."

<u>This</u> is how he approaches <u>philosophy</u> and the matter of undercutting all human knowledge.

I am also grateful to the many colleagues, friends, and associates with whom I discussed the work. The contribution of my daughter Louise should be mentioned: <u>many of her endless queries at the age of seven or eight went right to the heart of more than one question discussed here.</u>
   This book was written under trying circumstances. My father-in-law, Dr. Joseph Weinrebe, made it possible for me to write it in spite of them. The faith and love of my wife, children, and parents were an unfailing source of strength, as were many loyal friends and relatives. (xcvi)

(I'm sure he needed her—and I mean it!)

It is indecent to write the above in a scientific work: he does not speak of any intellectual or scientific helps, but of <u>emotional</u> reassurance. It is not facts and existence that interest him, but himself playing the role of a scientist. So he needed "faith and love" for the "strength" to write a 110-page book?

Chapter 2: Measurement and Communication

<u>When we make a measurement, we use some kind of procedure and apparatus for</u> choosing a <u>given result or results from the ensemble of possible results.</u> (8)

"Rube Goldberg" epistemology

He equates the discovery of a fact (such as the result of a measuring process) with a "<u>choice</u>." Thus, if given 2 + 2, he "<u>chooses</u>" the answer 4.

[*Ayn Rand's final comments on Chapter 2:*]
One clue to the epistemology of logical positivism: Instead of the Aristotelian, rational method of proceeding from concretes to an abstraction, they are literal Platonists who start with an undefined abstraction and then attempt to define (or Plato's "to recognize") concretes by means of that abstract Zero. The sole <u>psychological</u> meaning of such epistemology is: the <u>Wish</u> (as a realistically undefined, floating abstraction), then the thought (the perception of reality) as determined by that Wish (meaning: a selective or <u>censored</u> perception of reality).

This would explain the arbitrary "construct" idea: since the Zero-abstraction can be anything, they declare that human perception is only a matter of manipulating thought in such a way as to arrive at that non-A wish.

(One proof of this: the definition of a mathematical <u>unit</u> as part of a <u>group</u>.)

Chapter 3: Information and Thermodynamics

[W]e can observe a clock and acquire information about the passage of time. The paradox is only apparent, however, and is resolved as follows. When we make observations, our interest centers on objects forming but a part of the totality of things involved in the measurement. After the observation has been made, more information is available concerning the object of interest, but at the expense of an entropy increase in the wider totality of which the object is part. For example, looking at a clock involves illuminating it so that one can note its indication. The light used cannot be radiation in temperature equilibrium with the clock, for then the clock would be invisible. The entropy increase of the light more than compensates for the information gained about the clock. (15-16)

If I get this gibberish correctly, it seems to mean the following: every time you learn anything, you do so at the expense of things you have <u>not</u> learned, so that any gain in knowledge increases one's ignorance— ignorance of the unknown and unspecified; or you cannot learn <u>everything at once</u>.

[*Ayn Rand's Summary of Chapter 3:*]
Another clue: these gentlemen seem to proceed not from the known to further knowledge, but in reverse: they take the <u>unknown</u> as a start and deduce the known from that—by a kind of "<non> Heliotrope" method.

Chapter 4: Information, Logic, and Physics

<u>A fundamental distinction between science and other logical disciplines is the priority given by the former to observation.</u> (19)

Which are the "logical disciplines" that do <u>not</u> give priority to observation? And by <u>what means</u> is observation made in science?

The theory of relativity pointed this [i.e., the fact that a theory cannot be accepted if its predictions do not square with experience] out in a striking manner, showing that Euclidean geometry, hallowed by centuries of use, gave a less perspicacious description of the physical world than could be afforded by Riemannian geometry. It is now agreed that no geometry has a priori validity for physics, but rather that world geometry is a physical theory whose "truth" resides in successfully coordinating experience. (19-20)

> Oh bosh!

> Context-dropping

> By what means?

Much of the applicability of algebra can be ascribed to the empirical existence of objects in the world on which one can perform operations or transformations satisfying algebraic postulates, much as the rigid body satisfies the postulates of Euclidean geometry. (20-21)

> So algebra owes its success to the existence of objects that satisfy it—rather than: algebra owes its success to the objects. (Verbal cause-and-effect reversal.)

We feel that ascribing to observation as fundamental a role as logic itself is not putting the cart before the horse at all. We are born with both measuring and thinking equipment, and the latter does not develop without a tremendous information input provided by the former. Theories develop when a body of experimental data awaits rational explanation and organization. In their application to the world, logic and mathematics, like world geometry, are physical theories. (24)

> So "measuring" is a separate faculty and one measures without thinking? By what means does one measure or observe without logic or thought? ("Stolen concept" premise)

> !!!

Reichenbach has developed a three-valued logic for quantum mechanics admitting the truth values true, false, and indeterminate. His motivation is that if a component of the momentum of a particle say, is known, the corresponding co-ordinate cannot be considered as simultaneously having a definite (though unknown) selection from its possible values without encountering well-known difficulties of interference of probabilities. (25)

> If I got the hogwash correctly, logic must go when it interferes with "probabilities."

Destouches has shown that two theories can always be fused into one by modifying logic; the modifications have the sole effect of prohibiting certain arguments otherwise allowable. (26 n.4)

> There it is! "Allowable"? By whom? By what standard, once you "modify" logic? Any fact can always be explained by "modifying" language; any proof can be given by rewriting history!

We think it possible that extended or generalized logics may be useful in science should it ever be necessary to take into explicit account things which are operationally undefined, so that the usual class or ensemble defining properties are not at hand. (26-27)

(That's the defining by means of actions instead of entities.)

[O]ne might conclude that logics other than two-valued logics are superfluous as far as scientific reasoning is concerned. This impression is strengthened when one recalls how far the nature of measurement and communication goes in forcing a two-valued logic upon us. However, if the number of prohibited arguments grows sufficiently large, and the relations between them are sufficiently opaque, a new system in which they are automatically taken care of may become a tremendous "notional convenience" and therefore useful. The historical, heuristic, and practical importance of convenience must not be underestimated. One can preserve Euclidean geometry in general relativity, for example, by using a space of high enough dimensionality. (27 n.5)

Translation: "if the number of irrational arguments grows sufficiently large and the relations between them are sufficiently unintelligible, a new system which will automatically declare them to be rational will be tremendously convenient to the _empirical_ scientist who is thus set free of reality—as well as to any mystic, whim-worshipper and dictator."

Einstein's viewpoint is that quantum mechanics deals only with statistical aggregates or ensembles of similar systems, the concept of a single system with an objective existence in space and time having no place in the theory. He considers quantum mechanics to be an incomplete theory because he believes a complete theory would give a place to the "real" existence of a single system in space and time, and would yield present quantum mechanics as logical inferences. Bohr, and the majority of physicists with him, say that only the operationally defined has physical meaning: that the notion of physical reality must not be considered as independent of the means of observing reality; that Einstein's approach would entail the introduction of operationally undefined elements, and would be incompatible with quantum mechanics. Einstein thinks the majority viewpoint leads to a kind of sophisticated solipsism. (27-28 n.6)

Here is where the good empiricists become plain old fashioned "rationalists": if reality presents them with things which are "operationally undefined," reality must go— it must not touch the "system," it must fit one's whims ("definitions") or else.

One is tempted to speculate that fields such as the social sciences and psychology, where many fundamental phenomena are inaccessible to direct

Brother, are there plenty who are so tempted today. Soviet Russia, for one.

experimentation, might find some use for non-Aristotelian logic. (27-28)

Chapter 5: Language, Science, and Art

What is the meaning of a word? One cannot answer the intent of this question with a dictionary, for the problem then becomes that of ascribing meaning to words offered as substitutes for the original one. Semanticists say words have no meaning apart from the experiences they symbolize. . . . Experience—unsophisticated, unsystematic, groping and inexact in the child—is codified into the symbols of language and stored in his memory in a more systematic, exact way as he continues to live and learn.

> Boy, oh boy, oh boy! Really? What about building from primaries to complex abstractions?
>
> "Experience" instead of "perception."
> By whom? How?

    The meaning of physical concepts arise in the same way. The scientist develops extended senses by the use of measuring apparatus, capable of finer classifications, which gather his data (extensions of sense impressions). (30)

> I fully believe it—of him; his concepts are formed as by a child in a pre-language stage.
>
> Nice little equivocation! Sense impressions cannot be "extended" without thinking, which means: without abstractions, which means: without language (and without identity).

It is easy to see the parallelism between the descriptive and ordinary communicative functions of language and science; the analogue of artistic aspects is a little less obvious. I do not feel qualified to give a valid definition of what constitutes great art, but I do respond to much of it and have felt much the same response to many things in science. I find a great poem, for example, evokes far more than the mere sense of the words composing its text. . . . How often does a great poem seem to open up grand new vistas, to stir up thoughts we had never thought before, to give rise to a multitude of new cross references in the catalogue of our experience so that we see as if with new eyes, and to become thereby a memorable experience in itself! But does not a great scientific synthesis do the same thing? When one has labored long and finally grasps the scope of Maxwell's equations of the electromagnetic field

> And here is the union of the mystics of spirit and muscle—or "the drunken bookkeeper premise"—or simply the "Shyster premise," the "context-dropper" because it would be so "inconvenient" to try and identify every clause and step that goes into a work of art.

..., then he has had an essentially artistic vision, and the equations are the highest poetry rather than the dry, prosaic symbols of an uninspired text. (31-32)

Great syntheses and far-reaching theories do not exhaust the artistic elements in science by any means. Just as the composer needs the virtuoso to decipher the funny little marks he makes on oddly ruled paper and convert them into a vibrant experience for an audience of music lovers, so does the theorist need the experimentalist to translate his funny little marks into tangible apparatus serving to confront his concepts with quantitative test. The audience of scientists applauds the conclusive experiment and the successful theory, the scientific paper at a meeting or in a journal replacing the concert-hall performance. (32-33)

Good God!

And that is proof!

No, the vaudeville or burlesque performance.

Chapter 6: Information, Organization, and Systems

[Ayn Rand's comments on Chapter 6, much of which is devoted to entropy:]
Another clue: if "entropy" is a measure of unavailable energy, then what they seem to do is to start all their concepts and calculations with a zero, on some such pattern as: "I need all the energy to be available (with no definition of energy or availability), therefore I will start by calculating how far I am from that absolute (and undefined) Wish."

Chapter 7: Theory of Organization of Observation and a System for Prediction

The function of engineering ... is not so much to understand the world about us as to control it. .... (46-47)

To control without understanding?

Engineering is a system whose input is the world as the engineer finds it and whose output is the world as the engineer wants it. This last statement seems like an exaggeration and an oversimplification. But if one broadens the definition of engineering so that it is synonymous with all branches of applied science (a cattle raiser is a zoological engineer, a truck farmer a botanical engineer, etc.) and the practical arts, then the engineers include a large part of the human race and the statement is less open to criticism. (47)

"Beef stroganoff is made up of wood and gasoline. This statement seems inaccurate, but if one broadens the definition of wood to include all solid matter, and the definition of gasoline to include all liquids, the statement is less open to criticisms."

[*Ayn Rand's summary of Chapter 7:*]
Another clue: if it is true in psychological epistemology, that a mind can handle only so much material at one time, then these people seem to indulge in the exact opposite of the process achieved by the power of abstraction; abstractions permit a mind to cover a wider and ever wider range of thought by means of a certain number of units of thought (concepts); these people clutter up their thinking in such a manner (and, I believe, consciously) that they feel they've achieved a lot by the time they say in ten indirect strings of verbiage that "the cat is on the mat." And another purpose here is that by the time a student of theirs has understood that the cat is on the mat, his mind has no room for anything else.

Chapter 8: Skill as Organization

An important reason why we have been able to make so much progress in science and technology is because these fields are readily communicable, thus can become interpersonal (and so objective) and can be recorded and largely freed of dependence on the lives of individuals. (50)

(The substitution of the "collective" for the "objective." If "interpersonal" means "objective," then any fortune-teller and client are engaged in an objectively valid occupation, as objectively valid as that of any scientist.)

[The skillful person] cannot (yet) communicate his skill to posterity except through direct and rather prolonged contact, and only partially even then. His field thus has relatively little capacity for cumulative growth. (52)

Because there is no further place for it to grow, you idiot! It's limited by <definition>.

Clue and open confession: this gentleman thinks that the recorded knowledge of others, larger than his own brain's "storage capacity," can be used by him and become his "reflex." He hasn't the faintest idea of what the process of abstraction is and of the fact that knowledge is of no value whatever unless a mind grasps it and "stores" it from scratch. (The knowledge of others only helps us with the process of discovery.)

[The scientist's] long-and short-term memories, instead of being entirely contained in one brain and subject to the limitations on information storage capacity appertaining thereto, are as large as the labors and libraries of mankind care to make them. We hope the time will come when the same can be said for any skill, and think this possible in principle. For all skills are organized segments of experience and so should be representable in symbolic form, the meanings of the symbols being essentially operational, as in ordinary language or science. (53)

Language is not "operational," but exclusively Aristotelian (entity-based).

[*Ayn Rand's final comments on Chapter 8:*]
This whole chapter is the work of an amateur-savage running wild over the field that deals with human epistemology.

Chapter 9: Miscellaneous Applications of the Organization Concept

It is interesting to see what new insight can be gained about some of the subjects earlier considered, and a few new ones, when the idea of organization is used. Take language in its descriptive functions. Suppose I see something I want to describe to you. I map a set of visual impressions (after strong filtering action, for what I see depends on my previous experience) into a set of sounds; you hear the sounds and map them into a set of corresponding memory impressions which the sounds evoke. (54-55)

Another clue: these people take their "hunches," "stomach feelings" or any "back-seat-driving" notice as a scientific hypothesis and proceed to build "constructs" upon it.

Nice way to get around the concept of abstracting! Just how do "sound impressions" get to evoke "visual impressions"?

To say that nobody can ever tell precisely how another feels is to say something incapable of refutation or verification; furthermore, nobody can ever tell how someone else hears or sees any more than he can tell how someone else feels. Introduction of feelings, i.e., "subjective" elements, thus does not seem to affect the organizational aspects of language. (55-56)

What is this? An argument for simply evading the issue?

Yes, it can be "verified" (proved); just what is meant by "feeling" and by "knowledge."

To bring order into chaos, to separate the sea and dry land from some undifferentiated substrate, to form man from the dust of the earth, are part of a vivid poetic account of organizing the "formless void." (57-58)

Here's an example of "they want to be the God they invented who creates a universe out of a void by means of an arbitrary whim." When they approach a problem, they treat their material both as specific entities and as a non-A "void" to be shaped into something by their theory—correspondence to their theory being the standard of identification.

An important function religions perform for an adherent is to relate him to the universe and so to give him an inner security lacking in one who feels he is like a helpless cork aimlessly tossed by a blind tempest. In short, religion organizes him and his universe. It is easy to see from this

This passage is marvelous! Translation: science and religion had a common origin, in that they both use the same method, namely: to interpret reality according to their whims

how science and religion had a common origin, and why they often came later into conflict. Save for disputes involving fundamentalists (in both fields), the conflict seems to be largely resolved now by a kind of division of labor. Science deals with the universe insofar as it can be comprehended and measured, while religion is more concerned with purposes and values, i.e., determinants of conduct. Religion grapples with the problem of what is good for man no less than do medicine or engineering. (58)

("needs"). The division of labor now is as follows: science works to understand the universe, religion works to prescribe purposes and values without any understanding of the universe. Both activities are integrated by being "good for man." "Good," of course, requires no further definition.

Marilyn Van Derbur (a businesswoman and former Miss America) wrote Ayn Rand asking for information on motivation. In her letter of May 30, 1973, to Miss Van Derbur, Miss Rand wrote: "I recommend to your attention a very interesting book on this subject [i.e., 'inspiration']: How to Think Creatively by Eliot D. Hutchinson, which is a summation of his interviews with hundreds of writers, artists and scientists. The author is a psychologist; his thesis is: 'Inspiration comes only to those who deserve it.'"

Chapter 6: The Moment of Creation

What integrations of material they [i.e., creative minds] make, we can study. But what orients them toward the drama, poetry, the novel, what makes these the media in which their minds most freely move, we do not know except to equate them to the level of intuitive action and put a question mark after the expression. (152)

Their <u>basic premises</u>—their philosophical ideas about life and what they consider most important in life. They <u>would</u> have been equally good in <u>any other</u> creative field. But it is not a matter of "practicing" or "acquiring technique"—not a job which an average man could do by absorbing the techniques devised by others. It's a matter of <u>first-hand</u> judgment and independent rational connections. <u>This</u> is the point of difference between the creator and the second-hander.

Chapter 7: The Stage of Verification

The completion of the last part of a work is always difficult and never seems to come up to expectation. (190)

Completely untrue of me. The last part is always the easiest and best. The whole "dissatisfaction" business is untrue.

It is <u>not</u> a general rule.

[*Speaking of conferences, Hutchinson writes:*] To be effective the group must be small, with a submergence of individual ambition in the welfare of the whole. <u>Self-love</u> must be replaced by <u>sound and growing respect for the problem</u>, the conclusions of which must be accepted. (192)

<u>This</u> is an instance of the premise that "individual ambition" and "self-love" are not based on, but actually opposed to objective truth.

Creative thought is the history of effort, concep-

tion, attempt at solution, puzzlement, second be-
ginnings, gropings, drudgery, like the rough shaping of a block of marble. It is the story of new
and enheartening glimpses of the goal, of quick-
ening interest, of insight's mounting enthusiasm
and faster work—and then the difficult end. And
it is the history of these factors in multiple and
everchanging patterns. For this reason no one
will ever agree with his neighbor about the process. And for that reason in turn no one will ever
write the whole account, for it is written not in
words but in unfathomable experience. (196)

> This is nonsense. The details
> may vary, but the general
> principle can be discovered and
> stated. It's the whole essence of
> human consciousness that is
> involved here.

Chapter 8: Putting Insight to Work

Logic does not altogether suffice for establishing
formulations concerning the nature of ultimate
realities. The meaning of great truths is at times
best grasped through repeated insight. (197-198)

> Hell! Here's where he goes off
> into tripe. So far, he's spoken
> about insight as a grasp of
> logical reality—such as the
> solution of a scientific problem.
> An "insight" into something not
> verifiable by logic is pure drivel.
> How then do we know that it's
> true? Just because it "feels"
> true?

[O]ne may quite properly say that the formation
of belief, whether religious or not, employs the
principles of insight to a degree. The objects of
reference of such belief are always beyond proof
in the sense of exact demonstration. Belief to religion is what hypotheses is to science, the tool
by which further truth is unearthed. (225)

> Poor guy! He sure is honest,
> and doesn't know that he has
> here made mince-meat out of
> religion. There is no justification
> for religion or belief. At least
> this poor professor is a
> rationalist.

[S]uddenly in some moment when the larger
views seem unattainable and when certainty is
looked upon as the possession of the purely logical thinkers, comes a new insight into the nature
of experience, a new advance in personal conviction, an enheartening view of new reaches of
meaning. And that insight may reshape intellectual life or add stature and richness to one already growing. At any rate the task of testing the
insight is entered upon with enthusiasm, and
through it new levels of thought become the
background for further progress. The process will
yield nothing that is absolutely final, but an ever-
growing sub-structure of ideas which approach

> Here's the catch, brother!
> Creative insight produces a
> logical discovery. What happens
> in religious insight? If it
> produces a new thought that
> can be stated in logical terms—
> then it is merely a form of
> metaphysical thought. If not,
> then it is some form of essential
> self-fraud and self-indulgence,
> with pernicious results. A man
> merely got himself to feel
> certain about the unprovable,
> the vague, the wishful thinking

validity. It gathers no moss, though it may for the time being stand firm. (226-227)

of his original premises.

Unless a man will <u>sacrifice himself</u> *for* his own spiritual growth, he will sacrifice himself *of* it. He does not seek such achievement for prestige, for fame, or money, or any petty aim. He seeks it because he cannot help it, because his inner life finds self-realization therein. Art, science, religion—they are all ways to the interpretation of <u>that unity which is formed by the impingement of the *self* upon the *not-self*, the real</u>. (227)

He means here the creative action of the self in acquiring knowledge of objective reality and shaping it to his purposes. Why the talk about "sacrifice"? What can be more profoundly selfish? What in hell is the self without it?

John Hospers, *An Introduction to Philosophical Analysis* (New York: Prentice-Hall, Inc., 1953; 3rd ed., 1988)

John Hospers is a Professor of Philosophy who was interested in Objectivism in the early sixties, but who later became the first presidential candidate for the Libertarian Party. (There is an entire chapter devoted to Hospers in Letters of Ayn Rand, *edited by Michael Berliner.)*

In a letter to Hospers dated April 17, 1960, Ayn Rand wrote: "I am glad that you are reading Atlas Shrugged. *For my part, I am reading your* An Introduction to Philosophical Analysis. *I believe that this will give us both a firmer base for future discussions." In another letter (March 31, 1961) she wrote that although she disagreed with most of the content of his book, she noted a similarity in the way they presented their ideas.*

What follows are not, strictly speaking, marginal comments, but notes that Ayn Rand wrote while reading Hospers' book. To make them more intelligible, they are shown, where appropriate, alongside the passage she was commenting on. In other cases, they are presented separately as self-contained commentary as they were found in her notes.

Preface

In some cases the terms that have been introduced have been given a clarity and unambiguousness which they do not always possess in philosophical writing and discussion. . . . The only excuse for this is that without some definite pegs to hang his thoughts on, the reader who is new to philosophy would be lost. (vi)

What about the full-fledged philosopher? (re: "clarity and unambiguousness")

Chapter 1: Words and the World

I. The relation of words to things

Some things stand for others regardless of what human beings decide. [*Hospers calls these natural symbols.*] Clouds of a certain kind stand for rain—that is, they indicate that rain can be expected. . . . We have not invented or devised these relationships; they are already there—we merely find them and record them. (1)

"Clouds stand for rain"—plain equivocation. ("Natural symbols" is nonsense; "symbols" are a purely and exclusively epistemological matter.

Human beings have devised noises and made them into symbols. Unless people had taken and made them stand for things in the world, they would be *merely* noises, not words. (2)

Words as "noises." Why? Why not "sounds"?

The purest emotive words are the interjections:

(Look out! This is the definition

"hurrah," "phooey," "whoopee," and so on. Most emotive words are also used to stand for things, and therefore are impure examples of emotive words: "nasty," "beautiful," "contemptible." (3-4)

"Anybody can use any noise he wants to refer to anything he wants, as long as he makes clear what he is using the noise to refer to." This is the rule of freedom of stipulation. Its result . . . would be confusing if you made use of this freedom anywhere but on an island of which you were the sole inhabitant. (6)

"'Cats'" is a word which stands for the word "cats," which stands for cats. (10)

Words merely label things—they have no closer a relationship to the things than labels on bottles do to the bottles. Any label will do, so long as we agree upon it and use it consistently. (14)

II. Class words and classifications

Having class words is an enormous advantage from the point of view of economy of language. We can still talk about anything we want to with a language of a few thousand words that does not unduly tax our memory. (15-16)

Probably no two things in the universe are exactly alike in all respects. . . . Thus, even if two icicles were exactly alike in shape, size, and chemical structure . . . , we could call one, say, a "flep" and the other a "flup" because one was hanging from the north side of the house and the other from the west side. (18-19)

[T]here are probably no two things in the universe so different from one another that they do not have some characteristics in common which can be made the basis for membership in the

that will lead to making value-judgments "<u>emotive</u>" and subjective.)

"Freedom of stipulation"—<u>very</u> dubious concept (switch from <u>metaphysical</u> to <u>journalistic</u> issue). (Also: "confusion and inconvenience" are <u>not</u> the reasons for accepting "common usage." This is the removal of the man-made from the field of <u>objectivity</u>.)

When would <u>that</u> come up? (This is the infinite "<u>multiplication of entities</u>" in the realm of <u>consciousness</u>.) ("Metalanguage"?)

<u>Disaster</u>. (Words devised <u>only</u> for communication.) (Or: for economy, or for convenience.)

<u>Disaster</u>: "class words" (with "manageable language" as purpose)—instead of "abstractions" or "universals."

Consequences of disaster: words for "icicles"—we could <u>not</u> do that, neither neurologically, nor epistemologically. This is what happens when one takes language as a primary, without definition.

Here the subject goes haywire—"a special word for the fact that these things occurred to me in the last ten

same class. For example, a thought and a sandpile are vastly different, but both are "temporal entities," i.e., they occur in time. Triangles, trees, the square root of -1, running, and the relation of being above, though they belong in utterly different categories, have in common at least the fact that they have all been thought of by me in the last ten minutes! In practice this fact would hardly justify us in devising a class word to include all of them, but it could be done: we could use a noise, say "biltrus," and say that a biltrus is anything thought of by me. Often we do in fact build up wider and more inclusive classifications, such as "Guernsey," "cow," "mammal," "animal," "organism," "physical thing," "existing thing," each successive word applying to more and more particular things because the requirements for membership in the class are progressively fewer and less restrictive. (19)

> minutes!" —and this as a prelude to the widest universals, which are labeled as "less restrictive." (!)

Are there natural classes of things? The common characteristics which we take as criteria for the use of a class word are a matter of convenience. Our classifications depend on our interests and our need for recognizing both the similarities and the differences among things. (20)

> The "killer-tenet"—there are no natural classes of things—it's all arbitrary, it's a matter of "wishes" and "needs."

If we were more interested in the colors of creatures than in their shapes, or if animals always bred true to color but offspring of the same parents had a chaotic variety of shapes, sizes, number of legs, and so on, then, doubtless, we would consider classification by color more "natural" or more "right" than classification by any other means. (20)

> He mentions and rejects as "mere convenience" the classification we would use if color were the essential attribute of objects, on which other attributes "depended." (!) This is the "stolen concept."

Classes are in nature in the sense that the *common characteristics* can be found in nature, waiting (as it were) to be made the basis for a classification. On the other hand, classes are manmade in the sense that the *act of classifying* is the work of human beings, depending on their interests and needs. (21)

> Abstractions depend upon our "interests and needs"—curtains.

III. Defining characteristics and definitions

Of the two [i.e., denotation and designation], designation is by far the more important, for the

> "Package deal": how can one say that designation is more

characteristics which a word designates will determine what the particular things are which the word denotes. (25)

The issue, "When is it a table and when isn't it?" is a *verbal* issue—one which involves only the meanings of words, in this case the word "table." There is no dispute about the *facts*—whether the object can be painted, chopped to pieces, etc. Different people might witness the whole series of operations and yet disagree on "when it stopped being a table." Nor is the dispute clarified by assertions that "we are here searching for the *essence* of a table (or tablehood)" or that "we are trying to find *the real nature of* a table." (31)

To state a defining characteristic is to state a part of the meaning (definition) of a term; but to state an accompanying characteristic is to state some fact, not about the term itself (for the accompanying characteristic is no part of its meaning), but something about the thing named by the term. (34)

When you have stated the defining characteristics of X, you have proved nothing one way or the other about whether an X exists. In other words, if you know what the term "X" *designates*, you still know nothing about what the term "X" *denotes*. The word "horse" denotes many things, and the word "centaur" (a creature half man and half horse) denotes no things whatever, for there are no centaurs. But the meaning of the two words is equally clear. (36)

important than denotation— since, by his definition, the second is the result of the first and cannot be "unimportant," if it should contradict its own cause?

Disastrous equivocations: "when is it a table?" taken as merely a "verbal issue." Implications: definitions are arbitrary; the various states of the table cited have nothing to do with the dispute—that is, correspondence to the facts of reality is irrelevant.
(Throughout all of it, so far, the main equivocation is between the "noise" of words and the conceptual meaning.)

Enormous disaster! Issues of "defining characteristics" are verbal (!), but issues of accompanying characteristics are "factual." (The equivocations are too enormous to bother untangling!) The implication: defining characteristics are not factual (!!) (this is what comes from "context-dropping"!)

Boy, oh boy, oh boy! This is how equivocations grow: following the line that definitions are merely verbal issues, it is now stated that to state the defining characteristics of a thing is "to prove nothing about whether it exists." Example: centaurs. (What is dropped? —the fact that "characteristics" have to come from reality—that "definitions" are not "verbal and arbitrary" —and that concepts are hierarchical.) What a messy way to go about thinking! (Proof of the fact that one cannot start "analysis" in midstream or at any arbitrary point.)

You are the same person as you were ten years ago. . . , even though many things have happened to you in the interim, such as the replacement of every cell in your body by other cells. In general: many characteristics of a thing can change or disappear and be replaced by others, and the thing in question will still be that kind of thing as long as the defining characteristics continue to be present. (38)

To answer argument on this page: but if definitions are arbitrary, and if I choose the specific position of a molecule in a human body as my definition, then Heraclitus is right and language becomes metaphysically impossible.

In the case of organisms it is usually the form or shape of the thing that is defining: thus horses and cows have much the same chemical composition but differ in shape and contour, and this is the distinguishing mark between them. (39)

Horses and cows are distinguished by means of shape!!! Good God! (Are men and whales included in the category of mammals by means of shape?!)

[T]he meanings we give [words] are not clear and definite, only enough to suit our practical purposes, and sometimes hardly even that. We know roughly what characteristics we have in mind when we give a noise a designation, but we do not know as a rule *exactly* which ones we would consider essential and which we could do without. . . . "Don't the words really *have* more precise meanings, even if we don't know them?" The answer should now be obvious. Words have meanings only because we have *given* them meanings, otherwise they would be noises or pen-marks. And they have only *as much* meaning as we give them, no more. (47)

If the passage on vagueness (p. 47) were true, it would rule out all language as impossible, because subjective.

If someone defines "triangle" as a four-sided figure, meaning by this that the word "triangle" is used in English to stand for figures with four sides, this would be a false statement—it would be a false report about how a word in the English language is used. Reportive definitions are reports of word-usage, and there can be true reports and false reports. In this sense, then, definitions not only can be, but are, true or false. (52-53)

Here's the switch from the objective to the "collective": definitions can be true or false only when they are "reportive" of how "people" use words.

(In all these discussions, language is treated as if it were: "a thing plus a noise." The concept of "concepts" is evaded.)

No one ever found a definition that somebody before him had not given. (53)

This is preposterous! Infinite regress—without a "first physicist"? And what about a new science? What about a new invention, like TV? (Ask J.H. about this.) (The means to "find"—what meaninglessness!!)

Page 53: The abyss: in this casual, hasty, superficial manner—the objective meaning of words has been destroyed, i.e., language has been destroyed. First, he stated that words had to refer to things; now, after pages of overloading the reader with out-of-context details, he announces that definitions of words do not define things.

In this book . . . we shall speak only of defining words, not the things named by the words. There are, however, two kinds of definition of words which we may give: (1) word-word definitions, in which we say that a certain word means the same as a certain other word or words; (2) word-thing definitions, in which we say what characteristics a thing must have in order to be labeled by a word. It is word-thing definitions which we have been discussing so far. . . . In word-word definitions we merely relate the word to other words. For example, "dog" means the same as "chien." . . . [I]t is possible that someone might know about every word in one language and its equivalent in another language, without knowing what is designated by a single word in either. (54-55)

If so—what is language?

The concept of "word-word" definitions is nonsense. Finding synonyms is an accident of language and deals truly only with comparing noises; it is not a conceptual nor a philosophical issue. The concept of comparing words from two different languages, like "dog" means "chien," is pointless nonsense. And—to include the activity of a person who has memorized the translations of all the words from one language into another, without knowing what is designated by a single one of them, in the category of "language" is shameful equivocation (and context-dropping).

(In the above approach to the subject of language, the alleged "empiricists" are employing the methods of the worst of the primitive "rationalists": they pick up some concept at random and draw preposterous conclusions (by means of context-dropping), without referring to reality (or "experience"). If their analysis of language were true, language (i.e., thought, knowledge and communication) would be impossible; but they see that in reality language is possible, it exists and functions; yet this does not make them decide to check their premises and definitions—they decide that knowledge is impossible.)

The clearest and most precise way of relating a

He keeps talking of words in

word to the world is . . . to state what characteristics it designates. (55)

terms of "<u>characteristics</u>." How did we get to the stage of grasping "characteristics"?

Sometimes it is difficult or even impossible to state exactly what the word means, but we are able to take the whole sentence in which it is embedded and state what *it* means. Thus, we say what the word "brother" means if we say, "X is the brother of Y means that X is a male having the same parents as Y." This is known as a *contextual* definition of "brother.". . . (55)

Oh, good God almighty! "<u>Contextual definitions</u>" means that <u>some</u> words have no exact meaning outside of a context. . . . <u>This</u> is how they get around the fallacy of "the stolen concept."

IV. Sentences and propositions

Just as words are labels of things, think of sentences as labels of situations or *states-of-affairs*. (65)

(??) (Too vague a definition, which can become a "definition by non-essentials.")

Truth. A proposition is true when the state-of-affairs expressed by the sentence asserting it is *actual*, and false when it is not actual. The proposition expressed by the sentence "Snow is white" is true if, and only if, the situation it alleges is actual, that is, if snow really *is* white. . . . The mysterious-sounding question "What is truth?" asked by Pontius Pilate becomes the question "What are true propositions?" The answer is simply this: "A true proposition is one standing for a state-of-affairs which is actual.". . . There are different kinds of truth, that is, different kinds of true propositions, and the ways of discovering whether or not they are true are not always the same. (66)

<u>Center of the disaster</u>! The switch from: "What is true?" to "What are true propositions?" Next step: "What kind of truths (!) there are" depends on what kind of propositions men use. <u>This</u> is a reversal of cause and effect: instead of first defining how we perceive the truth and how we express it—the expressions are taken as a primary, as the given, and <u>then</u> we are asked to untangle their <u>truth</u> (their relation to reality) by "rules" of language. Right <u>here</u>, consciousness is given primacy over existence. (<u>Platonism and social metaphysics</u>.) <u>Truth</u> cannot be a matter of <u>propositions</u>, because it is a matter of <u>context</u>. Propositions have to conform to reality, <u>not</u> reality to propositions. And if it is claimed that our knowledge has to be held by means of <u>our</u> form of cognition, i.e., by means of words and propositions—then the first step is to define the

relation of our means and forms of cognition to reality, not to accept our forms as primaries and then attempt to adjust reality to them. Example: "Mathematical formulas express the truth about matter, when they are properly applied"— not: "Matter is that which fits mathematical formulas." (And more: to switch from: "What is true?" to: "What are true propositions?" means that we destroy context and expect the whole truth (omniscient truth) of any subject, issue or problem to be contained within one proposition. This is the root of their nonsense about: "The present king of France is bald.")

Ambiguity of the word "proposition." Do sentences stand for propositions? We have said that they stand for states-of-affairs. But propositions are true or false, and states-of-affairs are not true or false, they just *are*, exactly as tables aren't true or false, but simply are. Yet a sentence cannot stand both for what is true or false and what is not true or false. There must be something wrong here. Again, there is an ambiguity, this time in the word "proposition." The word can stand for (1) that which is true or false—not the sentence "Rover is a dog" but what this sentence has in common with all other sentences having the same meaning. But it can also stand for (2) what the sentence means: either what states-of-affairs it denotes, or what characteristics of states-of-affairs it designates. We are using the word "proposition" only in the first sense: thus, a proposition is true or false, but the sentence expressing it stands for states-of-affairs which either exist or do not exist. (66-67)

Total disaster. The sequence entitled "Ambiguity of the word 'proposition'" contains the essence of the switch, the equivocation, the evil and the nonsense of modern philosophy. (Take it in connection with the preceding sequence, entitled "Truth.") (Copy these two for reference—and also pp. 64-65, par. 2 and 3, of division "IV Sentences and propositions.") The switch is as follows: the distinction between "sentences" and "propositions" is first defined as the difference between the verbal-grammatical-linguistic form and the conceptual-reality-tied content. But it is stated as if it were a difference between a specific verbal sentence and a verbal sentence that has many verbal equivalents. (How are these equivalents grasped or identified—that is: how do we know that they are equivalents?

By the fact that they refer to the same facts of reality. But this is merely implied, it is not stated.) Then, on p. 67, the truth or falsehood of a proposition is said to be sought in "what this sentence has in common with other sentences having the same meaning"—and "a proposition is true or false, but the sentence expressing it stands for states-of-affairs which either exist or do not exist." (!!!) Thus the tie to reality is dropped, lost in the shuffle. We are not supposed to remember that without reference to reality we will not be able to know whether sentences have the same meaning. ("Stolen concepts"—and how! and how rapidly stolen!) (Also, "definitions-by-non-essentials"—and does it work fast!)

Would there still be propositions even if there were no human beings? In the second sense, yes; there would still be possible states-of-affairs, even if there were no world at all. (67)

Good God Almighty! There would be "possible states-of-affairs" in a zero? In a total vacuum? (This is where Parmenides is needed.) The gimmick of modern philosophers is as follows: first, split existence and consciousness altogether, as two independent, unrelated realms; then, unite them into "package-deals" whenever you happen to wish; and if anyone objects to the "package-deal" and attempts to analyze it into its components, yell: "But these are two separate realms!" (or: "We can never know 'things-in-themselves'!")

Emotive meaning. When someone says, "That

Major disaster! (inexcusably so):

dress is gorgeous," the sentence is in the form of an assertion, like "That dress is green." But it is difficult to say *what* the person who utters the sentence is asserting. . . . It is difficult to pin down . . . , because it is not clear what sort of a characteristic is designated by the word "gorgeous." (70)

One could restrict the use of the word "meaning" to what we have called cognitive meaning, saying that "the rest isn't meaning, just effects." In this sense, sentences having only what we called emotive meaning would be strictly meaningless. Or, one could include effects of sentences as meanings . . . , and say that there are different senses of the word "meaning," for example, cognitive meaning and emotive meaning. We shall adopt the latter terminology in this book, speaking of the emotional effects of sentences as meaning, but, of course, as emotive meaning, not meaning in the sense of designation. Sometimes the term "emotive meaning" is used to apply to sentences only when the sentences have a fairly *widespread, uniform* response, just as a noise is called a word only if there is a convention, a widespread use of an arbitrary symbol. (71)

The sequence entitled "Emotive meaning." Here "emotive" is equated with "meaningless" and "non-cognitive"—in as careless a manner as one could conceive of (which is shocking after all the hair-splitting precision on lesser issues). The word "gorgeous" is an "<u>evaluating</u>" term. It is much, much more complex than the word "green." Is it, therefore, to be regarded as "unclear"—and to be consigned to "<u>unclarity</u>" by its nature? Just because it is not a sensory primary? Should we, as philosophers, demand that people define their value-terms as precisely as their cognitive terms? <u>Or</u> should we decide that value-terms are undefinable, arbitrary, subjective and unrelated to reality? . . . <u>Nothing (nothing) can be "clear and manifest" without relation to reality (and, in that sense, without cognitive meaning.</u>)

<u>Ghastly confusion!</u> This is a good example of the consequences of "definitions-by-non-essentials": "Emotive" is (apparently) defined as "an <u>effect</u> in a person," and <u>not</u> as "value-judgment." Which, of course, opens the way to the ghastly collectivism of [*the last line of the passage cited*], where it is suggested that <u>only those</u> emotive sentences have meaning which create a "<u>widespread, uniform response</u>." (!!!) And <u>this</u> is compared to the "convention" of creating words (ascribing meanings to "noises"). Such a suggestion would, <u>in fact</u>, mean that only "<u>widespread, uniform</u>"

value-judgments <u>are</u> value-judgments. (Besides, <u>this</u> is an example of "emotions taken as a tool of cognition.")

If we keep in mind the distinction between cognitive and emotive meaning, we shall avoid many possible confusions. Do the two sentences "I am going away" and "Alas, I am going away" have the same meaning? This depends on whether we are talking about cognitive meaning only. Cognitively, the two sentences have the same meaning; they assert the same state-of-affairs, and the word "alas" adds nothing to the assertion. But in emotive meaning the two are quite different: the word "alas" adds an emotive effect to the sentence which the sentence would not have without it. (71)

Messily inexact. "Alas, I am going away" communicates the speaker's appraisal (value-judgment) of the fact of his going away. And the listener learns <u>two facts</u> cognitively: 1) that the speaker is going away, 2) that the speaker has a negative appraisal of his own going away. Value-judgments <u>have</u> cognitive meaning in regard to the valuer's code or standard of value—and the hearer of a value-statement learns something about the speaker's code. <u>Of course</u>, this is to be separated from "cognitive," as applied to learning something about the facts of reality or of nature—but the distinction is destroyed, rather than established, by this sort of definition.

Suppose the word "cultured" has come to mean "acquainted with the arts." This is a cognitive meaning. But suppose it is popular, and a mark of esteem, to be acquainted with the arts; then the word "cultured" acquires a favorable emotive meaning in addition to its cognitive meaning. Now someone comes along who does not like the arts; he makes an after-dinner speech in which he says, "*True* culture is not acquaintance with the arts, but with science and technology." <u>Of course there is no such thing as the true meaning of a word, there are only common and uncommon meanings, exact and inexact meanings.</u> His audience is not sensitive to these distinctions and he successfully uses the emotive meaning the word "culture" already possesses in order to make them respond favorably to science and technology, which he wants them to like. He has given a persuasive definition of "cultured." (72)

(???) (Ask J. H. about <u>this</u>!) Here is the destruction of language—and of concepts, and of man's power of abstraction. One cannot accept a fantastic term such as "<u>persuasive definitions</u>." (What a package-deal and what an equivocation!)

Pictorial meaning. . . . Sometimes a sentence is not intended to work on people's emotions (or to express those of the speaker), nor yet is it cognitive in its meaning. . . . [The speaker] may not have meant his sentence to convey any information at all; he may simply have wished to implant in his hearer's mind an interesting *picture.* Many fantasies, childhood stories, and more ambitious works of the imagination were not intended to be read for their cognitive meaning and tested on that basis. (73)

"Pictorial meaning"—more of the same vagueness of definition. (What's wrong with the concept of "metaphor"? What does the term "pictorial meaning" accomplish, except a dangerous and pernicious confusion?)

Page 75: "We mean, not sentences mean."—Here's the payoff! This is the ultimate result of the earlier statements about language being "man-made" and, therefore, totally arbitrary—the equivocation between "noise" and "meaning"—the reduction of language to gibbering subjectivity. If any man may ascribe subjective meanings to the words he uses, and if this is still to be regarded as a proper use of language, then how do his listeners determine his "criterion" (p. 76), etc.? What if their use and understanding of words is also subjective? Where is the objective criterion? The implications of this section lead straight to an "elite" of psychologists (Freudian ones) who will decree what a man means, whether he knows it or not. (This is the "Humpty-Dumpty" section—and the Tower of Babel—and the Lenin-Hitler plan to destroy language.) The epistemological method that leads to such a mess is as follows: here are philosophers, posturing as "empiricists," who do not start by identifying and defining what is language, but start, instead, by accepting the immediate, journalistic, statistical uses of language as the given, the irreducible primary, and then build some "theorizing" upon it, in hair-raisingly vague and sloppy terms; they "study" a man-made skill, such as language, as if it were a fact of physical nature—by cataloging indiscriminantly everything vaguely related to the subject, without even defining the subject, as they would have had to do in physical science. Such a method, applied to the man-made, can best be summarized as follows: if these philosophers were attempting to study and define automobiles, they would declare that an automobile is an object used for transportation, for running people over, for creating collisions, for providing the livelihood of garage-employees, for causing envy among married women, and for filling junk-yards—all of this indiscriminately, as of equal definitional validity, with the subjective uses of various people as the sole standard of conceptual knowledge. (The consequence: "What is an automobile for you, may not be an automobile for me.")

Page 76-79: "What is philosophy?" This section is a good illustration of all the above points—and of the futility of modern philosophy. (The arbitrary "starting-in-midstream"—the attempt to deal with the undefined, by the method of: "I am doing something, I don't know what, why or what for"—the acceptance of an enormous concept, such as "philosophy," as if it were a primary. They do not know that one cannot use any abstraction until one has the knowledge of the total chain of abstractions which it integrates and symbolizes.)

Chapter 2: Necessary Knowledge

<u>Page 86</u>: "Let us begin by asking simply, 'What do we know?' and 'How do we know it?' More specifically, what statements are there whose truth we can be said to know?" <u>This is the essence of my whole opposition to modern philosophy.</u> This is the act of taking <u>words</u> ("statements") as an irreducible primary. How do they dare jump from "truth" to "statements" without a single mention of the enormous subject of: what <u>are</u> statements? what <u>is</u> language? what <u>are concepts</u>? what <u>are</u> man's means of knowledge—and how does he get to the stage of <u>concepts</u>? They, the modern hair-splitters, simply evade and ignore the whole subject of <u>epistemology</u>—incredibly, they take it as the given and proceed to play the shyster-game of "No smoking allowed." (No wonder they omit the subject of "universals and particulars"!) If there is any way of discrediting philosophy and divorcing it from man's existence—this is it.

I. Rationalism and empiricism of concepts

There are other ideas with which the concept empiricist [i.e., one who holds that concepts come from experience] has a harder time. (1) Whence come the ideas of straightness, circularity, and other geometrical ideas, since we never see perfectly straight lines or perfect circles? . . . (2) Whence come our ideas of logical and mathematical relations, such as that of implication? When we say that "A is larger than B" implies "B is smaller than A," we do seem to employ the notion of implication, but whence comes this idea? (89)

The questions in this paragraph are answered by the Law of Identity.

"How do we know that our judgments are true?" Experience and experience alone enables us to know, says the empiricist, and the rationalist denies it. (90)

How many levels of <u>equivocation</u> are involved in this sort of "package-deal" use of the term "<u>experience</u>"? What is to be regarded as "experience" in this kind of context—a split second, an hour or a century? And what is the role of previous knowledge in relation to "experience"? (Also: it is impossible to go into the issue of "judgment rationalism" and "judgment empiricism" without an answer to the first problem raised here, namely: "concept rationalism" and "concept empiricism"—yet that problem is here dismissed in 3½ pages, plus a footnote (p. 86) stating

that it is not essential to
further understanding (!!?!).

II. Analytic and synthetic statements; tautologies

Page 92: example of tautology: "If you read this chapter long enough, you'll
understand it"—this being explained by the fact that the speaker equates "long
enough" with "understanding." Look out! Here is the trap and the "gimmick" of
modern philosophy: by making the use of words arbitrary and subjective, they here
prepare the ground for themselves to refute anything simply by rejecting any
consistency (and objectivity) of terms.
Nice little possibility:
  [1] Tautologies are not knowledge
  [2] Any consistent use of concepts is reducible to a tautology
  [3] Therefore anything that involves a consistent use of concepts is not knowledge
  [4] Therefore only the inconsistent (and the contradictory) is knowledge.
(Then, of course, all our "knowledge" is shaky, problematic, "relative," uncertain and
to be refuted at any moment.)
(This is the perfect pattern for the psychology of a whim-worshipper in philosophy.
Translate it: I can indulge in contradictions, defy the Law of Identity, oppose reality
and get away with it—until it suits my whim to decide to change my ideas or reverse
myself.)

Are definitions tautologies?

Complete definitions, as well as statements
of defining characteristics, are also tautologies:
for example, "A yard is three feet." Substitute the
defining phrase for the term to be defined, and
we have "Three feet is three feet," which is
clearly a tautology. . . .

But does this not conflict with what we said
in Chapter 1 [*about stipulative and reportive definitions not being tautologies*]?. . .

In neither case . . . is a definition a tautology.
In the case of a stipulative definition we have
'Let us use "yard" to mean . . .' which is not an
assertion at all, and therefore neither true nor
false; and in the case of a reportive definition we
have 'English-speaking people use "yard" to
mean . . .' which is a true synthetic statement. In
the first case a meaning is assigned; in the second
case it is reported. But in the present case it is
presupposed. In other words, if we presuppose
the truth of the synthetic statement that people
use "yard" to stand for three feet, then we get, *by
substituting* the defining phrase for the word to
be defined, a tautology: "Three feet is three feet."
93-94)

Boy, oh boy, oh boy!
The section "Are definitions
tautologies?" is the perfect
example of the cashing-in on
the fallacies set earlier. Here is
the result of taking definitions
as either "stipulative" or
"reportive"! And the "gimmick,"
of course, is the switch
between "words-as-concepts"
and "words-as-noise." Here, the
discussion is about concepts,
yet it is "solved" by a discussion
of "noise"—and thus concepts
are wiped out. If all definitions
are "synthetic" (the meaning
here is "arbitrary"), then of
course we can never know
anything for certain.

Observe the trick pulled

between the <u>first</u> and the <u>last</u> paragraphs of this section: definitions are tautologies, because they rest on a "presupposition" of the truth (and of <u>what</u> truth!—not the objective truth of <u>facts</u>, but the "truth" of whether "<u>people</u>" think so or not!—lovely little institutionalizing of social metaphysics!)—so here go all axioms, all self-evident knowledge and all reason! This is how they'll get to axioms being a matter of arbitrary choice.

III. Possibility

It is logically impossible for there ever to be a square circle: if it's a circle it can't be a square, and if it's a square, it can't be a circle. The "can't" here is a *logical* "can't," meaning that it's *logically* impossible for it to be so. On the other hand, it is logically possible for you to jump ten thousand feet into the air by your own unaided muscular power. If you said that you had done so, you would be making a false synthetic statement, but your statement would not be self-contradictory. (94)

Here the "logically possible" is openly made to be a matter of <u>definitions</u> (examples: the "square circle" vs. "I jumped ten thousand feet into the air"). Yet by all the preceding discussion, <u>definitions</u> are not and do not have to be <u>precise</u>—therefore, any sort of nonsense is <u>logically</u> possible. <u>This</u> is <u>the total split between logic and reality</u>, or logic and knowledge. (And if knowledge is unrelated to logic —there go reason, science and certainty, and the mystics have won: there is now no distinction between <u>knowledge</u> and <u>faith</u>.)

It is for science to tell us what is empirically possible. It is for *applied*, or practical, science to tell us what is technically possible. <u>Our chief concern here is what is logically possible</u>. The others are brought in here only to distinguish them from

Here the split between logic and reality is made complete. This means that philosophy is concerned with a game of words and rules, <u>unrelated to</u>

logical possibility. (96)

reality. The joke is on the modern philosophers: by the above premises, modern philosophers are pure Platonic rationalists, they make conclusions without any reference to empirical reality—they, who are so proud of being "empiricists"! (The concept of the "technically possible" only adds to the confusion and wipes out the metaphysical meaning of the concept "empirical.")

Page 96, 97: Good God Almighty! Logic is here openly equated with ignorance (!!!) "It seems to be empirically impossible for living things to exist without oxygen, nitrogen, carbon, and hydrogen. But it is logically possible that life in some form could exist without one or more of these." Translated, this means: since no attribute of an entity is essential, how do we know whether that entity will still preserve its identity without any or all of them? The gimmick is so blatantly contained in: what do we mean by the concept "life"? But they answer that we are free to mean anything we wish. And more: it is here made obvious that the logical vs. empirical distinction rests on taking the "single-attribute," primitive level of abstractions (the level corresponding to the first, visual abstractions of a child, one step above the level of perceptions) as the base, root, source, absolute, and irreducible primary of logic (!!!). Thus, logic is the discipline that belongs to the epistemology of those of "arrested mental development"—and to nobody and nothing above that level (!!!). Else why are "square circle" or "male aunt" logically impossible, but "life without oxygen" is not? Merely because "square," "circle," "male" and "aunt" use simple, almost single-attribute concepts, which do not require a long chain of prior, precise, specific concepts with unequivocal, absolute definitions? Logic, therefore, stops and breaks with reality at the point where a retarded mind (or an anti-effort mind) begins to waver, cloud and vacillate.

In the same passage: the unknown is taken as the license to unlimited invention, to the "playing it deuces wild." If we do not know whether the law of gravitation applies to other universes (which, in itself, is nonsense), this gives us license to claim anything as possible. This is the epistemology of a savage (and of a mystic). If we do not know the cause of the sun's movement, then we are logically entitled to claim that the cause is a sun-god (or green cheese)—and such a claim acquires the status of the "logically possible." (Here is where Parmenides is needed again: "that which is not, is not—and cannot be or be thought about." The unknown is, epistemologically, a zero; a zero leads to nothing and entitles us to nothing. A zero cannot be the cause of a non-zero, of an existent; if we do not know that "A" is impossible, this does not grant any epistemological validity whatever to the hypothesis that "A" is possible.)

In the same passage: the idea that the mathematical formula of Newton's law of gravitation could be mathematically different in "another universe" rests on a disintegrated view of the universe—on the failure to grant identity to the universe as a whole and, therefore, causality to any of its specific parts, attributes or relationships. The existing mathematical relationship is not <u>causeless</u>; therefore, it <u>could not</u> be different—<u>if</u> all the interrelated aspects and elements of the universe remained the same; but none of <u>these</u> aspects and elements is causeless, either. The concept of "another universe" is, in fact, illogical: it rests on the mystics' premise of "creation out of a void"—on the premise that the basic or essential nature of the universe came out of somebody's whim and "could have been" different.

    <u>Question</u>: why did they manufacture such a concept as "the logically possible"? Wouldn't the issue be thoroughly covered by the concepts of "<u>logical</u>" and "<u>illogical</u>," if formalistic correctness were the sole subject of that distinction? Obviously, the purpose here is to <u>institutionalize equivocation</u>, that is, to corrupt and invalidate the concept of "<u>logic</u>" by means of an in-built self-destroyer. Thus: the "illogical" is obviously a term pertaining to <u>epistemology</u>; the "logically <u>possible</u>" is a term pertaining to <u>metaphysics</u>; by the inappropriate, out-of-context, stolen-concept-like use of the term "possible," they open the way for <u>logic</u> to become the tool of mysticism, the tool of mystical invention—the tool not of <u>perceiving</u>, but of <u>creating</u> reality. (Observe such an expression as: the "logically possible universes.") This is the way in which <u>logic</u>, the heart and essence of reason, is appropriated by its enemy and destroyer: mysticism. This is the way in which reason is emasculated and made into a meaningless concept vaguely pertaining to some sort of Attila-like, range-of-the-moment, perceptual (non-conceptual) empiricism. This is the way in which modern philosophers are <u>epistemological neo-mystics</u>. (<u>The above is terribly important for my non-fiction book</u>.)

<u>Page 97, 98</u>: "<u>Conceivability</u>"—what a mess! Here are philosophers who find it unnecessary (and leave it to anybody's arbitrary whim) to define the exact meaning of the concept "to conceive" (and, therefore, of the concept of "concept"). There are too many equivocations to untangle here (all of them results of the preceding errors and evasions), but briefly:

    a) If "conceivable" is defined as a synonym of "logically possible," then <u>there</u> is the proof of my preceding notes, of logic in the service of mysticism.

    b) If "conceivable" is defined as a synonym of "imaginable"—then <u>why</u> is "imagination" equated with "visual imagination"? <u>This</u> is corroborating evidence of the fact that they freeze logic on the lowest level of abstraction—on the level of a child's first abstractions, which are <u>visual</u>. And what a sloppiness in regard to the <u>psychological</u> meaning of the term "imagination"! On what ground (with no specific definition of "imagination" whatever) do they decide that something can be "unimaginable because of the limitation of our powers of imagination"? (!) (What is the "unlimited" power of an undefined faculty?)

    c) If the meaning of the term "conceivable" is left to anyone's arbitrary whim in defining it (as is done in the last paragraph of this sequence), then what is the place, use or meaning of such a term in philosophy? (Or, of course, of <u>any</u> term?) What are we doing when we are studying or dealing with undefined terms of unspecified meaning? <u>Where is the Law of Identity in this context</u>?

    d) If an issue such as the nature and meaning of "<u>conception</u>" is left undefined, unspecified and indeterminate, then this is not merely a "philosophy without metaphysics," it is also a "philosophy without epistemology." What, then, is left of philosophy without <u>these</u> two branches? The answer: "to erect upon that plastic fog a single holy absolute: their <u>wish</u>." (Remember that <u>morality</u> has to rest on <u>metaphysics</u>

and epistemology. Now it's clear what morality is to rest on: their whim.)
("Logic without Ontology"? This is also "Logic without Epistemology.")

Examples. Let us now run through a few examples of logical possibility and impossibility. . . .
1. Is it logically possible for a solid iron bar to float on water? Of course it is. There is no contradiction at all in it. . . . You can even imagine it now . . . : you take a piece of iron . . . , you weigh it, then you plunge it into a vessel of water, and behold, it floats. (98)

Good God! The statement "Behold, it floats" is factually and stylistically worthy of a mystic's description of a miracle! The statement: "there is nothing logically impossible" about a fact that "does not actually occur," is the complete detachment of logic and science (and this from those science-worshipping "empiricists"!). This paragraph is a total and conscious "institutionalized evasion" or "context-dropping as a rule of logic" (!!!). (May the God they want to invent, forgive them!)

2. Is it logically possible to remember something that never happened? As in so many cases, the answer is "Yes" in one sense and "No" in another, depending on the sense of the word "remember" that is employed. It may be used in a *weak* sense, so that you remember something whenever you have "that recollective feeling" about it, regardless of whether it really happened or not. . . . Here someone might object, "Then you didn't *really* remember it, you only thought you did!" This person is using "remember" in the "strong" sense [in which case the event really occurred]. (99)

Re: "weak" and "strong" remembering. Well, here's "hard" and "soft" determinism. And if this is not a social metaphysician's cue-words elevated into logic, I'll eat his book! What's blatant here is: emotions as tools of cognition (and of definition)—"you remember something whenever you have that recollective feeling." (My, oh my!—the severe, modern, anti-mystical advocates of the scientific method!)

3. Is it logically possible for a cat to give birth to pups? Biologically impossible, doubtless . . . , but logically possible. . . . Once again, cats are distinguished from dogs and other creatures (somewhat vaguely, as we saw in Chapter 1) by their general appearance, and it is logically possible for something with all feline appearances to give birth to something with all canine appearances. (99-100)

Same tripe. The reference to Chapter 1, to the premise that definitions are (and have to be) "vague," is the proof of the awareness of the purpose for which definitions were destroyed.

Note on this whole sequence of "examples": Observe that logic is here made to be equated with the illogical, the irrational, the contradictory, the impossible, the preposterous, the miraculous. Logic, the guardian of reason and knowledge, the tool by which we are able to integrate the facts of reality, is made to serve irrationality, disintegration, context-dropping, equivocation. Thus the "logical" is the absurd (and what actually happens in reality has nothing to do with any of it). Could Tertullian have asked for anything more?

4. Is it logically possible to go from Chicago to New York without traversing the distance in between? Unless some unusual sense of the word is being employed, it is logically impossible to go from Chicago to New York (or anywhere else) without traversing distance, for to go from one place to another *is* to traverse distance; this is what "going" means. (100)

Why the sudden precision of definition? Why "to go from one place to another is to traverse distance"? Where is the epistemological line separating firm definitions from the sloppy fog? (The answer is probably that "philosophers" have to have a job and a chance to argue like medieval scholastics —and a chance to bring in an absolute when they need it.)

5. Is it logically possible for a creature to see without eyes? (101) [*This line is followed by a two-page dialogue that is meant to "bring out various facets of the issue." The opening of the dialogue follows:*]
A. Of course it's logically impossible [to see without eyes]. Seeing is by definition what comes by means of eyes, and through eyes.
B. Let's be careful here not to oversimplify the issue: let's not confuse a definition with a causal relation. . . . [W]hen I say I see I am only referring to . . . this awareness [i.e., a visual experience], but I am not saying anything about the sense organ which makes it possible for me to have this experience.

The return to medieval scholasticism is here complete. Observe three facts: 1. This is what happens in a discussion where words have no firm, objective definitions; 2. This is what would make all discussion, communication, agreement or co-operation among men impossible; 3. This is what causes people to become anti-intellectual Babbits and to believe that philosophy is a lot of useless, meaningless jabber.

Three unpublished papers by John Hospers: "Egoism," "Liberty" and "Some Aspects of My Conception of Freedom"

Professor Hospers sent these papers to Ayn Rand in the early 1960's. They were informal papers, not meant for publication, and thus he asks that the reader be made aware of his published works on these topics: Human Conduct *(2nd ed. Harcourt Brace 1982, 3rd ed. forthcoming);* Introduction to Philosophical Analysis *(3rd ed. Prentice-Hall 1988); and assorted articles in* The Freeman *through the years, especially 1984-88 and 1994.*

"Egoism"

There are aspects of egoism which are not clear to me; even where I think I know what your view would be, I am not sure what the reasoning would be by means of which you would defend it. Consider:

Here is a person who thinks only about herself and talks only about herself. In a social gathering she discusses only her aches and pains, her trivial problems, her relation to her employer, etc. She is not interested in anyone else's affairs nor in the affairs of the world. Everyone agrees that she is a social bore, and everyone agrees also on the reason: "She's completely selfish, she can't think of anybody except herself."

John, <u>why</u> do you ignore the meaning of "<u>rational</u>" selfishness?

"Selfishness" is not a <u>primary,</u> but a derivative of <u>rationality</u>.

I daresay you would disapprove of her behavior. But on what grounds?

I don't think you would call her selfish in your sense; but in any usual sense of "selfish" she would be considered virtually the paradigm case of a selfish person.

What <u>is</u> the "usual sense"?

Flyers in the Navy stayed on in the service during the '20's and '30's, at low pay and without the <u>notoriety</u> they could have had in private life engaging in <u>Lindbergh-like flights</u> across the Atlantic, etc. They did so to keep spurring the Navy on to get the aircraft which it needed, and which it was so desperately short of when World War II came. I would consider this action on their part noble and heroic; and it would ordinarily be called a case of "pure unselfishness" as well.

?!?
Who have you been talking to?

I take it that you would approve of their action, and that you would NOT call it unselfish— you would say they <u>would have been traitors to their OWN highest ideals if they had not done as</u>

Not necessarily: Why <u>did</u> they do it? I'm not even sure it was good.

they did.

True—but were these selfish ideals? Since they got very little (in either money or personal satisfaction) from pursuing these ideals, what entitles them to be called selfish?

If following whatever your own highest ideal is, is automatically to be called selfish, then any activity directed toward a long-range goal would be selfish, would it not? and then what distinctive meaning has "selfish" any longer? What then would be unselfish? NOT following your cherished goal? I should think that what distinguishes the selfish from the unselfish is not the fact that one pursues it, but the NATURE of the goal which one pursues.

> No!!!

> No!! Why one pursues it—the motive.

"Liberty"

People are sometimes said to be free when they have freedom of *action*, that is, they are able to act in accordance with their choices. Though this is a necessary condition, it is not a sufficient one: a person may choose to surrender his money at the point of a gun, or as a result of threats; he chooses to do what he does (rather than face a more unpleasant alternative), but he is still not doing what he wants to do, or what he would have done had there been no coercion upon him.

> Metaphysical confusion: When would this freedom be absent?

People are sometimes said to be free when they have freedom of choice, i.e., when they are able to choose in accordance with their desires. In this sense the man who acts at the point of a gun is not free, and the person who acts without coercion is. Certainly freedom requires the ability to choose as well as to act. But this too is necessary without being sufficient; not everyone who fulfills this requirement can be called free.

> This is a description of freedom (but not a definition).

Consider the population of a state ruled by a dictator, in which people are permitted to vote (and thus have freedom of action with respect to voting at least) and also are permitted to vote for the candidate they favor (they are free to choose in accordance with their preference for candidates). But the state controls the radio and newspapers, and presents the people with such a slanted view of the news/truth that the people have no rational

> Disastrous package-deal: intelligent choice and free choice are not synonyms. If "full and sufficient knowledge" is the standard of freedom, then no one can be free until men are omniscient.

basis for making an intelligent choice. Imagine also that the news is so cleverly slanted that the people do not know they are being duped: they think they are free, but they are not, because, although they have freedom of choice, they cannot choose the candidates they WOULD HAVE CHOSEN if they had had full or sufficient knowledge on which to base their choice. Such a people surely would not be free. They would be free only if they had available the wherewithal for making an intelligent choice—if they were able to choose in accordance with the best information available.

The ability to exercise a free choice is man's most important possession. It is his most characteristic activity of man, and it is his basic tool of survival. . . . So important is this ability to make free choices that I would like to enunciate the following moral principle and devote the rest of my time to applications of it: so act as to promote the maximum possible scope for free choices for the human beings affected by your action. In other words, act so as to *maximize* the range of voluntary actions.

> This rule would make us all into altruist collectivists.

Would I approve the practice of policemen forcibly preventing people who are trying to drown themselves? This is somewhat more complex: on the one hand, I might say that if that's what they want to do they should be left free to do it, and that one should not ask a policeman to risk his life to prevent forcibly someone from doing what he probably will do sooner or later. On the other hand, one might argue that by preventing the person from acting on a hasty choice, he will be saving his life and thus enabling him to survive to make future choices. The latter is felt to be the more important, and on these grounds, I suppose, the practice of forcing people to survive against their own (temporary?) wishes is continued.

> Confusion: save his life to make future choices. The last two sentences of this paragraph open the way for total dictatorship, by means of the concept of "hasty choice."

At first it might seem as if the maximum of liberty would be possible in a state of anarchy, in other words in Hobbes' state of nature. After all, in such a state there are no laws, no courts, no legal authorities to whom you have to defer, no authorities to exert compulsion on you in any

> Bad argument. It would hold only if one defined political freedom properly. But the impossible (such as traffic chaos) is not the "non-free."

way. But on second thought, this state of nature would be one in which most freedoms turn out to be impossible. Any person or group of people could gang up on you and rob you or snuff out your life without fear of legal authorities; your life would not be safe for a moment, your security would be zero, and you would have to spend most of your time, not in creative or productive effort, but in trying to defend yourself against aggressive acts by others. The maxim of freedom is possible only under law. Freedom cannot mean the absence of all restraints, for the obvious reason that it is not only you but others whose actions would be unrestrained, and there would be nothing to restrain them from killing you. Freedom is impossible without government in exactly the same way as, on a smaller scale, there is no freedom on the highway apart from law: if there were no traffic laws you would not be safe on the highway for a single moment; any fool who chose to drive at 120 m.p.h. or on the left side of the road, or to crash into you, could do so without penalty, and the much-desired freedom could not exist; even bad traffic laws would be better than no laws at all.

Assuming then that there must be some government, the only question is whether its power should be limited or unlimited.

> If one defined <u>why</u> men need a government, the limit would be <u>implicit</u>.

In a republic the sphere of government is LIMITED; there are certain things that it cannot do. It may not, for example, deprive any individual of the right to trial by jury.

> (Too small an example)

"Some Aspects of My Conception of Freedom"

So important is freedom in man's life, and in the development of his peculiarly human potentialities, that I would set forth the following criterion for evaluating actions and policies with respect to it: the acts and policies should be such as to MAXIMIZE THE SPHERE OF VOLUNTARY ACTION.

> There is no <u>involuntary</u> action in man's nature (in the sense here used), so <u>what</u> is there to <u>maximize</u>? "Maximizing" implies the existence of coercion to be removed.

When governmental (court) action makes segregation in public schools illegal, it could be argued that this act of compulsion reduces the

> "Public" is the only issue here.

sphere of voluntary action among whites; but also that it increases it among Negroes, who hitherto were prevented from attending the same schools. By giving these Negroes a *chance* for education equal to those of whites, <u>it increases their freedom</u>—a freedom which would never, probably, have been granted if the court had not intervened. This is a most difficult type of case—a case in which, unless *some* freedom is taken from Mr. A, Mr. B will never have a chance to achieve the same freedom for himself. (The fact that Mr. A does not grant B's right voluntarily, but must be made to do so by government coercion, is a moral loss. But so is the loss to B that results when government does not interfere and Mr. A does not do the act voluntarily.)

?

Here "<u>freedom</u>" loses all meaning. If I do not own a yacht, I "do not have the same freedom" as a millionaire, and I do not make the same choices which I "<u>would have made</u>" if I had a yacht—therefore, "some freedom (and some cash) has to be taken from the millionaire and given to me because otherwise I "will never have a chance to achieve the same freedom for myself."

Henry Sidgwick, *The Elements of Politics* (1891; 4th ed., London: Macmillan and Co., 1919)

In the early 1960's, John Hospers sent Ayn Rand six typed pages of selected passages from The Elements of Politics, *Chapter X: "Socialistic Interference." Her comments were written on those pages. For ease of reference, the given page numbers are from the fourth edition.*

The socialistic interference for which, in the present chapter, I propose to offer a theoretical justification, is here only recommended as a supplementary and subordinate element in a system mainly individualistic. (146)

No philosopher has the moral right to talk like <u>that</u>!

In the first place, it should be observed that the argument above given, even if fully granted, would only justify appropriation to the labourer, and free exchange of the utilities produced by labor; it affords no direct justification for the appropriation of natural resources, which private property in material things inevitably involves. Hence, so far as this appropriation of natural resources restricts other men's opportunities of applying labour productively, the appropriation is of doubtful legitimacy, from the point of view of the strictest individualism. It must, therefore, be regarded as theoretically subject to limitation or regulation, in the interest of the whole aggregate of individuals concerned. How far this limitation and regulation should go must be determined by experience in different departments; but it may be laid down generally that it is the duty of Government as representing the community to prevent the bounties of nature from being wasted by the unrestricted pursuit of private interest. Thus, for instance, Government may properly interfere to protect mines and fisheries from wasteful exhaustion, and save rare and useful species of plants from extermination. . . . (146-147)

Are we ghosts?!

This paragraph is the best illustration of why the "utilitarian" approach to morality killed competition.

Good God!

In how many thousands of years ahead?

Secondly, individuals may not be able to remunerate themselves by the sale of the utilities which it is for the general interest that they should render to society. This may be either because the utility is from its nature incapable of being appropriated, or because (though undeniably important from the point of view of the community) its value to any individual is too uncertain and remote to render it worth purchasing on grounds of private interest. . . . The [latter] case may be illustrated by scientific investigation generally; since most of the advances made in scientific knowledge, even though they may be ultimately the source of important material benefits to man's estate, would hardly remunerate the investigator if treated as marketable commodities, and only communicated to private individuals who were willing to pay for them. (148)

What about Edison, Westinghouse, etc.?

[T]here is an important class of cases in which the individuals have an adequate motive for rendering *some* service to society, but not for rendering as much service as it is in their power to render. These are cases in which competition is excluded by natural or artificial monopoly of the production or sale of a commodity. (149)

The "worker's speech" in "AS" [*Atlas Shrugged*]

The old "monopoly" argument

[M]odern governments universally monopolize coinage, and regulate in some degree the business of banking—interventions chiefly justified by the great public importance of giving security and stability to the current medium of exchange. (153)

This is what causes depression!

But the term "Socialistic" may be fairly applied to this kind of intervention, whatever its degree of intensity, if it is used in simple opposition to "Individualistic." This meaning of the term, however, must be carefully distinguished from another—and more common—meaning, in which "Socialism" is understood to imply a design of altering the distribution of wealth, by benefiting the poor at the expense of the rich. For though such effects on distribution may in some cases result from the measures above mentioned, their primary aim is not to give advantage to one section of the community at the expense of another, but to secure benefits to the community as a whole which tend to be distributed among its members generally. . . . (153-154)

The determination of what is or is not "socialistic" rests on the basic principle of: who has the primary right and why? Any request for the "common welfare" is socialistic.

No single example given <indicates> this—every one <invokes> <alleged> "majority" benefits and "minority" sacrifice.

Any great equalization of wealth would probably diminish the accumulation of capital, on which the progress of industry depends; and would deteriorate the administration of the capital accumulated; since the most economic organization of industry requires capital in large masses under single management, and the management of borrowed or joint-stock capital is likely to be, on the average, inferior to that of capital owned by the manager. . . . Still, I cannot doubt that at least a removal of the extreme inequalities, found in the present distribution of wealth, would be desirable if it could be brought about without any material repression of the free development of individual energy and enterprise, which the individualistic system aims at securing. . . . (161)

> Oh? So this is not his purpose.
>
> Men as Atlases and victims and serfs—not as possessors of rights.

[T]here are . . . other measures designed for the benefit of the poor . . . of which the primary aim is not to distribute compulsorily the product of labour, but to equalize the opportunities of obtaining wealth by productive labour, without any restriction on the freedom of adults. State aid to emigration is an example of this class, and a part at least of the expenditure on education must be held to belong to it. Now measures of this kind are not in their primary aim opposed to Individualism, since we obviously increase instead of diminish the stimulus to self-help and energetic enterprise by placing a man in a position to gain more than he could otherwise have done by the exercise of these qualities. (161-162)

> At whose expense?
>
> A subsidized parasite is not an individualist nor an exponent of individualistic enterprise.

[T]he institution of private property as actually existing goes beyond what the individualistic theory justifies. Its general aim is to appropriate the results of labour to the labourer; but in realizing this aim it has inevitably appropriated natural resources to an extent which, in any fully peopled country, has entirely discarded Locke's condition of "leaving enough and as good for others." (163)

> The "range-of-the-moment" bastard! All he sees is the interests of the day-laborer. Any form of savings and any industry is ruled out by this kind of reasoning.

[I]n so far as this [i.e., a certain socialistic program] is done without such heavy taxation as materially diminishes the stimulus to industry and thrift of the persons taxed, this expenditure of public money, however justly it may be called Socialistic, appears to be none the less defensible as the best method of approximating to the ideal of Individualistic justice. (163)

> This is the key to the "pragmatic" unprincipled approach of this bastard!

In most modern states an important percentage of

> ?

the population are, at any given time, temporarily or permanently incapacitated from providing themselves with the necessities of life. . . . [I]n an important minority of instances the affliction of indigence is due to misfortunes which the persons afflicted cannot reasonably be blamed for not foreseeing; and even where this is not the case, probably few individualists are able to regard starvation as the appropriate penalty for improvidence, or even for worse faults. . . . It seems, therefore, that the problem must be taken in hand by Government in some manner and degree. (164)

> I do!
> This means penalize Rearden [See Atlas Shrugged] for the bum—and nothing else.

This method [of insurance] involves government interference which is in one aspect greater than that entailed by the English method, since the provision compulsorily made extends to labourers generally, whereas the English system only provides for the destitute; on the other hand, the method of compulsory insurance is, from another point of view, less anti-individualistic, so far as the burden of the provision is thrown on the persons who receive the benefit of it. (165-166)

> This is too sickening epistemologically!

We actually find that the promotion of education and culture, and the cure of diseases, have been largely provided for in modern civilized communities by the donations and bequests of individuals. So far as needs can be adequately met in this way, there is an advantage in avoiding the necessity for additional taxation. . . . (166)

> Who decides this? By what standard?

[There are always] such disadvantages [to government interference] as (1) the danger of overburdening the government machinery with work, (2) the danger of increasing power capable of being used by governing persons oppressively or corruptly, (3) the danger that the delicate economic functions of government will be hampered by the desire to gratify certain specially influential sections of the community. . . . [W]e are not justified in concluding that governmental interference is expedient even when laissez faire leads to a manifestly unsatisfactory result; its expediency has to be decided in any particular case by a careful estimate of advantages and drawbacks, requiring data obtained from special experience. (167-168)

> These two points are enough to damn the total of government interference. But observe how he ignores them.

> By what standard?
> By what standard?
> By what standard?!!!

C.S. Lewis, *The Abolition of Man, or Reflections on Education with Special Reference to the Teaching of English in the Upper Forms of Schools* (New York: Macmillan, 1947)

The Innovator attacks traditional values (the *Tao*) in defense of what he at first supposes to be (in some special sense) 'rational' or 'biological' values. But as we have seen, all the values which he uses in attacking the *Tao*, and even claims to be substituting for it, are themselves derived from the *Tao*. If he had really started from scratch, from right outside the human tradition of value, no jugglery could have advanced him an inch towards the conception that a man should die for the community or work for posterity. (27)

> You bet he couldn't!

I am considering what the thing called 'Man's power over Nature' must always and essentially be. No doubt, the picture could be modified by public ownership of raw materials and factories and public control of scientific research. But unless we have a world state this will still mean the power of one nation over others. And even within the world state or the nation it will mean (in principle) the power of majorities over minorities, and (in the concrete) of a government over the people. And all long-term exercises of power, especially in breeding, must mean the power of earlier generations over later ones. (35-36)

> So in the pre-science age, there was no power of majorities over minorities—and the Middle Ages were a period of love and equality, and oppression began only in the U.S.A. (!!?!) The abysmal bastard!

> !!

[T]he later a generation comes—the nearer it lives to that date at which the species becomes extinct—the less power it will have in the forward direction, because its subjects will be so few. There is therefore no question of a power vested in the race as a whole steadily growing as long as the race survives. The last men, far from being the heirs of power, will be of all men most subject to the dead hand of the great planners and conditioners and will themselves exercise least power upon the future. (36-37)

> It is unbelievable, but this monster literally thinks that to give men new knowledge is to gain <u>power</u>(!) over them. The cheap, awful, miserable, touchy, social-metaphysical mediocrity!

> <u>This</u> is almost too unbearably obscene!

Each new power won *by* man is a power *over* man as well. Each advance leaves him weaker as well as stronger. (37)

> So when you cure men of TB, syphilis, scurvy, small pox and rabies—you make them <u>weaker</u>!!!

In the older systems both the kind of man the teachers wished to produce and their motives for

> And which brought such great joy, peace, happiness and moral

producing him were prescribed by the *Tao*—a norm to which the teachers themselves were subject and from which they claimed no liberty to depart. (38)

stature to men!! (The bastard!)

[Those who will replace traditional values] are . . . not men (in the old sense) at all. They are, if you like, men who have sacrificed their own share in traditional humanity in order to devote themselves to the task of deciding what 'Humanity' shall henceforth mean. (40)

So the state of being "man" is equated with tradition!(?)

[Those who reject tradition] are not men at all: they are artefacts. Man's final conquest has proved to be the abolition of Man. (41)

Meaning: if you choose your own values and drop blind faith, you are an "artefact"!

I am very doubtful whether history shows us one example of a man who, having stepped outside traditional morality and attained power, has used that power benevolently. I am inclined to think that the Conditioners will hate the conditioned. Though regarding as an illusion the artificial conscience which they produce in us their subjects, they will yet perceive that it creates in us an illusion of meaning for our lives which compares favourably with the futility of their own: and they will envy us as eunuchs envy men. (42)

What a confession of his own social-metaphysical soul this all is! He knows he "can be had" by anyone, and he's scared of his non-traditional masters!

[The non-traditionalists'] extreme rationalism, by 'seeing through' all 'rational' motives, leaves them creatures of wholly irrational behaviour. If you will not obey the *Tao*, or else commit suicide, obedience to impulse (and therefore, in the long run, to mere 'nature') is the only course left open.

The "rational" to him is blind faith!

At the moment, then, of Man's victory over Nature, we find the whole human race subjected to some individual men, and those individuals subjected to that in themselves which is purely 'natural'—to their irrational impulses. (42)

!!!

So man, by nature, is irrational—but faith makes him rational!!!

If the fully planned and conditioned world (with its *Tao* a mere product of the planning) comes into experience, Nature will be troubled no more by the restive species that rose in revolt against her so many millions of years ago, will be vexed no longer by its chatter of truth and mercy and beauty and happiness. (43)

—all of which are unnatural!?!

We do not look at trees either as Dryads or as beautiful objects while we cut them into beams: the first man who did so may have felt the price keenly, and the bleeding trees in Virgil and Spenser may be far-off echoes of that primeval sense of impiety. The stars lost their divinity as astronomy developed, and the Dying God has no place in chemical agriculture. To many, no doubt, this process is simply the gradual discovery that the real world is different from what we expected, and the old opposition to Galileo or to 'bodysnatchers' is simply obscurantism. But that is not the whole story. It is not the greatest of modern scientists who feel most sure that the object, stripped of its qualitative properties and reduced to mere quantity, is wholly real. Little scientists, and little unscientific followers of science, may think so. The great minds know very well that the object, so treated, is an artificial abstraction, that something of its reality has been lost. (44)

> This is really an old fool—and nothing more!

> Ad hominem!

> And what does he think an abstraction is, that great "advocate of reason"? Here's where the Korzybski comes out in him.

We are always conquering Nature, because 'Nature' is the name for what we have, to some extent, conquered. The price of conquest is to treat a thing as mere Nature. Every conquest over Nature increases her domain. The stars do not become Nature till we can weigh and measure them: the soul does not become Nature until we can psycho-analyse her. (45)

> This incredible, medieval monstrosity believes that "mere Nature" is the rationally intelligible!!!!

Either we are rational spirit obliged for ever to obey the absolute values of the *Tao*, or else we are mere nature to be kneaded and cut into new shapes for the pleasures of masters who must, by hypothesis, have no motive but their own 'natural' impulses. Only the *Tao* provides a common human law of action which can over-arch rulers and ruled alike. A dogmatic belief in objective value is necessary to the very idea of a rule which is not tyranny or an obedience which is not slavery. (46)

> The lousy bastard who is a pickpocket of concepts, not a thief, which is too big a word for him.

> Either we are mystics of spirit or mystics of muscle—reason? who ever heard of it?

> —such as in the Middle Ages?

In the *Tao* itself, as long as we remain within it, we find the concrete reality in which to participate is to be truly human: <u>the real common will and common reason of humanity, alive, and growing like a tree, and branching out, as the situation varies, into ever new beauties and dignities of application.</u> (46-47)

Such as starvation and babies dying at birth. "<u>Unenslaved</u>" by science!

Nothing I can say will prevent some people from describing this lecture as <u>an attack on science.</u> I deny the charge, of course: and real Natural Philosophers (there are some now alive) will perceive that in defending value I defend *inter alia* the value of knowledge, which must die like every other when its roots in the *Tao* are cut. (47)

And how!

What's <u>that</u>, brother?

<u>The serious magical endeavour and the serious scientific endeavour are twins: one was sickly and died, the other strong and throve. But they were twins. They were born of the same impulse.</u> (47-48)

The cheap, drivelling non-entity!

<u>There is something which unites magic and applied science while separating both from the 'wisdom' of earlier ages.</u> For the wise men of old the cardinal problem had been how to conform the soul to reality, and the solution had been knowledge, self-discipline, and virtue. For magic and applied science alike the problem is how to subdue reality to the wishes of men: the solution is technique; <u>and both, in the practice of this technique, are ready to do things hitherto regarded as disgusting and impious—such as digging up and mutilating the dead.</u> If we compare the chief trumpeter of the new era (Bacon) with Marlowe's Faustus, the similarity is striking. You will read in some critics that Faustus <u>has a thirst for knowledge. In reality, he hardly mentions it. It is not truth he wants from the devils, but gold and guns and girls</u>. 'All things that move between the quiet poles shall be at his command' and 'a sound magician is a mighty god.' In the same spirit Bacon condemns those who value knowledge as an end in itself: this, for him, is to use as a mistress for pleasure what ought to be a spouse for fruit. The true object is to extend Man's power to the performance of all things possible. <u>He rejects magic because it does not work, but his goal is that of the magician.</u> (48)

<u>This</u> is monstrous!

!!!

!!

So Bacon is a "magician"—but Christ performing miracles is, of course, a spectacle of pure, <u>rational</u> knowledge!!!

This monstrosity is <u>not</u> opposed to science—oh no!— not to <u>pure</u> science, only to <u>applied</u> science, only to anything that improves man's life on earth!

!!!

It might be going too far to say that the modern
scientific movement was tainted from its birth:
but I think it would be true to say that it was born
in an unhealthy neighbourhood and at an inauspi-
cious hour. (49)

!!! You bet your life, you God-
damn, beaten mystic: at the
Renaissance!

Is it, then, possible to imagine a new Natural Philosophy, continually conscious that the 'natural
object' produced by analysis and abstraction is
not reality but only a view, and always correcting
the abstraction? I hardly know what I am asking
for. (49)

That is true—but even here
he's lying. He knows what he
wants: a science subservient to
the Pope.

[Lewis claims we must stop at tradition if we wish to
avoid an infinite regress of rational explanations.]
You cannot go on 'seeing through' things for
ever. The whole point of seeing through something is to see something through it. It is good
that the window should be transparent, because
the street or garden beyond it is opaque. How if
you saw through the garden too? It is no use trying to 'see through' first principles. If you see
through everything, then everything is transparent. But a wholly transparent world is an invisible
world. To 'see through' all things is the same as
not to see. (50)

The abysmal caricature who
postures as a "gentleman and
scholar" treats subjects like
these by means of a corner
lout's equivocation on "seeing
through."! By "seeing through,"
he means: "rational
understanding."!
Oh, BS!—and total BS!

[Lewis ends his essay with the previous passage. On the next page (51), above the beginning
of the Appendix, Ayn Rand made her last comment, apparently a summary of the essence of
the whole essay:]
The bastard actually means that the more man knows, the more he is bound by
reality, the more he has to comply with an "A is A" existence of absolute identity and
causality—and that is what he regards as "surrender" to nature, or as nature's "power
over man." (!) What he objects to is the power of reality. Science shrinks the realm of
his whim. (!!) When he speaks of value judgments he means values set by whim—and
he knows that there is no place for that in nature, i.e., in reality. (The abysmal scum!)

Helmut Schoeck, *Envy: A Theory of Social Behavior*, translated from the German by M. Glenny and B. Ross (New York: Harcourt, Brace & World, Inc., 1969) Reprinted by Liberty Press (1987) *[Page numbers from both editions are given.]*

Chapter 1: Man the Envier

[P]otential envy is an essential part of man's equipment if he is to be able to test the justice and fairness of the solutions to the many problems which occur in his life. Very few of us, when dealing with employees, colleagues, etc. are able to take a position which consciously ignores the existence of envy. . . . No matter how mature, how immune from envy a personnel manager or plant manager may himself be, when he has to deal with the taboo subject of wages or staff regulations he must be able to sense exactly what sort of measures are tolerable, given the general tendency to mutual envy. (3/6)

What about <u>justice</u>?

The kind of maturity achieved by an individual which <u>enables him to conquer his own envy</u> does not seem to be a universally attainable attribute. The reasons for the varying role or effectiveness of envy in different societies must be sought, therefore, in the ethos of the respective cultures. Both the envier, who must somehow come to terms with observed inequalities in his life, and the envied person in trying to ignore the other's envy . . . , will <u>make use of creeds, ideologies, proverbs, etc. which tend to reduce the power of envy</u> and thus allow daily life to proceed with a minimum of friction and conflict. (6/8-9)

?

<u>This</u> is pure BS: he seems to substitute envy for Freud's sex or Marx's means of production, as a universal instinct and basic motive.

To anticipate one of the main theses of this work: the more both private individuals and the custodians of political power in a given society are able to act <u>as though there were no such thing as envy</u>, the greater will be the rate of economic growth and the number of innovations in general. The social climate best suited to the fullest, most unhampered deployment of man's creative faculties (economic, scientific, artistic, etc.) is one where accepted normative behavior, custom, religion, common sense and public opinion are more or less agreed upon an attitude which functions *as if* <u>the envious person could be ignored</u>. (11/15)

Good God Almighty!

Well, shouldn't he be?!

[M]any well-meant proposals for the 'good society' or the completely 'just society' are doomed
because they are based on the false premise that
this must be a society in which there is nothing
left for anyone to envy. This situation can never   Not because an independent
occur because, as is demonstrable, man inevita-   man will create something?
bly discovers something new to envy. (11/15)

[*At the end of Chapter 1, Ayn Rand wrote:*]
He doesn't understand principles at all, particularly not justice, morality or objectivity.

Chapter 2: Envy in Language.

[T]here are no objective criteria for what it is that   Oh no?!
stimulates envy. And herein lies the error of po-
litical egalitarians who believe that it is only nec-   Is that all?
essary to eliminate once and for all certain inequalities from this world to produce a harmoni-
ous society of equals devoid of envy. (19/25)

[*Schoeck quotes several proverbs from many
different cultures, e.g., "Envy looks at a swamp and
sees a sea," "Envy can see the ship well enough, but
not the leak." He then writes:*]
These proverbs explain, too, why in all cultures   He regards appeasement as
it is not just good taste but virtually a compulsion   normal. (?!?)
never to mention one's own advantage, new pos-
session or good luck to others unless in conjunc-
tion with a lack, a disadvantage or a mischance.
(21/27)

None lives in this world without envy. (21/27)   ?!

The more kindness is shown to an envious man,   True
the worse he becomes.
     This . . . observation is particularly impor-
tant because psychopathology has repeatedly
confirmed it. The more one seeks to deprive the
envious man of his ostensible reason for envy by   True
giving him presents and doing him good turns,
the more one demonstrates one's superiority and
stresses how little the gift will be missed. (21/28)

The envious man is perfectly prepared to injure
himself if by so doing he can injure or hurt the   True
object of his envy. (22/28)

Proverbs in many languages agree that the great-

est damage done by the envious man is to himself. (22/28)

True

In 1964 a woman journalist explained the partial
failure of the Ford Foundation's 'Artists-in-Resi-
dence Project' in Berlin, namely, the isolation of
the visitors and the remarkable reactions—
amounting to pure envy—of the local artists, and
quoted the revealing comments of a Berlin artist:
'No one rolls out the red carpet for me when I
arrive in London or Paris' and, 'My studio is
much smaller than the Ford artists' studios.'
Much envied, too, were the monthly stipends (up
to $1,250) of these people. No one but <u>Ameri-
cans, who so often cultivate a blind spot so far as
envy is concerned</u>, could conceivably have attempted such a project. (23/29-30)

Because they are <u>innocent</u>.

Chapter 3: The Envious Man and His Culture

[I]t is virtually impossible categorically to declare that in a given social situation or custom
none of those involved feels envy. (28/36)

To <u>prove</u> a negative?

Social life would be impossible if cultures did
not succeed within reason in forcing those <u>who
have real cause for envy</u> or jealousy to cooperate.
For after all, a society in which there was never
cause for envy, <u>a society of total and constant
equality</u>, would not be workable even as a theoretical experiment. (29/36-37)

What would he regard as a
"<u>real cause</u>"?!

He <u>grants</u> the egalitarian
premise.

<u>We can never say that in such and such a culture
and such and such a social situation none of the
participants is envious or jealous</u>. (29/37)

So what if some <u>are</u>?

Chapter 6: The Psychology of Envy

[T]he propensity for envy is chiefly acquired
through experiencing and suffering sibling jealousy. (62/77)

BS!

Unconsciously the envious one almost expects,
so to speak, that his emotion will be aroused by
minimal differences between himself and another,
just as it was during his childhood and adoles-
cence. (62/78)

B.S.!

The material obtained from dream analysis does at least provide evidence for my thesis that the feeling of envy and jealousy is experienced and learnt primarily in the sibling group and that these feelings, on reaching a certain intensity, have an exceptionally inhibited and destructive effect upon the personality. (68/85)

> What utter B.S.!

The way in which envy is linked with all these experiments becomes apparent as soon as we ask ourselves why a man is not prepared to trust his senses and to defy a group. What is he afraid of? What could the other students, whose identity he does not even know, do to him if he trusted himself and contradicted them? Why is he afraid of being himself? (81/100)

> What a reversal! They conform because they are "afraid of envy"—and not: they are second-handers and, therefore, afraid to be left on their own.

[T]he question as to why etiquette in most cultures regards boasting as a breach of good taste remains unasked [by the social psychologist Albert Pepitone in his "braggart experiment"]. (85/103)

> The issue of "boasting as too easy" (i.e., non-objective) does not even occur to him.

[E]nvy is chiefly directed against people within the same social group and at the same level, and very rarely at those considerably above us.(85/103-104)

> Untrue

In my opinion, the basic error in [the braggart] experiment is the actual concept of the boaster, the swaggerer, the vain man. For in themselves these words mean a man who, from the point of view of society, has a self-evaluation that is objectively false. But what can be made of a person—for instance, a Nobel Prize winner or some other internationally prominent figure—whose behavior corresponds to his position? (85/104)

> This is unintelligible gibberish! A man of achievement would not be a "boaster." (And issues of this kind cannot be studied by "group experiments.")

Chapter 7: Envy as Seen by the Social Sciences [On the title page of Envy, *Ayn Rand wrote: "Of special interest: pp. 87-89"—i.e., the first three pages of Chapter 7.]*
Without envy there could be no social group of any size. The other-directed process comprised in this concept consists of emotional, probably also endocrine processes which influence our perceptions as well as our rationalized cognitive acts. (87/106)

> This is his essence—the abysmal b.!

Often enough we conform whether or not the sympathy of the rest is, or should be, of especial importance to us: we fear what they might do—or not do—if we were to arouse their envy of our courage to deviate from the norm. (87-88/107)

Appeasement as a law of human nature?!!

Despite some influential social theories, it may be that man experiences his membership of a group not as fulfilment but as diminution. Thus membership of the group would be for man a compromise with his true being, not the culmination of his existence but its curtailment. This is a necessary experience for nearly everyone if he is to acquire certain values such as economic security, the acceptance of his children into society etc. But even in the most 'socially minded' man there is a residue of stubborn, proud individualism, the core of his existence as a human being which fills him with *Schadenfreude* when he is able to help impose upon others the same loss of individuality that he himself has painfully experienced. (89/108)

Well, that depends on what kind of man!

He is a total appeaser and second-hander, all the way down! (Only an individualist is fit for society.)

ananke, emphasizes the fact that the implication is true for all values of the variables: in our modern terminology, it is a universal quantifier. Aristotle defines a proposition, a *protasis*, as "a statement affirming or denying something of something." Its elements he calls "terms," *horoi*, the "limits" or "boundaries," the "termini" of the statement. He avoids all psychological or metaphysical overtones, all words like "notion," "concept," in their Greek equivalents. Aristotle's analysis of propositions into "terms" in the *De Interpretatione* is the most "nominalistic" book of the *Organon*.

?!!?

The outcome of Łukasiewicz's close textual analysis may be stated in historical terms. Aristotle's own "logic," in the *Prior Analytics*, is best presented in the "terminism" of William of Ockham, as Ernest Moody has contended in his study of Ockham's logic,[16] and not in the Platonizing reconstructions of the Aristotelian position to be found in Thomas Aquinas or Duns Scotus.

?

Aristotle's syllogistic is thus a consistent, purely formal "dialectic." But Aristotle is no advocate of a logic without ontological implications—quite the contrary! This is the instrument of proof, of demonstration, of science. In what kind of world can you use it successfully? What kind of structure of things can be so expressed?

(In reverse.)

The syllogism will operate in a world exhibiting "kinds" of thing, *eide*, and more inclusive "kinds," *gene*, a world in which are to be found real species and genera, a world in which individual things are what they are because they are of a certain kind, because they belong to a certain species. And this species is what it is because it in turn belongs to a more inclusive kind, to a certain genus. In such a world, science is not concerned with the individual or particular thing as such, with all its "accidental" or incidental qualities and relations. It is concerned rather with this structure of kinds, with what a given species is, and what

This is the root of all his intellectual problems of Aristotle!

[16] Ernest A. Moody, *The Logic of William of Ockham* (New York, 1935).

This is the total inversion (the primacy of consciousness): the universe consists of species and genera because logic demands it — not logic establishes these categories because such is the nature of the universe.

1. See "Review of Randall's *Aristotle*," *The Voice of Reason* (New York: New American Library, 1988), p. 9.

2. See "Review of Randall," p. 10.

3. See "Review of Randall," p. 10.

4. See "Review of Randall," p. 10.

5. See "Review of Randall," p. 11.

6. See "Review of Randall," pp. 8-9.

7. Ayn Rand regarded this as the best chapter of the book. See "Review of Randall," p. 10.

8. See "Review of Randall," p. 11.

9. "Review of Randall," p. 11 : "The blackest patch in this often illuminating book is Chapter XII." In her notes, Ayn Rand wrote: "All hell breaks loose in this chapter."

10. See "Review of Randall," p. 11.

11. See "Review of Randall," pp. 11-12.

12. Ayn Rand reacted here to Randall's interpretation. What Aristotle actually described were two ways in which a tyranny can preserve itself: one, to become more tyrannical and oppressive; the other, to become moral (or to approach being moral). After discussing the first way, Aristotle says, in *Politics* V 9 (quoted by Randall on p. 265): "Such are the arts of the tyrant, and such are the means he uses in order to maintain his authority; but they plumb the depth of wrongdoing." Ayn Rand commented in the margin: "A. is not an amoralist in politics."

Part II
Economics

we get it? *This* is the main place where the question of motive comes in. A man may earn money to support his family, to send his son to college, to pursue abstract scientific studies, to contribute to some public cause in which he deeply believes, to found a new charity. Now most working people are unselfish in this sense. Most of them support with their earnings not simply themselves, but others—a wife, children, aged parents, a sister or brother, and so on. A man works for his family—not so that he alone, but that *they* can have more. In brief, he works not merely for himself but for those he loves."

"But socialism, chief, argues that he ought to love *everybody*, and ought to work for everybody."

"But the simple fact is, Adams, that he *doesn't* love everybody, and you can't *force* him to love everybody. And if you try to force him to love and support everybody, you merely kill his incentives and impoverish everybody. Of course under a regime of freedom you can persuade or exhort a man to widen voluntarily the circle of his love or at least his good will. And if a man here or there under our free market system *does* love everybody, and *does* want to produce for everybody and give to everybody, there is nothing to prevent him from doing so to the limit of his capacity."

"Then your point," said Adams, "is that while we may regret that more people are not more charitable than they are, the fault is not that of the free market or of the private enterprise system, but of human nature?"

"Precisely," said Peter. "My point is that the nature of human beings primarily determines the nature and working of the economic and social system under which they live—and not, as Karl Marx supposed, the other way round."

"But wouldn't your argument apply also to communism, chief? Aren't its faults also primarily the faults of the people who adopted and operate it?"

"The people first embraced communism, Adams, under a delusion; but then were held to it by bayonets. I am talking about systems that people are still free to change peaceably. Communism is infinitely worse than the potential human nature of

332

Marginalia (handwritten):
- Why? What for?
- !!! / ' ' '
- Then if men were communists, that would be their virtue?
- !!! ! ! !
- And if he doesn't support any parasite whatever? If he is not a sacrificial beast of burden for anyone — do you grant him

Ludwig von Mises, *Human Action* **(New Haven, Conn.: Yale University Press, 1949)**
[Presently, the most accessible version is the Third Revised Edition (Chicago: Contemporary Books, Inc., 1966). In a few cases, the passage Ayn Rand was commenting on changed slightly in the later edition. When the page numbers of the two editions differ, both are given.]

Human Action *was favorably reviewed in* The Objectivist Newsletter, *vol. 2, no. 9 (September 1963), and was included in the Recommended Bibliography at the end of* Capitalism: The Unknown Ideal. *The review, which praises Mises' economic theories, ends with the following remarks: "In justice to Prof. Mises' position and our own, it must be mentioned that there are many sections of* Human Action *with which Objectivists cannot agree. These sections pertain, not to the sphere of economics as such, but to the philosophical framework in which his economic theories are presented. . . . Notwithstanding these reservations, the book is of the first rank of importance, eminently deserving of careful study." It is important to keep these remarks in mind, given the critical nature of what follows, and given that most of the marginalia on* Human Action *appear in the philosophical parts of the book.*

Introduction

1. Economics and Praxeology

[E]conomics opened to human science a domain previously inaccessible and never thought of. The discovery of a regularity in the sequence and interdependence of market phenomena went beyond the limits of the traditional system of learning. It conveyed knowledge which could be regarded neither as logic, mathematics, psychology, physics, nor biology. (1)

? Not true.

It was philosophy and psychology.

Philosophers had long since been eager to ascertain the ends which God or Nature were trying to realize in the course of human history. . . . [*They failed, Mises says, because of their faulty method.*] They dealt with humanity as a whole or with other holistic concepts like nation, race, or church. They set up quite arbitrarily the ends to which the behavior of such wholes is bound to lead. <u>But they could not satisfactorily answer the question regarding what factors compelled the various acting individuals to behave in such a way that the goal aimed at by the whole's inexorable evolution was attained.</u> (1)

<u>Equivocation!</u>
a) even if the methods were wrong, this is still the province of philosophy, by his own definition in paragraph 1.
b) since when is the teleology of "the whole" to be taken as a fact or a legitimate question, let alone as a primary?

Other philosophers were more realistic. They did

<u>Equivocation:</u> The discovery of

not try to guess the designs of Nature or God. They looked at human things from the viewpoint of government. . . . But all were fully convinced that there was in the course of social events no such regularity and invariance of phenomena as had already been found in the operation of human reasoning and in the sequence of natural phenomena. They did not search for the laws of social cooperation because they thought that man could organize society as he pleased. (2)

Bewildered people had to face a new view of society. They [i.e., those whose view depended on God or Nature, and those who looked at human action from "the viewpoint of government"] learned with stupefaction that there is another aspect from which human action might be viewed than that of good and bad, of fair and unfair, of just and unjust. In the course of social events there prevails a regularity of phenomena to which man must adjust his action if he wishes to succeed. It is futile to approach social facts with the attitude of a censor who approves or disapproves from the point of view of quite arbitrary standards and subjective judgments of value. One must study the laws of human action and social cooperation as the physicist studies the laws of nature. (2)

[The general theory of choice and preference] is the science of every kind of human action. Choosing determines all human decisions. . . . All human values are offered for option. All ends and all means, both material and ideal issues, the sublime and the base, the noble and the ignoble, are ranged in a single row and subjected to a decision which picks out one thing and sets aside another. . . . The modern theory of value widens the scientific horizon and enlarges the field of economic studies. Out of the political economy of the classical school emerges the general theory of human action, praxeology. (3)

"regular laws" is here equated with the goals of mystics or statists. The fact that he is dealing with the Law of Identity is ignored.

Good God, what equivocation! Now the moral is equated with the mystical. Are all standards and judgments of value "arbitrary" and "subjective"? All he has said in this paragraph, in fact, is that man ought to be studied as objectively as anything else. But this is not what he means nor implies.

??? What is this? An "easy" way of defining free will? Or, rather, of evading it?

So he is going to deal with values, choices, free will and action—but this is not the province of philosophy, morality, politics or psychology?

2. The Epistemological Problem of a General Theory of Human Action

[According to Mises, all men before Marx had accepted logic (or "the immutability of the logical structure of the human mind") as a given. Marx, Mises says, was the first to deny it. (4-5)]

Untrue! Marx was not the first to deny the validity of logic. Every other mystic had done it before him.

The technology of Soviet Russia utilizes without scruple all the results of bourgeois physics, chemistry, and biology just as if they were valid for all classes. The Nazi engineers and physicians did not disdain to utilize the theories, discoveries, and inventions of people of "inferior" races and nations. The behavior of people of all races, nations, religions, linguistic groups, and social classes clearly proves that they do not endorse the doctrines of polylogism and irrationalism as far as logic, mathematics, and the natural sciences are concerned.

> He is saying that the other sciences can ignore the destruction of their philosophical and epistemological base because the destroyers are still willing to use their products!!!
>
> This is near-sighted, and sounds like delusions of persecution!

But it is quite different with praxeology and economics. The main motive for the development of the doctrines of polylogism, historicism, and irrationalism was to provide a justification for disregarding the teachings of economics in the determination of economic policies. (5-6)

> The "main motive"—to escape from the Law of Identity— would not occur to him, since he is shunning it himself!

[A scientist] is bound to reply to every censure without any regard to its underlying motives or its background. (6)

> Example of his kind of equivocation: It is true that one should answer every censure regardless of its motives. It is not true that one should answer every censure. (What's missing? The concept of objectivity.)

The system of economic thought must be built up in such a way that it is proof against any criticism on the part of irrationalism, historicism, panphysicalism, behaviorism, and all varieties of polylogism. (7)

> !!! Try and do it! (He means: build a system that will embrace, include and defeat the irrationalists and the polylogists. He treats them, in effect, as legitimate errors of knowledge.)

3. Economic Theory and the Practice of Human Action

[T]o live implies both imperfection and change. (7)

> Oh no, philosophy's not necessary and he is not affected by it in his "scientific" approach, is he?

It is common with narrow-minded people to reflect upon every respect in which other people differ from themselves. The camel in the fable takes exception to all other animals for not having a hump. . . . (8)

> I thought he was going to answer criticisms without reference to motives (!?)

For him [i.e., the research worker in a laboratory] economics cannot be anything but a form of mechanics. (8)

And for M. von Mises, morality cannot be anything but a form of economics.

What is commonly called the "industrial revolution" was an offspring of the ideological revolution brought about by the doctrines of the economists. (8)

And **what** brought about the doctrines of the economists? Aristotle had nothing to do with it, did he? Economics is a primary, is it?

4. Résumé

It was necessary to make these preliminary remarks in order to explain why this treatise places economic problems within the broad frame of a general theory of human action. (10)

What has he explained? Only that a lot of socialists and fools are attacking his pet science, economics, which he treats as a primary in a vacuum. Does this constitute an objective explanation for the establishment of any new system of categories for sciences?

Part One: Human Action

Chapter 1: Acting Man

1. Purposeful Action and Animal Reaction

[*Mises contrasts neurotics and psychopaths with "we who consider ourselves normal." (12)*]

Epistemological agnosticism.

[A]cting man chooses, determines, and tries to reach an end. Of two things both of which he cannot have together he selects one and gives up the other. Action therefore always involves both taking and renunciation. (12)

!!!?

2. The Prerequisites of Human Action

The incentive that impels a man to act is always some uneasiness. A man perfectly content with the state of his affairs would have no incentive to change things. He would have neither wishes nor desires; he would be perfectly happy. He would not act; he would simply live free from care. (13/13-14)

??!!
This is Nirvana-worship! So happiness is the absence of desire?!

In colloquial speech we call a man "happy" who
has succeeded in attaining his ends. A more adequate description of his state would be that he is   ?!
happier than he was before. (14)

What makes a man feel uneasy and less uneasy is   Pure motivation by fear.
established by him from the standard of his own
will and judgment, from his personal and subjective valuation. Nobody is in a position to decree
what should make a fellow man happier. (14)

In the praxeological terminology the proposition:
man's unique aim is to attain happiness, is tauto-   ??!
logical. (15)

The idea that the incentive of human activity is   Fear!
always some uneasiness and its aim always to
remove such uneasiness as far as possible, that is,
to make the acting men feel happier, is the essence of the teachings of Eudaimonism and He-
donism. (15)

To punish criminal offenses committed in a state   Typical. He thinks that _fear_ is
of emotional excitement or intoxication more   practical.
mildly than other offenses is tantamount to en-
couraging such excesses. The threat of severe
retaliation does not fail to deter even people
driven by seemingly irresistible passion. (16)

3. Human Action as an Ultimate Given

[Science] is aware of the limits of the human   Perfection and "unlimited"
mind and of the human search for knowledge. It   knowledge would consist of
aims at tracing back every phenomenon to its   perceiving a reality of infinite
cause. But it realizes that these endeavors must   regress, without any axioms!
necessarily strike against insurmountable walls.
There are phenomena which cannot be analyzed
and traced back to other phenomena. (17)

Concrete value judgments and definite human   ?!
actions are not open to further analysis. We may
fairly assume or believe that they are absolutely
dependent upon and conditioned by their causes.
But as long as we do not know how external   His view of the nature of
facts—physical and physiological—produce in a   consciousness: "external facts
human mind definite thoughts and volitions re-   _produce_ thoughts"!!?
sulting in concrete acts, we have to face an insur-
mountable *methodological dualism*. (17/18)

Reason and experience show us two separate realms: the external world of physical, chemical, and physiological phenomena and the internal world of thought, feeling, valuation, and purposeful action. No bridge connects—as far as we can see—these two spheres. Identical external events result sometimes in different human responses, and different external events result sometimes in different human responses. We do not know why. (18)

What a mess! What equivocation and "concept-salad"!

Human action is one of the agencies bringing about change. . . . As—at least under present conditions—it cannot be traced back to its causes, it must be considered as an ultimate given and must be studied as such. (18)

He thinks that since the actions of consciousness cannot be reduced to physical causes, they must be accepted as an irreducible primary![2]

4. Rationality and Irrationality; Subjectivism and Objectivity of Praxeological Research

Human action is necessarily always rational. The term "rational action" is therefore pleonastic and must be rejected as such. When applied to the ultimate ends of action, the terms rational and irrational are inappropriate and meaningless. (18/19)

???!!!
Nobody can get anywhere with such a terminology!

No man is qualified to declare what would make another happier or less discontented. The critic either tells us what he believes he would aim at if he were in the place of his fellow; or, in dictatorial arrogance blithely disposing of his fellow's will and aspirations, declares what condition of this other man would better suit himself, the critic. (19)

And this, of course, is the standard of rationality!—the damn whim-worshipper!

The impulse to live, to preserve one's own life, and to take advantage of every opportunity of strengthening one's vital forces is a primal feature of life, present in every living being. However, to yield to this impulse is not—for man—an inevitable necessity. (19)

He means this more profoundly than in this superficial context.

The opposite of action is not *irrational behavior*, but a reactive response to stimuli on the part of the bodily organs and instincts which cannot be controlled by the volition of the person con-

He indulges in constant equivocation on the subject of "instincts," speaking of them as if he meant physical reflexes—

cerned. . . . With regard to the problem involved in the antithesis, rational and irrational, there is no difference between the natural sciences and the social sciences. Science always is and must be rational. (20/20-21)

but not quite.

How can a psychotic's choice of "means" be called rational? Or "deliberated"?

The human mind is not even capable of conceiving a kind of knowledge not limited by an ultimate given inaccessible to further analysis and reduction. The scientific method that carries the mind up to this point is entirely rational. The ultimate given may be called an irrational fact. (20-21/21)

Good God Almighty! Thus "A is A" is an irrational fact!!!

The teachings of praxeology and economics are valid for every human action without regard to its underlying motives, causes, and goals. . . . Praxeology deals with the ways and means chosen for the attainment of such ultimate ends. Its object is means, not ends. (21)

Let's see how many times he'll contradict this.[3]

[I]t is in this subjectivism [i.e., the subjectivism of the science of human action, which does not pass value judgments] that the objectivity of our science lies. Because it is subjectivist and takes the value judgments of acting man as ultimate data not open to any further critical examination, it is itself above all strife of parties and factions. . . . (21/22)

Hello, polylogist!

That's his idea of objectivity— and it's the substitution of the "collective" for the "objective."

[C]ausality is a category of action. (22)

?

[M]an raises the question: who or what is at the bottom of things? He searches for the regularity and the "law," because he wants to interfere. Only later was this search more extensively interpreted by metaphysics as a search after the ultimate cause of being and existence. Centuries were needed to bring these exaggerated and extravagant ideas back again to the more modest question of where one must interfere or should one be able to interfere in order to attain this or that end. (22)

I'm sick of this logical-positivist-like equation of metaphysics with mystical metaphysics!

The philosophical, epistemological, and metaphysical problems of causality and of imperfect

What becomes of "praxeology" if he makes a perfect case for it,

induction are beyond the scope of praxeology. (23)

> except that philosophers prove to him that there is no knowledge and no reality and no causality, and, therefore, everything is a "subjective" delusion, including his "praxeology"?

[T]he evidence that we have correctly perceived a causal relation is provided only by the fact that action guided by this knowledge results in the expected outcome. (23)

> Really, dear pragmatist?

6. The Alter Ego

It may be admitted that it is impossible to provide conclusive evidence for the propositions that my logic is the logic of all other people and by all means absolutely the only human logic. . . . (24)

> Well, if this is not polylogism, what in all hell is it?

What cannot be brought under either of these categories [i.e., teleology and causality] is absolutely hidden to the human mind. An event not open to an interpretation by one of these two principles is for man inconceivable and mysterious. (25)

> Hello, neo-mystic!

Both principles of cognition—causality and teleology—are, owing to the limitations of human reason, imperfect and do not convey ultimate knowledge. Causality leads to a *regressus in infinitum* which reason can never exhaust. Teleology is found wanting as soon as the question is raised of what moves the prime mover. (25)

> He is fighting the modern philosophers like Russell Kirk is fighting the socialists—by pleading "human infirmity"!!!

He who seeks this [i.e., perfect cognition] must apply to faith and try to quiet his conscience by embracing a creed or a metaphysical doctrine. (25/25-26)

> Logical positivist!

Praxeology and history are manifestations of the human mind and as such are conditioned by the intellectual abilities of mortal men. Praxeology and history do not pretend to know anything about the intentions of an absolute and objective mind, about an objective meaning inherent in the course of events and of historical evolution, and about the plans which God or Nature or Weltgeist

> ? Equating these two categories again, isn't he? He certainly considers objectivity as mystical. Who on earth, after reading all

or Manifest Destiny is trying to realize in direct-
ing the universe and human affairs. (28/28-29)

this, can consider him an
advocate of reason?

The subject matter of praxeology is human action. It is not concerned with human beings who
have succeeded in suppressing altogether everything that characterizes man as man: will, desire,
thought, and the striving after ends. It deals with
acting man, not with man transformed into a
plant and reduced to a merely vegetative existence. (29)

Break No.1 of the claim on p.
21: Here he excludes a certain
kind of version of "happiness."
Why aren't these "vegetative
mystics" entitled to their view
of happiness—since he claims
to pass no judgment on
"ends"—and since he included
"non-action <is> the free of
possibilities" in the category of
what he calls "action." (See
p.13)?[4] This definition on p.13
and the above are a blatant
contradiction.

Chapter 2: The Epistemological Problems of the Sciences of Human Action

1. Praxeology and History

The subject matter of all historical sciences is the
past. They cannot teach us anything which would
be valid for all human actions, that is, for the future too. (30)

What??!!

The information conveyed by historical experience cannot be used as building material for the
construction of theories and the prediction of future events. Every historical experience is open
to various interpretations, and is in fact interpreted in different ways. (31)

??!

So? And what isn't?

Complex phenomena in the production of which
various causal chains are interlaced cannot test
any theory. Such phenomena, on the contrary,
become intelligible only through an interpretation
in terms of theories previously developed from
other sources. In the case of natural phenomena
the interpretation of an event must not be at variance with the theories satisfactorily verified by
experiments. In the case of historical events there
is no such restriction. (31)

By what standard? What is
"satisfactory" verification? How
many theories have been
exploded, with or without
alleged experimental
verification, particularly when
the problems are complex?

[Praxeology's] cognition is purely formal and
general without reference to the material content
and the particular features of the actual case. It

This is the real motive of the
whole structure. There is no "a
priori" knowledge. There is no

aims at knowledge valid for all instances in which the conditions exactly correspond to those implied in its assumptions and inferences. Its statements and propositions are not derived from experience. They are, like those of logic and mathematics, a priori. They are not subject to verification or falsification on the ground of experience and facts. (32)

knowledge not derived from experience—but "experience" does not mean what the pragmatists intend it to mean.

[The statements and propositions of praxeology] are both logically and temporally antecedent to any comprehension of historical facts. They are a necessary requirement of any intellectual grasp of historical events. Without them we should not be able to see in the course of events anything else than kaleidoscopic change and chaotic muddle. (32)

Really? What about the philosophy of history?

2. The Formal and Aprioristic Character of Praxeology

Metaphysicians were eager to discover by intuition moral precepts, the meaning of historical evolution, the properties of soul and matter, and the laws governing physical, chemical, and physiological events. (32)

He hates morality, doesn't he?

There is no doubt that empiricism and pragmatism are right as far as they merely describe the procedure of the natural sciences. (32)

He does not understand philosophy at all!

With regard to praxeology the errors of the philosophers are due to their complete ignorance of economics and very often to their shockingly insufficient knowledge of history. (32-33)

Oh, dear me!

There is a history of logic as there is a history of technology. Nothing suggests that logic as we know it is the last and final stage of intellectual evolution. (33-34/33)

Huh?

God, oh God, oh God! And this is not polylogism?

We feel with them [i.e., animals, who lack reason] because we ourselves are in a similar position: pressing in vain against the limitation of our intellectual apparatus, striving unavailingly after unattainable perfect cognition. (34)

There's the desire for automatic omniscience!

The human mind is not a tabula rasa on which the external events write their own history. It is

What "concept-salad"!

equipped with a set of tools for grasping reality. Man acquired these tools, i.e., the logical structure of his mind, in the course of his evolution from an amoeba to his present state. But these tools are logically prior to any experience. (35)

[T]he category of action is logically antecedent to any concrete act. (35)

??

The fact that man does not have the creative power to imagine categories at variance with the fundamental logical relations and with the principles of causality and teleology enjoins upon us what may be called *methodological apriorism.* (35)

!!!—the power to create a reality of whim?!

He who addresses his fellow men, who wants to inform and convince them, who asks questions and answers other people's questions, can proceed in this way only because he can appeal to something common to all men—namely, the logical structure of human reason. (35)

Kant—and all the consequent disasters![5]

It does not matter for man whether or not beyond the sphere accessible to the human mind there are other spheres in which there is something categorically different from human thinking and acting. No knowledge from such spheres penetrates to the human mind. It is idle to ask whether things-in-themselves are different from what they appear to us, and whether there are worlds which we cannot divine and ideas which we cannot comprehend. These are problems beyond the scope of human cognition. Human knowledge is conditioned by the structure of the human mind. (36/35-36)

Green-gremlin premise!

It is true that Lévy-Bruhl himself maintains that the mentality of primitive peoples is essentially "mystic and prelogical" in character; primitive man's collective representations are regulated by the "law of participation" and are consequently indifferent to the law of contradiction. However, Lévy-Bruhl's distinction between prelogical and logical thinking refers to the content and not to the form and categorical structure of thinking. (36)

This is important and true. Von Mises' criticism is wrong—it's based on the premise of an automatic consciousness, functioning one way or another, with logic proceeding from some sort of "logical structure of the mind."

A peasant eager to get a rich crop may—according to the content of his ideas —choose various methods. He may perform some magical rites, he may embark on a pilgrimage, he may offer a candle to the image of his patron saint, or he may employ more and better fertilizer. But whatever he does, it is always action, i.e., the employment of means for the attainment of ends. Magic is in a broader sense a variety of technology. Exorcism is a deliberate purposeful action based on a world view which most of our contemporaries condemn as superstitious and therefore as inappropriate. (37)

> Here we go! This is what "definitions by non-essentials" will do. Mysticism is just an error of knowledge, is it?

No facts provided by ethnology or history contradict the assertion that the logical structure of mind is uniform with all men of all races, ages, and countries. (37-38/38)

> He wants logic to be innate!

3. The A Priori and Reality

The theorems attained by correct praxeological reasoning are not only perfectly certain and incontestable, like the correct mathematical theorems. They refer, moreover with the full rigidity of their apodictic certainty and incontestability to the reality of action as it appears in life and history. Praxeology conveys exact and precise knowledge of real things. (39)

> Really?

> How? When he does not concede our capacity to perceive reality?

There is nothing which only approximately or incompletely fits the economic category of an exchange. There are only exchange and nonexchange. . . . (40)

> Really? But "A is A" is only a "structure of our mind" which cannot be proved to have any connection to reality?

Unaided by praxeological knowledge we would never learn anything about media of exchange. If we approach coins without such preexisting knowledge, we would see in them only round plates of metal, nothing more. Experience concerning money requires familiarity with the praxeological category medium of exchange. (40)

> Good God!
> Praxeology is here made to be a form of "mystique" unrelated to plain rational perception and identification.

4. The Principle of Methodological Individualism

As the whole is both logically and temporally prior to its parts or members, the study of the in-

> Neatest trick of the week, whatever this means!

dividual is posterior to the study of society. (42)

A collective whole is a particular aspect of the actions of various individuals and as such a real thing determining the course of events. (43)

> What sort of superficiality and arbitrary assertion is this? A collective whole is not "an action" nor "an aspect of action"!

The *Ego* is the unity of the acting being. (44)

> "Definition by non-essentials."

6. The Individual and Changing Features of Human Action

When [a man] is born, he does not enter the world in general as such, but a definite environment. The innate and inherited biological qualities and all that life has worked upon him make a man what he is at any instant of his pilgrimage. They are his fate and destiny. His will is not "free" in the metaphysical sense of this term. It is determined by his background and all the influences to which he himself and his ancestors were exposed. (46)

> Is this Dewey and the anti-abstraction premise? Is it improper to conceive of his "entering the world" and of conditions that would exist in any "environment"??
>
> Here goes the whole possibility and sense of any sort of "praxeology." It is a "word-salad" to talk about the choices of a being who has no free will. And this is what he considers an irrefutable (!!!) science?!

Common man does not speculate about the great problems. With regard to them he relies upon other people's authority. . . . Yet the common man does choose. He chooses to adopt traditional patterns or patterns adopted by other people because he is convinced that this procedure is best fitted to achieve his own welfare. And he is ready to change his ideology and consequently his mode of action whenever he becomes convinced that this would better serve his own interests. (46)

> How? If his will is not free, but determined by the background which he is now supposed to reject?

7. The Scope and the Specific Method of History

It has been asserted that the historian himself cannot avoid judgments of value. No historian — not even the naïve chronicler or newspaper reporter—registers all facts as they happen. He must discriminate. . . . This choice, it is said, implies in itself a value judgment. It is necessarily conditioned by the historian's world view and

> This is the result of the revolt against definitions. If definitions are not made objectively and by essentials, then no judgment of "what is relevant" is possible— and any reporter's or historian's whim takes over.

thus not impartial. . . . History can never be anything else than distortion of facts. . . . (48)

There always remains at the bottom of each of [the historian's] problems something which resists analysis at the hand of these teachings of other sciences. It is these individual and unique characteristics of each event which are studied by the understanding. (49)

What on earth is <u>this</u>?

The uniqueness or individuality which remains at the bottom of every historical fact, when all the means for its interpretation provided by logic, mathematics, praxeology, and the natural sciences have been exhausted, is an ultimate datum. (49)

If it were <u>metaphysically</u> unique, it would have no relevance to anyone else anywhere.

But whereas the natural sciences cannot say anything about their ultimate data than that they are such, history can try to make its ultimate data intelligible. Although it is impossible to reduce them to their causes—they would not be ultimate data if such a reduction were possible—the historian can understand them because he is himself a human being. In the philosophy of Bergson this understanding is called an intuition, viz., "la sympathie par laquelle on se transporte a l'intérieur d'un objet pour coïncider avec ce qu'il a d'unique et par conséquent d'inexprimable." German epistemology calls this act *das spezifische Verstehen der Geisteswissenschaften* or simply *Verstehen* [understanding]. . . . The discovery and the delimitation of understanding was one of the most important contributions of modern epistemology. (50/49-50)

Contradictions. <u>This</u> is the "law of participation" mentioned on p.36 —the "law" of losing one's identity and becoming something else, the method of savages and mystics.

Pure and total mysticism! "Understanding" as an epistemological means apart from reason?

The scope of understanding is the mental grasp of phenomena which cannot be totally elucidated by logic, mathematics, praxeology, and the natural sciences to the extent that they cannot be cleared up by all these sciences. It must never contradict the teachings of these other branches of knowledge. (50)

What does he think <u>logic</u> is? Now here he has a "non-logical" means of understanding.

Why must it not? A value judgment, Dr. von Mises?

[N]o appeal to understanding could justify a historian's attempt to maintain that the devil really existed and interfered with human events otherwise than in the vision of an excited human

How does <u>he</u> know this? Did mathematics or the natural sciences prove it to him?

brain. (51)

[Some historians] try to oppose to the theorems of economics an appeal to documents allegedly proving things incompatible with these theorems. They do not realize that complex phenomena can neither prove nor disprove any theorem and therefore cannot bear witness against any statement of a theory. Economic history is possible only because there is an economic theory capable of throwing light upon economic actions. (51)

> The revolt against facts. "Theory" is above reality. This is a neat gimmick: reverse cause and effect, and claim that there is no perception without a "theory"—an innate, a priori, Platonic theory.

8. Conception and Understanding

[History] faces its own specific problem: the elucidation of the unique and individual features of the case by means of the understanding. (51)

> Non-conceptual?

[T]he problem which these differences of interpretation [among historians] offer must not be confused with the intentional distortion of facts by propagandists and apologists parading as historians. (52)

> Why not? How does he know which is which? Facts? How does he know them?

The facts of the French Revolution are presented in a quite different manner by those who believe in the sacred rights of the anointed king and those who hold other views. . . . Only those who believe that facts write their own story into the tabula rasa of the human mind blame the historians for such differences of opinion. (53)

> Innate or automatic—he had no other view of the mind.

Changes in the teachings of the nonhistorical sciences consequently must involve a rewriting of history. (53)

> Stalin would agree with him.

The divergences referred to above [i.e., differences in opinions among historians based on differences in outlook] must not be confused:
   1. With purposeful ill-intentioned distortion of facts.
   2. With attempts to justify or to condemn any actions from a legal or moral point of view.
   3. With the merely incidental insertion of remarks expressing value judgments in a strictly objective representation of the states of affairs. (54)

> 1. How can he know which is which?
> 2. What are "Catholic" or "Protestant" histories but a "moral point of view"?

To every historical factor understanding tries to assign its relevance. In the exercise of understanding there is no room for arbitrariness and capriciousness. The freedom of the historian is limited by his endeavor to provide a satisfactory explanation of reality. His guiding star must be the search for truth. But there necessarily enters into understanding an element of subjectivity. (57)

??!!
"Subjectivity" is not "arbitrary" or "capricious"? A non-objective mind is a tool in the search for truth?

The a priori sciences—logic, mathematics, and praxeology—aim at a knowledge unconditionally valid for all beings endowed with the logical structure of the human mind. The natural sciences aim at a cognition valid for all those beings which are not only endowed with the faculty of human reason but with human senses. The uniformity of human logic and sensation bestows upon these branches of knowledge the character of universal validity. Such at least is the principle guiding the study of the physicists. Only in recent years have they begun to see the limits of their endeavors and, abandoning the excessive pretensions of older physicists, discovered the "uncertainty principle." They realize today that there are unobservables whose unobservability is a matter of epistemological principle. (57)

"Automatism."

The "collective" instead of the "objective."

??!!

As far as understanding aims at assigning its relevance to each factor, it is open to the influence of subjective judgments. Of course, these are not judgments of value, they do not express preferences of the historian. They are judgments of relevance. (57)

Where is his definition of the difference? By implication, it is that the "judgments of relevance" are non-volitional, automatic and therefore reliable, while the "judgments of value" are arbitrary. The sole motive for any such division is hatred of morality.

But as far as historians disagree with regard to judgments of relevance it is impossible to find a solution which all sane men must accept. (58)

Social metaphysics.

Acting man looks, as it were, with the eyes of a historian into the future. (58)

Nice little metaphor—and how scientific!

9. On Ideal Types

Although unique and unrepeatable, historical

Epistemological equivocation of

events have one common feature: they are human action. (59)

the anti-abstraction premise: if historical events are unique in the sense of concrete existents, so are laboratory experiments. If we cannot form abstractions about historical events, neither can we form them about physics or anything else. What proof has he given for his anti-history contentions? Only that historical events are "complex" and that historians disagree. (Anti-effort and social metaphysics.)

Ideal types are the specific notions employed in historical research and in the representation of its results. They are concepts of understanding. As such they are entirely different from praxeological categories and concepts and from the concepts of the natural sciences. . . . An ideal type cannot be defined. . . . (59-60)

!!! Agnosticism! A "concept" that "cannot be defined"?!

The ideal type itself is an outcome of an understanding of the motives, ideas, and aims of the acting individuals and of the means they apply. (60)

These are outside logic and definitions!

No historical problem can be treated without the aid of ideal types. Even when the historian deals with an individual person or with a single event, he cannot avoid referring to ideal types. If he speaks of Napoleon, he must refer to such ideal types as commander, dictator, revolutionary leader. . . . (60)

Boy, oh boy, oh boy! What he is describing are abstractions—so what is the purpose of a concept such as "ideal type"? Well, see above: these are abstractions which are outside the bounds of logic and definition!!!

Whether or not the employment of a definite ideal type is expedient and conducive to an adequate grasp of phenomena can only be decided by understanding. It is not the ideal type which determines the mode of understanding; it is the mode of understanding that requires the construction and use of corresponding ideal types. (61/60)

Expediency as a standard of perception!!!

Translation: it is not objective abstractions that determine our approach to history; it is our subjective approach that determines our abstractions.(!!!)

The economic concept "entrepreneur" belongs to a stratum other than the ideal type "entrepreneur"

Good Lord! Intentional non-integration and "thinking in

as used by economic history and descriptive economics. (On a third stratum lies the legal term "entrepreneur.") (61)

squares." !!!

History has little use for a general ideal type of entrepreneur. It is more concerned with such types as: the American entrepreneur of the time of Jefferson, German heavy industries in the age of William II, New England textile manufacturing in the last decades preceding the first World War, the Protestant *haute finance* of Paris, self-made entrepreneurs, and so on. (61-62)

But no general and precise abstraction is possible? It is by such means as these that one creates an alleged "new science." (Straw-man premise—and the need of Occam's razor: don't multiply sciences!)

It will be shown at a later stage of our investigations that the distinction between "economic" and "noneconomic" motives of human action is untenable. (63)

???!

10. The Procedure of Economics

No special experience is needed in order to comprehend these theorems, and no experience, however rich, could disclose them to a being who did not know a priori what human action is. (64)

The mystic's formula.

Like logic and mathematics, praxeological knowledge is in us; it does not come from without. (64)

It ain't in me!

It would be possible to deal with this second task by delineating all thinkable conditions and deducing from them all inferences logically permissible. . . . It would deal no less with hypothetical acting such as would take place under the unrealizable conditions of imaginary worlds. (64-65)

Such is his idea of logic!

[Praxeology] examines unreal and unrealizable conditions if such an inquiry is needed for a satisfactory grasp of what is going on under the conditions present in reality. (65)

What a definition!

[T]he real world is conditioned by the disutility of labor. Only theorems based on the assumption that labor is a source of uneasiness are applicable for the comprehension of what is going on in the world. (65)

This is the end for me, as far as any possible agreement with praxeology is concerned. And this is what he calls "irrefutable"!

Economics does not follow the procedure of

Platonic and Kantian

logic and mathematics. It does not present an integrated system of pure aprioristic ratiocination severed from any reference to reality. (66)

"rationalist."

How does he know when he "comprehends reality"?

In the face of all this frenzied agitation it is expedient to establish the fact that the starting point of all praxeological and economic reasoning, the category of human action, is proof against any criticisms and objections. No appeal to any historical or empirical considerations whatever can discover any fault in the proposition that men purposely aim at certain ends. No talk about irrationality, the unfathomable depths of the human soul, the spontaneity of the phenomena of life, automatisms, reflexes, and tropisms, can invalidate the statement that man makes use of his reason for the realization of wishes and desires. (67)

!!?!

Some men do. This is sloppy definition-by-non-essentials or else equivocation.

With no definition of what is reason—and with all those schools who claim that there is no reason and with whom he agrees?

Most men do not use reason about their means. Why would they or could they do it, if they do not or can not use it about their ends? Besides, every means is a sub-end.

Precisely defining assumptions and conditions, they construct a system of concepts and draw all the inferences implied by logically unassailable ratiocination. With regard to the results thus obtained only two attitudes are possible: either one can unmask logical errors in the chain of the deductions which produced these results, or one must acknowledge their correctness and validity. (67)

Really? And what about challenging the "assumptions"?

Man is not infallible. He searches for truth—that is, for the most adequate comprehension of reality as far as the structure of his mind and reason makes it accessible to him. Man can never become omniscient. He can never be absolutely certain that his inquiries were not misled and that what he considers as certain truth is not error. (68)

This is a good example of how an irrationalist, while paying all the lip-service to reason, will leave himself a crack for the irrational—and then announce the non-absolutism of human knowledge. Always look for that crack. It will always be stated explicitly—and as unobtrusively as here.

[The empirical sciences] can deal with segments without paying attention to the whole field. (69)

Really?

[Historians] sometimes fail to realize that it is impossible to abstract any causal relations from the study of complex phenomena. (69)

Really?

11. The Limitations on Praxeological Concepts

The praxeological categories and concepts are devised for the comprehension of human action. They become self-contradictory and nonsensical if one tries to apply them in dealing with conditions different from those of human life. (69)

How did he know that which applies to the "conditions of human life" a priori? He would have to know those conditions a priori also.[6]

[A]ction can only be imputed to a discontented being, and repeated action only to a being who lacks the power to remove his uneasiness once and for all at one stroke. An acting being is discontented and therefore not almighty. (69)

A priori knowledge, eh?

"Discontentment" is his irreducible primary.

For an all-powerful being there is no pressure to choose between various states of uneasiness; he is not under the necessity of acquiescing in the lesser evil. (69)

This is not me nor my philosophy. Evil? By what standard?

Action is a display of potency and control that are limited. It is a manifestation of man who is restrained by the circumscribed powers of his mind, the physiological nature of his body, the vicissitudes of his environment, and the scarcity of the external factors on which his welfare depends. It is vain to refer to the imperfections and weaknesses of human life if one aims at depicting something absolutely perfect. The very idea of absolute perfection is in every way self-contradictory. The state of absolute perfection must be conceived as complete, final, and not exposed to any change. . . . But the absence of change—i.e., perfect immutability, rigidity and immobility—is tantamount to the absence of life. Life and perfection are incompatible, but so are death and perfection. (70)

He is "restrained" by identity.

But what standard?

Why?

By what standard?!!!

Where there are conditions, there are limitations

And this is the confession:

and not perfection; there are endeavors to conquer obstacles, there are frustration and discon-
tent. (70)

"perfection" is a universe
without "conditions" or
"limitations"—a universe of
non-A. And this is what happens
—and must happen—when you
start with emotions as a
primary ("an ultimate given")!

After the philosophers had abandoned the search
for the absolute, the utopians took it up. They
weave dreams about the perfect state. They do
not realize that the state, the social apparatus of
compulsion and coercion, is an institution to cope
with human imperfection and that its essential
function is to inflict punishment upon minorities
in order to protect majorities against the detrimental consequences of certain actions. With
"perfect" men there would not be any need for
compulsion and coercion. But utopians do not
pay heed to human nature and the inalterable
conditions of human life. [*Mises proceeds to describe some especially ridiculous utopian views of
Godwin, Fourier, Marx and Trotsky. (70/70-71)*]

He is making a package-deal of
the issue of absolutes
(epistemology), perfection
(morality) and crank-notions—
on the premise that the
reader's inferiority complex will
prevent him from breaking up
the package. What is his
absolute in this paragraph? The
evil of human nature and the
malevolent universe of the
"unalterable conditions of
human life."

Chapter 3: Economics and the Revolt Against Reason

1. The Revolt Against Reason

[Utopian writers] failed to realize that what they
called absolute reason and manifest truth was the
fancy of their own minds. They blithely arrogated
to themselves infallibility. . . . (72)

Doesn't he?

The revolt against reason, the characteristic mental attitude of our age, was not caused by a lack
of modesty, caution, and self-examination on the
part of the philosophers. (73)

It was caused by the
philosophers.

2. The Logical Aspect of Polylogism

Lenin dispersed by force the Constituent Assem-
bly elected, under the auspices of his own government, by universal franchise for men and
women, because only about one-fifth of its members were Bolshevik. (76)

Factually untrue! It was under
the Kerensky government. (Is
this the nature of his
erudition?!)

No further proof is needed of the insincerity of
the whole doctrine. (77/76)

!! Is "sincerity" relevant to
proof?

3. The Praxeological Aspect of Polylogism

It is paradoxical to assert that a vicious theory is from any point of view more useful than a correct one. (77)

> Why not—if "end" may properly be "subjective" i.e., not related to reality?

[Marxist historicism] is a purely mystical doctrine. The only proof given in its support is the recourse to Hegelian dialectics. Capitalist private property is the first negation of individual private property. It begets, with the inexorability of a law of nature, its own negation, namely common ownership of the means of production. (80)

> ?? This is not the way communists teach that triad. (?)

It is useless to argue with mystics and seers. They base their assertions on intuition and are not prepared to submit them to rational examination. (83)

> And what about his so-called "understanding"?

4. Racial Polylogism

[Mises makes the following claim in opposition to those ethnologists who hold that "other races have been guided in their activities by motives other than those which have actuated the white race":] The Asiatics and the Africans no less than the peoples of European descent have been eager to struggle successfully for survival and to use reason as the foremost weapon in these endeavors. They have sought to get rid of the beasts of prey and of disease, to prevent famines and to raise the productivity of labor. (85)

> Nonsense! That the lowest savage uses reason if he survives at all—is true. But from that to the supremacy of reason is a distance of light-years. This is not the way to refute racism.

The categories of human thought and action are neither arbitrary products of the human mind nor conventions. They are not outside of the universe and of the course of cosmic events. They are biological facts and have a definite function in life and reality. . . . They are therefore appropriate to the structure of the external world and reflect properties of the world and of reality. They work, and are in this sense true and valid. (86/85-86)

> Really?
>
> Is this his way of skirting around the concept of "objectivity"?

The fundamental logical relations and the categories of thought and action are the ultimate source of all human knowledge. (86)

> ??? Not the senses?

5. Polylogism and Understanding

What use could a champion of Protestantism derive from misunderstanding the tremendous power and prestige of Catholicism, or a liberal from misunderstanding the relevance of socialist ideas? In order to succeed a politician must see things as they are; whoever indulges in wishful thinking will certainly fail. Judgments of relevance differ from judgments of value in that they aim at the appraisal of a state of affairs not dependent on the author's arbitrariness. (88)

Judgments of value, therefore, depend on a man's "arbitrariness" by definition. Here is his whim-worship officially stated.

As has already been pointed out, the serious discrepencies to be found in historical studies are an outcome of differences in the field of the nonhistorical sciences and not in various modes of understanding. (88-89/88)

What superficial nonsense—as a means to avoid the concept of "objectivity."

Part Two: Action Within the Framework of Society

Chapter 10: Exchange Within Society

1. Autistic Exchange and International Exchange

Action always is essentially the exchange of one state of affairs for another state of affairs. If the action is performed by an individual without any reference to cooperation with other individuals, we may call it autistic exchange. An instance: the isolated hunter who kills an animal for his own consumption; he exchanges leisure and a cartridge for food. (195/194)

Sloppy metaphor, at best. (He exchanges action for food. "Leisure" would not provide the food.)

Within society cooperation substitutes interpersonal or social exchange for autistic exchanges. Man gives to other men in order to receive from them. Mutuality emerges. Man serves in order to be served. (195/194)

Sloppy! Man "serves" himself.

Although the emergence of interpersonal exchange was the result of a long evolution, no gradual transition is conceivable between autistic and interpersonal exchange. There were no intermediary modes of exchange between them. The step which leads from autistic to interpersonal exchange was no less a jump into something entirely new and essentially different than was the

Precisely! Therefore, what is the purpose of so grotesque a definition as "autistic exchange"? And—using Mises' terms—isn't the Communists' goal a society in which everybody is engaged in "autistic exchange" for the sake of his neighbors? Are you

step from automatic reaction of the cells and nerves to conscious and purposeful behavior, to action. (196/195)

by any chance going to conclude that Communism leads to "autistic selfishness" and Capitalism to "social service"?

2. Contractual Bonds and Hegemonic Bonds

The state as an apparatus of compulsion and coercion is by necessity a hegemonic organization. So is the family and its household community. (198/197)

???!

Right or law is the complex of rules determining the orbit in which individuals are free to act. (199/198)

Good Lord! Look at what the premise of "definitions by negatives" will do! "Everything which is not permitted by law is forbidden"? (See "Anthem")

3. Calculative Action

Modern civilization is above all characterized by the fact that it has elaborated a method which makes the use of arithmetic possible in a broad field of activities. This is what people have in mind when attributing to it the—not very expedient and often misleading—epithet of rationality. (200/199)

Oh, is it? Only arithmetic is rational?

Part Three: Economic Calculation

Chapter 11: Valuation Without Calculation

2. The Barter-Fiction of the Elementary Theory of Value and Prices

Now, we must realize that valuing means to prefer *a* to *b*. (205/204)

No, it doesn't! "Choice" means this. "Value" and "choice" are not the same concepts. (Typical equivocation.)

("Valuing" means measurement by means of a standard.)

"Value" cannot exist where there is no choice. But it is not the fact of choice that determines a value, it is the standard of value. Example: the "value" of a girl to a lover is not that he prefers her to other girls; he had to have a standard which made him prefer her; he could have chosen none if none filled his standard.

There is no method available to construct a unit of value. (206/205)

Values are measured by a process of "final causation," not by "units."

In the market society there are money prices. Economic calculation is calculation in terms of money prices. . . . It is a fictitious assumption that an isolated self-sufficient individual or the general manager of a socialist system, i.e., a system in which there is no market for means of production, could calculate. (206/205)

Oh boy! Nice little package deal! An isolated self-sufficient individual <u>can</u> calculate. A social "manager" cannot.

3. The Problem of Economic Calculation

Technology tells how a given end could be attained by the employment of various means which can be used together in various combinations, or how various available means could be employed for certain purposes. But it is at a loss to tell man which procedures he should choose out of the infinite variety of imaginable and possible modes of production. What acting man wants to know is how he must employ the available means for the best possible—the most economic—removal of felt uneasiness. (208/207-208)

Since when is <u>this</u> the province of technology?

<u>Who</u> wants to know it? About <u>whose</u> uneasiness?

Technology and the considerations derived from it would be of little use for acting man if it were impossible to introduce into their schemes the money prices of goods and services. The projects and designs of engineers would be purely academic if they could not compare input and output on a common basis. The lofty theorist in the seclusion of his laboratory does not bother about such trifling things; what he is searching for is causal relations between various elements of the universe. But the practical man, eager to improve human conditions by removing uneasiness as far as possible, must know whether, under given conditions, what he is planning is the best method, or even a method, to make people less uneasy. He

This is getting to be ridiculous! No <u>practical</u> man thinks that way. <u>This</u> is the thinking of a socialist planner. And this whole approach is a perversion of the actual meaning of money. Money <u>is</u> an <u>objective</u> means of measuring <u>economic value</u>. The standard in passages such as this is the preposterous one of <u>the divine right of collective whims.</u>

must know whether what he wants to achieve will be an improvement when compared with the present state of affairs and with the advantages to be expected from the execution of other technically realizable projects which cannot be put into execution if the project he has in mind absorbs the available means. Such comparisons can only be made by the use of money prices. (209/208)

Where there are no money prices, there are no such things as economic quantities. There are only various quantitative relations between various causes and effects in the external world. There is no means for man to find out what kind of action would best serve his endeavors to remove uneasiness as far as possible. (210/209)

What is the logical connection between these two [underlined] statements?

Who cares?

For [self-sufficient farmers] no calculation was needed, as they could directly compare input and output. (210/209)

Isn't that calculation?

4. Economic Calculation and the Market

The qualitative treatment of economic problems must not be confused with the quantitative methods applied in dealing with the problems of the external universe of physical and chemical events. The distinctive mark of economic calculation is that it is neither based upon nor related to anything which could be characterized as measurement. (210/ 209)

Calculation without measurement?

The last decades have witnessed a revolution in the traditional epistemological setting of physics, chemistry, and mathematics. We are on the eve of innovations whose scope cannot be foreseen. (210/209)

Now do you see what he is philosophically?

Perhaps [the coming generation of physicists] will be forced to drop the idea that there is something unaffected by cosmic changes which the observer can use as a standard of measurement. (211/210)

"Straw-man setting" type of dishonesty.

Chapter 12: The Sphere of Economic Calculation

2. The Limits of Economic Calculation

Honor, virtue, glory, and likewise vigor, health,

He here admits that there are

and life itself play a role in action both as means and as ends; but they do not enter into economic calculation. (216/215)

values <u>other</u> than economics.

Neurotic reformers, mentally unbalanced literati, and ambitious demagogues take pleasure in indicting "rationality" and in preaching the gospel of the "irrational." (216-217/215-216)

Doesn't <u>he</u>?

<u>The prices are not measured in money; they consist in money.</u> (218/217)

They are, and do, <u>both</u>.

3. The Changeability of Prices

With [classical economists] value was something objective, i.e., a phenomenon of the external world and a quality inherent in things and therefore measurable. They utterly failed to comprehend the purely human and voluntaristic character of value judgments. (220/219)

Equivocation—or else ignorance: he means "<u>intrinsic</u>," and offers us the old choice between "intrinsic" and "subjective."

4. Stabilization

Stability, the establishment of which the program of stabilization aims at, is an empty and contradictory notion. The urge toward action, i.e., improvement of the conditions of life, is inborn in man. Man himself changes from moment to moment and his valuations, volitions, and acts change with him. In the realm of action there is nothing perpetual but change. There is no fixed point in this ceaseless fluctuation other than the eternal aprioristic categories of action. (220/219)

Heraclitian universe (or—Hegalian).

Sloppy thinking.
??

What <u>are</u> they?

Look at who's opposed to metaphysics and "philosophical presumption"!

[*Twice in one paragraph Mises refers to "<u>demand and supply</u>." (223/222)*]

Observe the reversal.

Where quantities are measured, all further <u>doubts and disagreements</u> concerning their dimensions cease. These questions are settled. (224/223)

His standard of objectivity.

5. The Root of the Stabilization Idea

The state . . . offered to the citizen an opportunity to put his wealth in safety and to enjoy a stable income secure against all vicissitudes. It opened a way to free the individual from the necessity of risking and acquiring his wealth and his income anew each day in the capitalist market. He who invested his funds in bonds issued by the government and its subdivisions was no longer subject to the inescapable laws of the market and to the sovereignty of the consumers. He was no longer under the necessity of investing his funds in such a way that they would best serve the wants and needs of the consumers. He was secure, he was safeguarded against the dangers of the competitive market in which losses are the penalty of inefficiency; the eternal state had taken him under its wing and guaranteed him the undisturbed enjoyment of his funds. . . . He was no longer a servant of his fellow citizens, subject to their sovereignty; he was a partner of the government which ruled the people and exacted tribute from them. (226/225)

> This is sickening. Are we all to regard ourselves as blindly dependent slaves of the "sovereign consumers'" whims? (Note: in a free economy, the irrational consumer soon ceases to consume.)

The fact that economic calculation in terms of money is unequal to the tasks which are assigned to it in these illusory schemes for establishment of an unrealizable realm of calm removed from the inescapable limitations of human action and providing eternal security cannot be called a deficiency. There is no such things as eternal, absolute, and unchanging values. The search for a standard of such values is vain. Economic calculation is not imperfect because it does not correspond to the confused ideas of people yearning for a stable income not dependent on the productive processes of men. (229)

> Basic contradiction in Mises' theory: if it is true, as he here argues about economics, that human life has to be constant motion, then the concept of man as a being constantly seeking the Nirvana of stagnation and constantly pushed by "uneasiness"—is wrong. On what ground would we assume—"as an apriori praxeological absolute"—that man, by nature, is set against reality? If life is motion, then action is man's proper state— and only abstinence from action (the opposition to reality and to one's own nature) can cause "uneasiness." What Mises blanks out totally in his assumption of a happy Nirvana-seeker is the phenomenon of ambition.

Chapter 13: Monetary Calculation as a Tool of Action

1. Monetary Calculation as a Method of Thinking

[In the opening paragraph of this section, Mises refers to "the sovereign consumer." (230/229)]

Nice term—and nice altruist-parasite implication!

The measurements of physics and chemistry make sense for practical action only because there is economic calculation. It is monetary calculation that made arithmetic a tool in the struggle for a better life. It provides a mode of using the achievements of laboratory experiments for the most efficacious removal of uneasiness. (231/230)

Pathological anxiety now taken for granted and used as a matter of fact.

[Monetary calculation] makes success and failure, profit and loss ascertainable. (231/230)

Doesn't this mean "objective"?

There are people to whom monetary calculation is repulsive. They do not want to be roused from their daydreams by the voice of critical reason. Reality sickens them. . . . (231/230)

What reality? The reality that we cannot perceive? A Kantian can't talk about reality.

2. Economic Calculation and the Science of Human Action

[Classical economics] drew implicitly the borderline between what is to be considered economic and what extra-economic along the line which separates action calculated in monetary terms from other action. Starting from this basis the economists were bound to widen step by step the field of their studies until they finally developed a system dealing with all human choices, a general theory of action. (232/231)

And that was the proper delimitation of the field and science of economics.

This is the definition of the province of morality. Isn't it clear by now that "praxeology" is intended as a substitute for morality? What is morality, if it is not the science of "all human choices"?

Part Four: Catallactics of Economics of the Market Society

Chapter 14: The Scope and Method of Catallactics

1. The Delimitation of the Catallactic Problems

There have never been any doubts and uncertain-

Social-metaphysics.

ties about the scope of economic science. Ever since people have been eager for a systematic study of economics or political economy, all have agreed that it is the task of this branch of knowledge to investigate the market phenomena, that is, the determination of the mutual exchange ratios of the goods and services negotiated on markets, their origin in human action and their effects upon later action. (233/232)

No.
"Market" only? Distribution, but not production?

In studying interpersonal exchange one cannot avoid dealing with autistic exchange. But then it is no longer possible to define neatly the boundaries between the kind of action which is the proper field of economic science in the narrower sense, and other action. Economics widens its horizon and turns into a general science of all and every human action, into praxeology. The question emerges of how to distinguish precisely, within the broader field of general praxeology, a narrower orbit of specifically economic problems. (233/232)

Translation: in dealing with interpersonal exchange, one cannot avoid dealing with individual motivation. Then one invades the field of philosophy by inventing a new science whose boundaries one cannot define.

Every action is motivated by the urge to remove a felt uneasiness. It does not matter for the science of action how people qualify this uneasiness from a physiological, psychological, or ethical point of view. It is the task of economics to deal with all commodity prices as they are really asked and paid in market transactions. (233/232)

God damn this!

Well, here is his definition of economics. What else is he after?

Whether it is possible to separate neatly those actions which aim at the satisfaction of needs exclusively conditioned by man's physiological constitution from other "higher" needs can be left undecided. (234/233)

Can it?

A market in which there is direct exchange only is merely an imaginary construction. (235/234)

Not true. It exists in any period of economic collapse, such as inflation.

He who contests the existence of economics virtually denies that man's well-being is disturbed by any scarcity of external factors. (235/234)

No! "He" denies that man has to produce and that production is a science. Mises' definition proceeds from the premise of "the goods are here."

[Mises quotes half of Marx's famous saying: "to each

Why does he so conveniently

*according to his needs," thus leaving out "from each
according to his ability." (236/235)]*

       omit the other half of this
slogan?

There is in the vast flood of Marxian writings
not the slightest allusion to the possibility that a
communist society in its "higher phase" might
have to face a scarcity of natural factors of production. (236/235)

Is the mind "a natural factor of
production"?

The fact of the disutility of labor is spirited away
by the assertion that to work, under communism
of course, will no longer be pain but pleasure,
"the primary necessity of life." (236/235)

God damn him! So Rearden's
[See Atlas Shrugged] motive
power is the "disutility of
labor"? ! . . . Besides,
praxeology here contradicts
itself: since "ends" do not
matter, why wouldn't men be
motivated by "collective" glory
or prestige?

Such is the myth of potential plenty and abundance. Economics may leave it to the historians
and psychologists to explain the popularity of
this wishful thinking and indulgences in daydreams. . . . It deals with action, i.e., with the
conscious endeavors to remove as far as possible
felt uneasiness. It has nothing to assert with regard to the state of affairs in an unrealizable and
for human reason even inconceivable universe of
unlimited opportunities. In such a world, it may
be admitted, there will be no law of value, no
scarcity, and no economic problems. (236-237/
235)

Such as what? He has not
answered the socialists.

God damn this!

What does he mean by this? . . .
Anyway, the whole issue, which
he is here evading, is the fact
that collectivists simply want
the able to serve the unable.

If ever such a world [i.e., the kind of world described in the last passage] were to be given to
the descendants of the human race, these blessed
beings would see their powers to think wither
away and would cease to be human. For the primary task of reason is to cope consciously with
the limitations imposed upon man by nature, to
fight against scarcity. Acting and thinking man is
the product of a universe of scarcity in which
whatever well-being can be attained is the prize
of toil and trouble, of the conduct popularly
called economic. (237/236)

On what basis does he call it
"scarcity," except on the
Garden of Eden" premise—or
the premise that wishes do not
automatically produce
satisfaction?

What limitations? The law of
identity?

This last sentence is my proof
of the fact that Mises' basic
premise, metaphysically and

morally, is the anti-effort and anti-mind one of the "Garden of Eden."

2. The Method of Imaginary Constructions

[*Mises refers to:* "imaginary constructions *which are* inconceivable." *(237/236)*]

Blatant contradiction in terms.

The imaginary constructions of praxeology can never be confronted with any experience of things external and can never be appraised from the point of view of such experience. Their function is to serve man in a scrutiny which cannot rely upon his senses. In confronting the imaginary constructions with reality we cannot raise the question of whether they correspond to experience and depict adequately the empirical data. We must ask whether the assumptions of our construction are identical with the conditions of those actions which we want to conceive. (238/237)

George! What other proof do you need? If it weren't for you, I would drop, then and there, any book containing that sentence.[7]

By means other than those based on the senses?

Thus we conceive the category of action by constructing the image of a state in which there is no action. . . . (238/237)

This is more than "definitions by negatives"! This is "perception by negatives"!!! Things cannot be perceived, but a zero can!

[The method of imaginary construction] is, to be sure, a method very difficult to handle because it can easily result in fallacious syllogisms. It leads along a sharp edge; on both sides yawns the chasm of absurdity and nonsense. Only merciless self-criticism can prevent a man from falling headlong into these abysmal depths. (238/237)

Now this I agree with fully!!!

Well, he did fall.

3. The Pure Market Economy

The imaginary construction of a pure or unhampered market economy assumes that there is division of labor and private ownership (control) of the means of production and that consequently there is market exchange of goods and services. (238/237)

This is merely a process of abstract thought. Why call it "imaginary construction"??

To buy in the cheapest market and to sell in the dearest market is, other things being equal, not

conduct which would presuppose any special assumptions concerning the actor's motives and
morality. It is merely the necessary offshoot of
any action under the conditions of market exchange. (241/240)

It __does__ presuppose rationality
and self-interest.

In his capacity as a businessman a man is a servant of the consumers, bound to comply with
their wishes. He cannot indulge in his own whims
and fancies. But his customers' whims and fancies are for him ultimate law, provided these customers are ready to pay for them. He is under the
necessity of adjusting his conduct to the demand
of the consumers. If the consumers, without a
taste for the beautiful, prefer things ugly and vul-
gar, he must, contrary to his own convictions,
supply them with such things. (241/240)

This is unspeakably
contemptible—and untrue.
What he describes here is a
Peter Keating [See The
Fountainhead] or the kind of
businessman who fails—or,
worse, the __European__ view of a
businessman.

Even an action directly aiming at the improvement of other people's conditions is selfish. The
actor considers it as more satisfactory for himself
to make other people eat than to eat himself. His
uneasiness is caused by the awareness of the fact
that other people are in want. (243/242)

And __this__ is precisely the aim of
socialism. If Mises claims that
the market __can__ operate
regardless of "ends," then all
that the socialists want is to
preserve the market, but to
give everyone an altruist
motive. So "praxeology" has not
refuted them.

7. The Integration of Catallactic Functions

The term entrepreneur as used by catallactic
theory means: acting man exclusively seen from
the aspect of the uncertainty inherent in every
action. In using this term one must never forget
that every action is embedded in the flux of time
and therefore involves a speculation. The capital-
ists, the landowners, and the laborers are by necessity speculators. So is the consumer in providing for anticipated needs. There's many a slip
'twixt cup and lip. (254/253)

What childish nonsense! __This__ is
what happens when you
abandon Aristotelian
epistemology! __This__ is "cue-
words" and equivocation built
into an epistemological system.

It is awkward that the same term [i.e., "entrepreneur"] should be used to signify two different
notions. It would have been more expedient to
employ another term for this second notion—for
instance, the term "promoter." (256/255)

And how! It would have been
more expedient to use
Aristotelian Epistemology!

It is to be admitted that the notion of the entre-

Not "idea" or "abstraction"?

preneur-promoter cannot be defined with
praxeological rigor. (256/255)

The inequality of men, which is due to differ-   ???!
ences both in their inborn qualities and in the vicissitudes of their lives, manifests itself in this
way too. There are in the market pacemakers and
others who only imitate the procedures of their   Is this learned "a priori"?
more agile fellow citizens. (256/255)

Chapter 15: The Market

1. The Characteristics of the Market Economy

The market economy is the social system of the   Equivocation—in the "purpose"
division of labor under the private ownership of   sense of the word.
the means of production. Everybody acts on his
own behalf; but everybody's actions aim at the
satisfaction of other people's needs as well as at
the satisfaction of his own. Everybody in acting
serves his fellow citizens. Everybody, on the
other hand, is served by his fellow citizens. Ev-
erybody is both a means and an end in himself;   Ghastly definition!
an ultimate end for himself and a means to other
people in their endeavors to attain their own
ends. (258/257)

The state, the social apparatus of coercion and
compulsion, does not interfere with the market
and with the citizens' activities directed by the
market. It employs its power to beat people into   ??? This(?!) about the
submission solely for the prevention of actions   government of a free society?!!
destructive to the preservation and the smooth
operation of the market economy. (258/257)

There is no mixture of the two systems [i.e., a   What is it that we have today?
market economy and a planned economy] pos-
sible or thinkable; there is no such thing as a
mixed economy, a system that would be in part
capitalistic and in part socialistic. (259/258)

These publicly owned and operated enterprises   Oh hell! No!
are subject to the sovereignty of the market.
(259/258)

[Publicly owned and operated enterprises] must   No! Do they?

strive for profits or, at least, to avoid losses. (259/258)

Nothing that is in any way connected with the operation of a market is in the praxeological or economic sense to be called socialism. The notion of socialism as conceived and defined by all socialists implies the absence of a market for factors of production and of prices of such factors. (260/259)

The existence of and the prices charged by the government post office, or roads, or monopolistic "public utilities" based on exclusive franchises— are not determined by a free market and free competition. How does he classify them?

8. Entrepreneurial Profit and Loss

Profit and loss in the original sense are psychic phenomena and as such not open to measurement and a mode of expression which could convey to other people precise information concerning their intensity. A man can tell a fellow man that *a* suits him better than *b*; but he cannot communicate to another man, except in vague and indistinct terms, how much the satisfaction derived from *a* exceeds that derived from *b*. (287/289)

Hell!

So what?

If an action neither improves nor impairs the state of satisfaction, it still involves a psychic loss because of the uselessness of the expended psychic effort. The individual concerned would have been better off if he had inertly enjoyed life. (287/290)

???!!

The only source from which an entrepreneur's profits stem is his ability to anticipate better than other people the future demand of the consumers. (288/290)

No!
("Definition-by-consequences")

The specific entrepreneurial function consists in determining the employment of the factors of production. (288/290-291)

If this is the meaning of the term "entrepreneur," as used by Mises, then it is an arbitrary definition that should not be used by us. A businessman is more than a "box-office chaser" or "demand guesser." If that were all he is, then of course there would be no need for him in a planned economy—and not much need in our economy. (Proof? Peter Keating.)*[See The*

Fountainhead]

12. The Individual and the Market

Without exception all political parties [*and every pressure group, says Mises in the previous paragraph*] promise their supporters a higher real income. There is no difference in this respect between nationalists and internationalists and between the supporters of a market economy and the advocates of either socialism or interventionalism. If a party asks its supporters to make sacrifices for its cause, it always explains these sacrifices as the necessary temporary means for the attainment of the ultimate goal, the improvement of the material well-being of its members. (315/318)

Superficial—and "selective perception." The fact that people do want material well-being is no proof that that is their main motive. They act on it? Well, they act on altruism, too, and much more consistently.

What is wrong with the producers' policies is their faulty economics. (315/319)

Really?

[Modern man] fails to realize that he is an undivided and indivisible person, i.e., an individual, and as such no less a consumer than a producer. (315-316/319)

Hell! What about the desire for the unearned? What about consumers who are not producers and do not wish to be?

If a statement were not exposed as logically erroneous, psychopathology would not be in a position to qualify the state of mind from which it stems as pathological. If a man imagines himself to be the king of Siam, the first thing which the psychiatrist has to establish is whether or not he really is what he believes himself to be. Only if this question is answered in the negative can the man be considered insane. (316/319)

He really is? But we have no means to perceive reality, according to Kant and Mises. It's just "the structure of our minds" etc. What sort of process is he describing here? The perception of reality by means of logic?

Chapter 23: The Data of the Market

3. The Historical Role of War and Conquest

Civilization is an achievement of the "bourgeois" spirit, not the spirit of conquest. (645/650)

"Definition by consequences"

This is an example of the basic

error of "praxeology": The ideas expressed in this sequence are true, in the main—and totally off-focus, and, therefore, ineffectual. It is not the "bourgeois" spirit that creates civilization, but the rational spirit. It is not trade that is primary here, but production. And the base of production is thought. And the base of productive action is the pursuit of rational values. Before there could be any "bourgeois," there had to be all the enormous philosophical thinking that led to individualism and private property.

Ludwig von Mises, *Bureaucracy* (New Haven: Yale University Press, 1944)

This book is included in the Recommended Bibliography at the end of Capitalism: The Unknown Ideal.

Chapter 2: Bureaucratic Management

2. Bureaucracy Within Democracy

The definition of democratic government is: A system of government under which those ruled are in a position to determine, directly by plebicite or indirectly by election, the exercise of the legislative and executive power and the selection of the supreme executives. (41 n. 1)

> Bad!
>
> ("Those ruled"—this is probably right for a democracy and that is precisely why America was not and is not a "democracy")

[Concerning executive power] there is only the alternative between the arbitrary rule of despotic officeholders and the rule of the people enforced by the instrumentality of law abidance. (42)

> Bad!
>
> (The law is not "the rule of the people," but of a principle of justice. Who determines justice? It can't be determined at all, except on the basis of inalienable individual rights as an axiom.)

The characteristic feature that distinguishes [the constitutional state] from despotism is that not the authorities but the duly elected people's representatives have to decide what best serves the commonweal. (43)

> Rot! In a proper country nobody has the right to decide anything for the "commonweal."

Chapter 4: Bureaucratic Management of Private Enterprises

4. Unlimited Dependence on the Discretion of Government Bureaus

It would be mistaken to place the blame for this corruption on the system of government interference with business and bureaucratism as such. It is bureaucraticism degenerated into racketeering in the hands of depraved politicians. (73)

> ?!
>
> Why, the damn fool!

Chapter 5: The Social and Political Implications of Bureaucratization

1. The Philosophy of Bureaucratism

The citizen may reply [to the "bureaucratic radicals" whose mentalities are a step away from to-

> God damn the fool!

talitarianism]: You may be excellent and lofty men, much better than we other citizens are. We do not question your competence and your intelligence. But you are not vicars of a god called "the State." You are servants of the law, the duly passed laws of our nation. (76)

By their very natures, bureaucrats are neither intelligent nor competent, but <parasites>. The competent do not go in for government service.

The State is the only institution entitled to apply coercion and compulsion <u>and to inflict harm upon individuals</u>. (76)

Good God!

2. Bureaucratic Complacency

There are, of course, men and women serving in <u>an altruistic and entirely detached way</u>. Mankind would never have reached the present state of civilization without <u>heroism and self-sacrifice on the part of an elite</u>. . . .

Rot!

It was a purposeful confusion on the part of the German metaphysicians of statolatry that they clothed all men in the government service with the gloriole of such <u>altruistic self-sacrifice</u>. From the writings of the German etatists the civil servant emerges as a saintly being, a sort of monk who forsook all earthly pleasures and all personal happiness in order to serve, to the best of his abilities, God's lieutenant, once the Hohenzollern king and today the Führer. (78)

It is this goddamn altruism that permits such excuses!

This is a marvelous proof of how collectivism and altruism worked together to bring the world to where it is today!

The incentive offered by the civil service in Europe consisted not only in the level of the salary and the pension; many applicants, and not the best ones, were attracted by the ease of the work and by the security. As a rule government jobs were less exigent than those in business. (79)

This is the perfect description of the parasite and of mediocrity—and the <u>proof of what kind of people</u> go in for government service and why.

4. The Bureaucratization of the Mind

Economics is a theoretical science and as such does not tell man what values he should prefer and what ends he should aim at. It does not establish ultimate ends. This is not the task of the thinking man but that of the acting man. Science is a product of thought, action a product of will. (81)

Rotten definition. How are you going to have action or will without thought? Action proceeds from thought—and bad action from bad thought.

5. Who Should Be the Master?

In the economic sphere the right to acquire and to own property is not a privilege. It is the principle that safeguards the best satisfaction of the wants of the consumers. He who is eager to earn, to acquire, and to hold wealth is under the necessity of serving the consumers. The profit motive is the means of making the public supreme. The better a man <u>succeeds</u> in supplying the consumers, the greater become his earnings. It is to everybody's advantage that the entrepreneur who produces good shoes at the cheapest cost becomes rich. . . . (88)

Good—except: why must we justify an inalienable right by the "social good" it does? What about the man's right? Property <u>does</u> serve the public, but that is <u>not</u> its moral justification. (It's interesting how scared von Mises is of altruism, how saturated with it and muddled because of it.)

Chapter 7: Is There Any Remedy Available?

1. Past Failures

All learned criticisms [of bureaucracy] and witty satires are of no avail because they do not hit the core of the problem. Bureaucratization is only a particular feature of socialization. The main matter is: Capitalism or Socialism? Which? (110)

They have failed because capitalism never stated its moral basis. The defenders of capitalism have betrayed it on moral grounds—just as von Mises betrays it. (As far as literature goes, satire won't do it. It's not enough. What is needed is inspiration—an uplifting ideal—<u>Roark</u>.)[See The Fountainhead]

The supporters of socialism contend that capitalism is an unfair system of exploitation, that it is extremely detrimental to the welfare of the masses. . . . On the other hand, they depict their socialist utopia as a promised land of milk and honey in which everybody will be rich. Are they right or are they wrong? <u>This is the question</u>. (110)

<u>No</u>. This is <u>not all</u> of the question.

In a letter to Rose Wilder Lane (August 21, 1946), Ayn Rand wrote: "Now to your second question: 'Do those almost with us do more harm than 100% enemies?' I don't think that this can be answered with a flat 'yes' or 'no,' because the 'almost' is such a wide term and can cover so many different attitudes. I think each particular case has to be judged on his own performance, but there is one general rule to observe: those who are with us, but merely do not go far enough, yet do not serve the opposite cause in any way, are the ones who do us some good and who are worth educating. Those who agree with us in some respects, yet preach contradictory ideas at the same time, are definitely more harmful than 100% enemies . . . . As an example of the kind of 'almost' I would tolerate, I'd name Ludwig von Mises. . . . As an example of our most pernicious enemy, I would name Hayek. That one is real poison."

Foreword, by John Chamberlain

The alternative to "planning" is the "rule of law." Hayek is no devotee of laissez faire; he believes in a design for an enterprise system. Design is compatible with minimal-wage standards, health standards, a minimum amount of compulsory social insurance. It is even compatible with certain types of government investment. But the point is that the individual must know, in advance, just how the rules are going to work. (vi-vii)

Here is where the whole case is given away. How are these things "compatible" with the principle of inalienable individual rights? And if this principle is not observed—how is there going to be any "rule of law"? What law, based on what? How is the individual going to know in advance "how the rules are going to work"? An untouchable principle remains untouched. A principle broken to the extent of an inch, can be broken to the extent of a mile tomorrow.

Preface

Though this is a political book, I am as certain as anyone can be that the beliefs set out in it are not determined by my personal interest. (ix)

The damn fool! He's crawling to begin with. Why should a man apologize for a "personal interest"?

For those who, in the current fashion, seek interested motives in every profession of a political opinion, I may, perhaps, be allowed to add that I have every possible reason for *not* writing or publishing this book. (ix)

This is an example of how a denial of "interested motives" leads to a denial of all personal motives and, therefore, of personal rights.

Chapter 1: The Abandoned Road

[T]he essential features of that individualism which, from elements provided by Christianity and the philosophy of classical antiquity, was first fully developed during the Renaissance and has since grown and spread into what we know as Western civilization—are the respect for the individual man *qua* man, that is, the recognition of his own views and tastes as supreme in his own sphere, however narrowly that may be circumscribed. . . . (14)

Rotten definition! A collectivist could subscribe to it. You can circumscribe "a man's own sphere" to mere breathing— and not too much of that. <u>Who</u> decides on what a man's "own sphere" is?

If a defender of individualism can offer no better definition than this—it's proof of why the cause of individualism has failed. It had no real base, no moral base. <u>This is why my</u> book is needed.

Wherever the barriers to the free exercise of human ingenuity were removed, man became rapidly able to satisfy ever widening ranges of desire. And while the rising standard soon led to the discovery of <u>very dark spots in society</u>, spots which men were no longer willing to tolerate, there was probably no class that did not substantially benefit from the general advance. (16)

?
Here's the kind of point where they all lose their way. What "dark spots"? Who isn't willing to tolerate what? If they mean something like slums—at whose expense are they to be "untolerated"?

What in the future will probably appear the most significant and far-reaching effect of this success is the new sense of power over their own fate, the belief in the unbounded possibilities of improving their own lot, which the success already achieved created among men. With the success grew ambition—and man had every right to be ambitious. What had been an inspiring promise seemed no longer enough, the rate of progress far too slow. . . . (17)

Ambition—for what? Man moved forward because he was ambitious <u>for himself</u>. Being ambitious for others—as I think Hayek implies here—is quite another thing. Again—the contradiction and the muddle.

There is nothing in the basic principles of liberalism to make it a stationary creed; there are no hard-and-fast rules fixed once and for all. The fundamental principle that in the ordering of our affairs we should make as much use as possible

God damn the fool! <u>Here</u> is the whole case given away for good. If principles aren't "hard-and-fast"—what is? What do we go by? Who decides what is

of the spontaneous forces of society, and resort as little as possible to coercion, is capable of an infinite variety of applications. There is, in particular, all the difference between deliberately creating a system within which competition will work as beneficially as possible and passively accepting institutions as they are. (17)

"beneficial" and what is "possible"?

There were many obvious tasks, such as our handling of the monetary system and the prevention or control of monopoly, and an even greater number of less obvious but hardly less important tasks to be undertaken in other fields, where there could be no doubt that the governments possessed enormous powers for good and evil. . . . (18-19)

When and how did governments have "powers for good"?

But while the progress toward what is commonly called "positive" action was necessarily slow, and while for the immediate improvement liberalism had to rely largely on the gradual increase of wealth which freedom brought about, it had constantly to fight proposals which threatened this progress. (19)

What "positive" action? And just on what can you rely except on the increase of wealth?

He actually thinks—on expropriation. He talks like a god damn socialist himself, right here.

All we are here concerned to show is how completely, though gradually and by almost imperceptible steps, our attitude toward society has changed. What at every stage of this process of change had appeared a difference of degree only has in its cumulative effect already brought about a fundamental difference between the older liberal attitude toward society and the present approach to social problems. (20)

Doesn't he realize that this is unavoidable if we go about prattling that "there are no hard-and-fast rules"?

Chapter 2: The Great Utopia

[*Hayek quotes Peter Drucker, who writes that Russia is following the same road Germany travelled. Drucker says:*] Not that communism and fascism are essentially the same. Fascism is the stage reached after communism has proved an illusion, and it has proved as much an illusion in Stalinist Russia as in pre-Hitler Germany. (29)

Why do the goddamn fools say and repeat things like that? Not "essentially" the same? Then what do they mean by essence?

[Fascists and communists] competed for the support of the same type of mind and reserved for

Because the issue here is basic: individualism or collectivism in each other the hatred of the heretic. But their practice showed how closely they are related. <u>To both, the real enemy, the man with whom they had nothing in common and whom they could not hope to convince, is the liberal of the old type.</u> (29-30)

philosophy, the creator vs the second-hander parasite in human type.

[*At the end of Chapter 2, Ayn Rand wrote:*]
(Nineteenth Century Liberalism made the mistake of associating liberty, rights of man etc. with the ideas of "fighting for the people," "for the downtrodden," "for the <u>poor</u>," etc. They made it an altruistic movement. But altruism is collectivism. That is why collectivism took the liberals over.)

Chapter 3: Individualism and Collectivism

[T]he "economic planning" which is the prime instrument of socialist reform, can be used for many other purposes. . . . Whether we should wish that more of the good things of this world should go to some racial elite, the Nordic men, or the members of a party or an aristocracy, the methods which we shall have to employ are the same as those which could insure an equalitarian distribution. (33)

Doesn't he know that the fault here lies in the idea that society has no <u>right</u> to distribute incomes. Therefore there can be no "just" planned distribution. It is a contradiction in terms.

It must also not be forgotten . . . that it is socialism which has persuaded liberal-minded people to submit once more to that regimentation of economic life which they had overthrown because, in the words of Adam Smith, it put governments in a position where "to support themselves they are obliged to be oppressive and tyrannical." (34)

Because of altruism—the idea of placing others above self, therefore above freedom, decency, and justice.

What our planners demand is a central direction of all economic activity according to a single plan, laying down how the <u>resources of society</u> should be "consciously directed" to serve particular ends in a definite way. (35)

(<u>Society</u> has no resources.)

The dispute between the modern planners and their opponents is, therefore, *not* a dispute on whether we ought to choose intelligently between the various possible organizations of society; it is not a dispute on whether we ought to employ foresight and systematic thinking in planning our common affairs. It is a dispute about what is the best way of so doing. The question is whether for this purpose it is better that the <u>holder of coercive</u>

Extremely dangerous rot! He gives away the basic premise— that "society" owns its "resources."

The "holder of coercive power"

power should confine himself in general to creating conditions under which the knowledge and initiative of individuals are given the best scope so that *they* can plan most successfully. . . . (35)

It is important not to confuse opposition against this kind of planning with a dogmatic laissez faire attitude. The liberal argument is in favor of making the best possible use of the forces of competition as a means of co-ordinating human efforts, not an argument for leaving things just as they are. It is based on the conviction that, where effective competition can be created, it is a better way of guiding individual efforts than any other. It does not deny. . . that, where it is impossible to create the conditions necessary to make competition effective, we must resort to other methods of guiding economic activity. (36)

To prohibit the use of certain poisonous substances or to require special precautions in their use, to limit working hours or to require certain sanitary arrangements, is fully compatible with the preservation of competition. The only question here is whether in the particular instance the advantages gained are greater than the social costs which they impose. (37)

In all these instances there is a divergence between the items which enter into private calculation and those which affect social welfare; and, whenever this divergence becomes important, some method other than competition may have to be found to supply the services in question. Thus neither the provision of signposts on the roads nor, in most circumstances, that of the roads themselves can be paid for by every individual user. Nor can certain harmful effects of deforestation, of some methods of farming, or of the smoke and noise of factories be confined to the owner of the property in question or to those who are willing to submit to the damage for an agreed compensation. In such instances we must find some substitute for the regulation by the price mechanism. (39)

An effective competition system needs an intelli-

doesn't create any conditions— he must merely keep his paws off!

The God damned abysmal fool!

The damn fool is talking the language of collectivism! Who is "making use"? What conditions "as they are"? Who creates competition?

Once you "guide" economic activity—where are you? Who guides whom? By what principle?

Who—in such an example— decides what are the "advantages" and what are the "costs" and who pays?

What is "social welfare"? Others? Everybody but oneself? But then oneself is "others" to the others. So who sacrifices to whom?

Why not? The gas tax did it and more. If the "individual user" doesn't pay for what he uses— who pays for it?

The God damn fool! Who decides all that? By what standard? The fool is so saturated with all the bromides of collectivism that it is terrifying!

gently designed and <u>continuously adjusted legal framework</u> as much as any other. Even the most essential prerequisite of its proper functioning, the prevention of fraud and deception (<u>including exploitation of ignorance</u>), provides a great and by no means yet fully accomplished object of legislative activity. (39)

> If so, what becomes of "laws known in advance"?
>
> Who defines that?

[P]lanning and competition can be combined only by <u>planning for competition</u> but not by planning against competition. (42)

> And <u>this</u> implies "planning" <u>can</u> work. The damn fool is lost in socialistic word-mongering. He can't give up "planning" himself.

[W]e cannot, within the scope of this book, enter into a discussion of the very necessary planning which is required to make competition as effective and beneficial as possible. (42)

> Oh yeah? And that's what I'd like to see him define!

Chapter 4: The "Inevitability" of Planning

[The argument for freedom applies] no less when, on the basis of our present knowledge, compulsion would seem to bring only advantages, and although in a particular instance it may actually do no harm. (52)

> Compulsion <u>always</u> does harm.

Chapter 5: Planning and Democracy

We are not concerned here with the question whether it would be desirable to have such a complete ethical code. It may merely be pointed out that up to the present the growth of civilization has been accompanied by a steady diminution of the sphere in which individual actions are bound by fixed rules. (58)

> How can any fool say that? He doesn't know what a moral code is if he doesn't know whether such a collectivist code "would be desirable."

The essential point for us is that no such complete ethical code exists. (58)

> No, you fool!
> That it <u>can't</u> exist!

Not only do we not possess such an all-inclusive scale of values: it would be impossible for any mind to comprehend the infinite variety of different needs of different people which <u>compete for the available resources</u> and to attach a definite weight to each. (58)

> They don't <u>compete</u> for the available resources—they <u>create</u> the resources. Here's the socialist thinking again.

The point which is so important is the basic fact that it is impossible for any man to survey more

> Only of his own—and then the trouble is that most fools don't

than a limited field, to be aware of the urgency of
more than a limited number of needs. (59)

know even that!

This is the fundamental fact on which the whole
philosophy of individualism is based. It does not
assume, as is often asserted, that man is egoistic
or selfish or ought to be. It merely starts from the
indisputable fact that the limits of our powers of
imagination make it impossible to include in our
scale of values more than a sector of the needs of
the whole society, and that, since, strictly speaking, scales of value can exist only in individual
minds, nothing but partial scales of values exist—scales which are inevitably different and often inconsistent with each other. From this the
individualist concludes that the individuals
should be <u>allowed, within very defined limits</u>, to
follow their own values and preferences rather
than somebody else's; that within these spheres
the individual's system of ends should be supreme and not subject to any dictation by others.
It is this recognition of the individual as the ultimate judge of his ends, the belief that as far as
possible his own views ought to govern his actions, that forms the essence of the individualist
position. (59)

Oh God damn the total,
complete, vicious bastard! This
means that man does exist for
others, but since he doesn't
know how to do it, the masters
will give him some "defined
limits" for himself.

If <u>that</u>'s the essence—this is
why individualism has failed.

Democratic control *may* prevent power from becoming arbitrary, but it does not do so by its mere
existence. If democracy resolves on a task which
necessarily involves the use of power which cannot be guided by fixed rules, it must become arbitrary power. (71)

If the fool understands this
much—why the hell does he
prattle about democracy?

He's right, <u>this</u> is what
democracy is—and this is why
America is <u>not</u> a democracy,
nor is any free country.

Chapter 6: Planning and the Rule of Law

Stripped of all technicalities, [Rule of Law]
means that government in all its actions is bound
by rules fixed and announced beforehand. . . .
(72)

Lousy definition!

The first type of rules can be made in advance, in
the shape of *formal rules* which do not aim at the
wants and needs of particular people. They are
intended to be merely instrumental in the pursuit
of people's various individual ends. And they are,

The man is an ass, with no
conception of a free society at
all. Laws do not "assist" anyone.
If he understood the nature of
<u>law</u>, he'd "know in advance."

or ought to be, intended for such long periods that it is impossible to know whether they will assist particular people more than others. (73)

The planning authority cannot confine itself to providing opportunities for unknown people to make whatever use of them they like. (73)

That's not the purpose of law, either!

To be impartial means to have no answer to certain questions—to the kind of questions which, if we have to decide them, we decide by tossing a coin. In a world where everything was precisely foreseen, the state could hardly do anything and remain impartial. (76)

?????!
(What, actually, is the fool's idea of justice or principles?)

Those most immediately interested in a particular issue are not necessarily the best judges of the interests of society as a whole. To take only the most characteristic case: when capital and labor in an industry agree on some policy of restriction and thus exploit the consumers, there is usually no difficulty about the division of the spoils in proportion to former earnings or some similar principle. The loss which is divided between thousands or millions is usually either simply disregarded or quite inadequately considered. (77)

What in hell does he really know about capitalism? The ass. Such a thing is impossible under laissez-faire capitalism.

To produce the same result for different people, it is necessary to treat them differently. To give different people the same objective opportunities is not to give them the same subjective chance. It cannot be denied that the Rule of Law produces economic inequality—all that can be claimed for it is that this inequality is not designed to affect particular people in a particular way. (79)

??!

!!!
?!

Oh, the goddamn fool! Is it inequality if an able man earns more than an incompetent one? Would paying them the same be equality?

The idea that there is no limit to the powers of the legislator is in part a result of popular sovereignty and democratic government. It has been strengthened by the belief that, so long as all actions of the state are duly authorized by legislation, the Rule of Law will be preserved. But this is completely to misconceive the meaning of the Rule of Law. (82)

Yes! And that's what's wrong with democracy! Doesn't he know any other possibility?

To say that in a planned society the Rule of Law cannot hold is, therefore, not to say that the actions of the government will not be legal or that such a society will necessarily be lawless. It means only that the use of the government's coercive powers will no longer be limited and determined by pre-established rules. The law can, and to make a central direction of economic activity possible must, legalize what to all intents and purposes remains arbitrary action. (82)

Chapter 7: Economic Control and Totalitarianism

[S]ome freedom in choosing our work is, probably, even more important for our happiness than freedom to spend our income during the hours of leisure. (94)

No doubt it is true that even in the best of worlds this freedom will be very limited. Few people ever have an abundance of choice of occupation. (94)

[Socialist economists] advocate planning no longer because of its superior productivity but because it will enable us to secure a more just and equitable distribution of wealth. This is, indeed, the only argument for planning which can be seriously pressed. (99)

Chapter 8: Who, Whom?

[C]ompetition and justice may have little else in common. . . . (101)

Inequality is undoubtedly more readily borne, and affects the dignity of the person much less, if it is determined by impersonal forces than when it is due to design. (106)

[I]t is the extent of the activities of the government which decides whether everything that any

---

?! What does he think law is?

The law must "legalize" illegality?

Some? The damn idiot!

Oh, the ass! Again, what does he think freedom is? Freedom is unlimited for every man. His abilities are not. That is quite a different thing.

Any half-way competent person always has an overabundance— in a free society.

The fool actually does not believe that when each man earns what he deserves—and no more—it is just and equitable.

He doesn't really believe in competition, in capitalism or in individualism.

Why call it "inequality"? Poverty for a man who isn't worth much is not inequality. Unearned payment would be.

Here is the whole case given away again. If the difference is

person gets any time depends on the government, or whether its influence is confined to whether some people will get some things in some way at some time. Here lies the whole difference between a free and a totalitarian system. (108)

> only of degree, there's nothing to talk about.

Most people find it difficult to admit that we do not possess moral standards which would enable us to settle these questions—if not perfectly, at least to greater general satisfaction than is done by the competitive system. Have we not all some idea of what is a "just price" or a "fair wage"? (110)

> The damn fool again! Competition is the moral standard—and the only one— because it's based on the voluntary decision of every man involved.

It is because successful planning requires the creation of a common view on the essential values that the restriction of our freedom with regard to material things touches so directly on our spiritual freedom. (113)

> The fool! Because material things are needed to live on— and if your physical life is only by permission, you can't have any spiritual freedom.

Chapter 9: Security and Freedom

Like the spurious "economic freedom," and with more justice, economic security is often represented as an indispensable condition of real liberty. In a sense this is both true and important. Independence of mind or strength of character is rarely found among those who cannot be confident that they will make their way by their own effort. (119)

> What the hell is he talking about? If a person cannot make his way by his own effort—who must give him "security" and why?

That anyone should suffer a great diminution of his income and bitter disappointment of all his hopes through no fault of his own, and despite hard work and exceptional skill, undoubtedly offends our sense of justice. The demands of those who suffer in this way, for state interference on their behalf to safeguard their legitimate expectations, are certain to receive popular sympathy and support. (123)

> Why? No fault of his own—but no fault of anyone else, either.

> The ass! Nobody has a "legitimate" expectation to be paid for something which others do not want any longer.

The problem of adequate incentives which arises here is commonly discussed as if it were a problem mainly of the willingness of people to do their best. But this, although important, is not the whole, nor even the most important, aspect of the problem. (124)

> The ass! The problem is moral. It is whether a man has the right to his own happiness or not.

The problem is, of course, even more important because in the <u>world as it is</u> men are, in fact, not likely to give their best for long periods unless their own interests are directly involved. (125)

And what else should it be, you damn collectivist?

[The military type of society] is the only system in which the individual can be conceded full economic security and through the extension of which to the whole of society it can be achieved for all its members. (127)

But it can't! An army is non-productive.

It is essential that we should re-learn frankly to face the fact that freedom can be had only at a price and that as individuals we must be prepared to make severe material sacrifices to preserve our liberty. (133)

The fool! He talks as if by giving up liberty people really did achieve "material security." Again, he has accepted the socialist premise. Only liberty does and <u>can</u> give any kind of security.

Chapter 10: Why the Worst Get on Top

<u>[T]he desire for a collectivist system springs from high moral motives.</u> . . . . (136)

There is no hope at all so long as would-be defenders of individualism spout things like that! God damn the bastard!

[T]he desire of the individual to identify himself with a group is <u>very frequently</u> the result of a feeling of inferiority and that therefore his want will be satisfied only if membership of the group confers some superiority over outsiders. (142)

Not "very frequently"—<u>always</u>.

When German philosophers again and again represent the striving for personal happiness as itself immoral and only the fulfillment of an imposed duty as praiseworthy, they are perfectly <u>sincere,</u> however difficult this may be to understand for those who have been brought up in a different tradition. (149)

"Sincere" does not mean <u>moral</u>.

Chapter 11: The End of Truth

We have seen that agreement on that complete ethical code, that all-comprehensive system of values which is implicit in an economic plan, does not exist in a free society but would have to be created. (155)

(The trouble with this book is that Hayek discusses totalitarians on the basis of their own estimate of themselves—that is, as a serious school of thought concerned with such things

as morals and philosophy—
instead of treating them for
what they are—total
viciousness on the loose.)

Totalitarian control of opinion extends, however, also to subjects which at first seem to have no political significance. Sometimes it is difficult to explain why particular doctrines should be officially proscribed or why others should be encouraged, and it is curious that these likes and dislikes are apparently somewhat similar in the different totalitarian systems. (161)

There's no secret about this at all. Everything pertaining to individualism is proscribed and for a good reason. All abstract thought pertains exclusively to individualism.

[At the end of Chapter 11, Ayn Rand wrote:]
Good God, what a mixture of ideas! The mind, then, is a collective attribute—or collective process, according to the damn fool. The "growth of reason" does not depend on any collective. The progress of human knowledge is the sum of individual work of many individual minds—each step in it strictly an individual act. If collectivists wish to have everything "consciously planned by reason"—the mistake lies only in forgetting that reason is an attribute of the individual—and if his life is planned by another or number of men, it is not planned by reason—not by his reason, which is the only thing that can plan for him. (Besides, you cannot "plan by reason" if you start with the premise that man exists for others. On what "reason" is that based?)

Chapter 12: The Totalitarians in Our Midst

As was also true in Germany, most of the works which are preparing the way for a totalitarian course in the democracies are the product of sincere idealists. . . . (185)

Well? Isn't it then the fault of the "ideal"? Of altruism?

I shall deliberately choose as illustrations authors whose sincerity and disinterestedness are above suspicion. (185)

When the hell will they stop worrying about motives and consider ideas? A well-meaning fool is still a fool.

Even more surprising, perhaps, is the remarkable tenderness which many socialists are likely to show toward the *rentier* bondholders to whom monopolist organization of industry frequently guarantees secure incomes. That their blind enmity to profits should lead people to represent effortless fixed income as socially or ethically more desirable than profits, and to accept even monopoly to secure such a guaranteed income to,

That's because what they hate is not the rich, but the competent. (This is a very good example of it.)

for example, railway bondholders, is one of the most extraordinary symptoms of the perversion of values which has taken place during the last generation. (196-197)

The probability is that wherever monopoly is really inevitable, the plan which used to be preferred by Americans, of strong state control over private monopolies, if consistently pursued, offers a better chance of satisfactory results than state management. . . . Even if this should have the effect (as it sometimes had with American public utilities) that the services of the monopolistic industries would become less satisfactory than they might be, this would be a small price to pay for an effective check on the powers of monopoly. (198)

All this nonsense means is that he would have to use a certain service and that this service would be rotten (much as the New York Subway).

Twenty-five years ago there was perhaps some excuse for holding the naïve belief that "a planned society can be a far more free society than the competitive laissez faire order it has come to replace" [from *The Old World and the New Society: An Interim Report of the National Executive of the British Labour Party on the Problems of Reconstruction*]. But to find it once more held after twenty-five years of experience and the re-examination of the old beliefs to which this experience has led, and at a time when we are fighting the results of those very doctrines, is tragic beyond words. . . . That the advances of the past should be threatened by the traditionalist forces of the Right is a phenomenon of all ages which need not alarm us. But if the place of the opposition, in public discussion as well as in Parliament, should become lastingly the monopoly of a second reactionary party, there would, indeed, be no hope left. (200-201)

Because the issue is not, and never has been, between the rich and the poor—but between the individual and the collective, between the competent and the parasite, between the creator and the second-hander.

Chapter 13: Material Conditions and Ideal Ends

It was men's submission to the impersonal forces of the market that in the past has made possible the growth of a civilization which without this could not have developed; it is by thus submitting that we are every day helping to build something that is greater than any one of us can fully comprehend. (204)

Oh, fudge! There's totalitarian language again.

Lousy argument! When at a loss for principles, the fool resorts to "submission," like all the rest of them.

The crucial point is that it is infinitely more difficult rationally to comprehend the necessity of submitting to forces whose operation we cannot follow in detail than to do so out of humble awe which religion, or even the respect for the doctrines of economics, did inspire. It may, indeed, be the case that infinitely more intelligence on the part of everybody would be needed than anybody now possesses, if we were even merely to maintain our present complex civilization without anyone's having to do things of which he does not comprehend the necessity. The refusal to yield to forces which we neither understand nor can recognize as the conscious decisions of an intelligent being is the product of an incomplete and therefore erroneous rationalism. (205)

> Lousy argument! It is not a matter of submitting to what one doesn't understand. Once the free market is understood, there is no necessity to know the specific reasons of every particular fluctuation—the general process is clear.

[I]t is sensible temporarily to sacrifice freedom in order to make it more secure in the future; but the same cannot be said for a system proposed as a permanent arrangement. (206)

> Again, the damn fool! You cannot sacrifice freedom "temporarily"—and it won't do any good in practice.

It is, in fact, in this field that the fascination of vague but popular phrases like "full employment" may well lead to extremely shortsighted measures, and where the categorical and irresponsible "it must be done at all cost" of the single-minded idealist is likely to do the greatest harm. (206)

> When will they stop calling fools "idealists"? They've made idealism a synonym for lunacy.

Our hopes of avoiding the fate which threatens must indeed to a large extent rest on the prospect that we can resume rapid economic progress which, however low we may have to start, will continue to carry us upward; and the main condition for such progress is that we should all be ready to adapt ourselves quickly to a very much changed world, that no considerations for the accustomed standard of particular groups must be allowed to obstruct this adaptation, and that we learn once more to turn all our resources to wherever they contribute most to make us richer. (210)

> The fool uses all the collectivist techniques again. It's funny how fearfully and resentfully he speaks about the workers—that they should be dispossessed for the common good—just the way they used to talk about the rich.

It is, however, more than doubtful whether a fifty years' approach toward collectivism has raised our moral standards, or whether the change has not rather been in the opposite direction. Though

> "More than doubtful" hell! Isn't the general corruption glaringly self-evident?

we are in the habit of priding ourselves on <u>our</u> <u>more sensitive social conscience, it is by no</u> <u>means clear that this is justified by the practice of</u> <u>our individual conduct. On the negative side, in</u> <u>its indignation about the inequities of the existing</u> <u>social order, our generation probably surpasses</u> <u>most of its predecessors.</u> But the effect of that movement on our positive standards in the proper fields of morals, individual conduct, and on the seriousness with which we uphold moral principles against the expediences and exigencies of social machinery, is a very different matter. (211)

> <u>There</u> is practically the best proof of my case against altruism.

Chapter 14: The Prospects of International Order

What these dangerous <u>idealists</u> do not see is that where the <u>assumption of a moral responsibility</u> involves that one's moral views should by force be made to prevail over those dominant in other communities, the assumption of such responsibility may place one in a position in which it becomes impossible to act morally. To impose such an impossible moral task on the victorious nations is a certain way morally to corrupt and discredit them. (228-229)

> Oh hell!
> The fool doesn't even see that to assume power over others cannot be a "moral responsibility," that it is the essence of immorality. But—it <u>is</u> consistent with the morality of altruism—and there's the real trap of altruistic philosophy.

[T]here must be a power which can restrain the different nations from action harmful to their neighbors, a set of rules which defines what a state may do, and an authority capable of enforcing these rules. The powers which such an authority would need are mainly of a negative kind; it must, above all, be able to say "No" to all sorts of restrictive measures. (233)

> And who is going to define what is "harmful" to neighbors, and how?

Far from its being true that, as is now widely believed, we need an international economic authority while the states can at the same time retain their unrestricted political sovereignty, almost exactly the opposite is true. What we need and can hope to achieve is not more power in the hands of irresponsible international economic authorities but, on the contrary, a superior political power which can hold the economic interests in check, and in the conflict between them can truly hold the scales, because it is itself not mixed up in the economic game. (233)

> Oh God! A political power which "can hold economic interest in check" <u>is not</u> "mixed up in the economic game"???

Federalism is, of course, nothing but the application to international affairs of democracy, the only method of peaceful change man has yet invented. <u>But it is a democracy with definitely limited powers</u>. (234)

And <u>that's</u> a contradiction in terms.

When we want to prevent people from killing each other, we are not content to issue a declaration that killing is undesirable, but we give an authority power to prevent it. (234)

Nonsense! The police have no power to <u>prevent</u> killing—the law merely has the power to punish a murderer.

It is, in fact, one of the main advantages of federation that it can be so devised as to make most of the harmful planning difficult while leaving the way free for all desirable planning. (235)

"Good" planning and "bad" planning? And who decides which is which?

<u>We shall never prevent the abuse of power if we are not prepared to limit power in a way which occasionally may also prevent its use for desirable purposes</u>. (237)

We shall never get anywhere so long as we think that power can achieve any "desirable purposes."

Henry Hazlitt, *The Great Idea* (republished as *Time Will Run Back*) (New York: Appleton-Century-Crofts, Inc., 1954)

In a letter to Harry Hazlitt (February 26, 1951), Ayn Rand wrote: "I do envy you for the fact that your novel [The Great Idea] is finished and is about to come out. . . . I am looking forward to reading it." Ayn Rand recommended The Great Idea to Leonard Peikoff as a work in economics, but added that one should beware of Chapters 34 and 39. Four of Hazlitt's books (though not this one) are included in the Recommended Bibliography at the end of Capitalism: The Unknown Ideal.

As The Great Idea is a novel, one must keep in mind that Ayn Rand was usually commenting on the remarks of characters in the novel—remarks that may not represent positions endorsed by Hazlitt.

Chapter 33

But only a comparatively few people seemed to have the consistency or generosity to admire the exceptional competence, ingenuity and adventurousness of the enterprisers who made big profits because they were exceptionally successful in meeting the wants of consumers. (271)

> There's a sentence that starts well and ends in a total contradiction.

In other words, by what looks at first like an amazing coincidence the individual enterpriser makes the same kind of decision that an economic dictator—if he could take into consideration all the needs of consumers and all branches of production—would try to make. (277)

> So the best justification of a private enterpriser is that he's as good as an ideal economic dictator?

> This is fudging. Capitalism certainly does not consider "all the needs" of consumers. "Needs" are not the yardstick. Nobody gets anything on the basis of his needs—under capitalism.

Chapter 34

We must absolutely forbid coercive monopoly. Perhaps that was the central evil of state socialism. The state's monopoly of power, and its monopoly of production. But we must do more than fight monopoly and encourage competition. We must draft our laws in such a way as to raise the level of competition. We must so draft them that a man who seeks his personal profit cannot attain that selfish goal *except* by promoting the public welfare. (280-281)

> ?
>
> ??
> ?
>
> ??! (If this is not moral communism, what is?)

We must not allow a private industry to thrive at
the cost of killing or maiming its workers, or in-
juring consumers of its products, or menacing the
public health, or polluting public streams, or polluting the air. . . . (281)

??! Can it thrive that way?

[I]f we make it impossible for people to grow
rich by violence or force or theft or fraud or
sharp practice, then the only way in which they
will be able to succeed in business will be precisely by competition and rivalry in serving the
consumers. (281)

(Is "serving" the only way? Is
that all that's involved in
success?)

"I'll admit this much, even now [Smith says
to Adams]. I'm not sure that men will accept and
abide by a moral code, however rational, based
on purely utilitarian grounds. Perhaps the masses
of mankind will never abide by a moral code unless they feel a deep sense of *reverence* for something. . . ."

Here's the collapse of the
whole book!

"For the universe itself?" [asks Adams].
"At least a deep sense of humility" [Smith
replies], "a recognition of their own littleness in
the universe, a profound sense of their own bot-
tomless ignorance before the mystery and the
miracle of existence. . . . Perhaps we need at least
a conviction, a faith, that beyond the seemingly
blind forces of nature there may be, there must
be, some Great Purpose, forever inscrutable to
our little minds." (283)

Oh God! This is a blueprint to
make man a worm.

Chapter 35

Before people had economic liberty, you and I
and the Central Planning Board laid down the
central economic plan. And from then on nobody
else had any function or duty but that of slavishly
carrying out, to the last detail, the plan that we
bureaucrats had laid down. Now *everybody* can
plan. Now everybody is a center of planning.
(285)

"Plan"? Or is it that everybody
can "think"?

Everyone tends to be rewarded by the consumers
to the extent that he has contributed to the needs
of the consumers. (286)

Why "tends"? What would he
consider exact?

For Marx's unworkable dictum: *From each according to his ability; to each according to his*

??! "Unworkable"? Is that all?

needs, we have substituted a new, workable principle: *To each what he creates*. (287)

But the moment we substitute the principle of 'to
each what he creates' we automatically solve the
problem of getting 'from each according to his
ability.' (287)

Getting? By what right?

"But you can't consistently apply the principle of
'to each what he creates,' " said Adams. "How do
you solve the problem of invalids, the crippled,
the blind, the helpless; the problem of mothers
bearing children, the problem of children themselves." (287)

Oh, you can't? And if I don't
want to work for cripples?

"To say that each worker or enterpriser *gets* what
he creates is not necessarily to say that each
keeps the market value of what he creates merely
for himself," [said Smith]. "He is free to distribute what he creates or what he earns as he sees
fit. He may provide for his family, or he may give
part of his earnings to the helpless or to charity."
    "But what you are saying, chief, is that the
helpless or non-productive should be provided
for only if the productive are generous enough to
provide for them. We can't depend on that. The
State should give everyone a minimum." (287-
288)

Is this moral communism or
not? Has man a right to exist
or not?

And if he doesn't, then he's
immoral?

Who can't? Who has any right
in the matter, except the
productive?

So the effort of our government must be to encourage the maximum of healthy competition, to
keep every field of competition constantly open
to newcomers. (290-291)

How? Is this the province of
government?

Then it isn't the generosity of the employers,
chief, but their selfishness and cupidity that leads
them to keep bidding up wages to the point
where they correspond with the worker's marginal productivity? (293)

"Cupidity"—to create and
produce?!

[An employer who had a monopoly in his field]
would certainly have to compete with other industries at least for *new* labor, or for common
labor. He might be able to some extent, perhaps,
to exploit his *skilled* labor—provided he did not
have to employ any additional skilled labor and
provided it would take his skilled workers a long
time to acquire other skills. (294)

What "exploitation"? What
"monopoly"? Are there any
private "monopolies"? Or is this
Marxism?

Chapter 37

Under our new system the *real* decisions are made by the whole body of consumers. The enterprisers merely try to guess what the wants and preferences of the consumers are going to be. (308-309)

Oh, rubbish! They are made by reason.
(?!)

But the competition of enterprisers in keeping up the prices of the factors of production means that in order for an individual enterpriser to make a profit, he must have *better* foresight than his competitors in meeting the wants of consumers. (312)

Why speak of "foresight"? It's creative intelligence.

When we have allowed for the wages of labor, the rental of land, the interest on capital and the wages—or presumptive or imputable wages—of management, then there is no net sum left over for profits. (312)

What's the difference between that and profits?

You have invented, chief—or made possible—a wonderful economic system. And one of its chief merits, I now agree, is that it rewards people in proportion to their foresight and their production—their ability to provide others with what those others want. (316)

Moral communism.

How will we be able to protect this system, for instance, against the incessant criticism of the unproductive and the unsuccessful? (316)

You won't be able to—because you yourself have conceded that the moral and social purpose of the productive and the successful is to serve the unproductive and unsuccessful.

But won't the successful, Adams—or, as I hope, the disinterested—always be there to answer the criticisms of the unsuccessful? (317)

The "disinterested" are morally superior to the successful—is that it?

Nearly everybody wants to be a writer; and therefore writers will seldom get the monetary rewards of speculators and enterprisers; and therefore the writers will be envious of these rewards; and the writers will always be more articulate, more plausible, than the successful businessmen. . . . (317)

It's not money-envy that prompts writers to attack capitalism—it's the altruist morality, since writers are concerned with ideas.

And then there's another point. Success is relative. Measured in wealth and income, everybody

Of course, everyone will feel that way—so long as wealth is

will be less successful than somebody else, except the one richest man in the world. And therefore even those who have much more than the average wealth and income will be unable to understand why others, surely no more intelligent, industrious or farseeing than themselves, have more wealth and income still. Everyone will be willing to take it for granted that those who have less than himself have less because they have contributed less value to the world. But almost no one will be willing to admit that those who have *more* wealth and income than himself have it because they have contributed *more* value to the world. (317)

justified by "contributions to the world"—so long as men are not taught to understand a man's inalienable right to his own production.

Chapter 38

Every sale was also a confirmation of the foresight in making or stocking certain goods, in correctly anticipating the wishes of consumers, or in anticipating these wishes better than their competitors did. (319)

Capitalism can't work on that sort of an attitude.

Neither the good nor the bad guesses of the commissars were considered to be the concern of the local storekeeper himself. (319)

How can one call the function of intelligence "a guess"?

The decision what to make or stock, and the task of persuading the customer that this article was as good as or better than what one's competitors had to offer (a task in the long run impossible unless the article actually *was* good or better), had all the adventure and excitement of playing a fascinating game. And though success, as in a good card game, might be sometimes due to luck—to the fall of the cards—in the long run it was the result of shrewd anticipation and skill in playing one's hand. (319-320)

If so, then isn't this proof of an objective, rational standard of value?

Is this any sort of view to hold of the capitalist system? Is Las Vegas a symbol of capitalism?

Time and the consumers kept weeding out what was merely meretricious and selecting what was best. (320)

Yeah? Or time and reason?

There was also competition in advertising; and the sometimes extravagant contentions of rival sellers were also the butt of Bolshekov's propaganda and of writers in Freeworld. But the Freeworld government kept this to a minimum by

Why help perpetuate the communistic confusion of mixing advertising and fraud? Are laws to control advertising proper?

tightening the laws against fraud and the misrepresentation of goods. (320)

And Peter, though he knew that the motives of
the individual advertisers were not disinterested,
and though he personally disliked the blatancy of
most of their methods, conceded that the basic
contention of the advertisers was ultimately right.
(321)

> Moral communism. Is it then
> improper to be interested in
> one's own success?

The contrast [between communism and the
West], Peter found, was not quite so striking in
certain realms—music, dancing, chess, mathematics. (324)

> Not true! Why did you fall for
> Soviet propaganda?

But in nearly all other realms the cultural and
spiritual contrast was glaring. It showed itself in
novels and plays, in criticism and poetry, in
painting, sculpture and architecture, in political
and economic thinking, in most sciences, in philosophy and religion. (324)

> If so, then how can spiritual
> progress come from a moral
> evil—from selfishness? Is
> selfishness evil?

Peter saw that this [i.e., that literature under communism was nauseating and based on the whims
of a dictator] was inevitable under any system in
which the livelihood of every author and artist
depended on the "planners" at the center, on any
one individual or compact ruling group. (324)

> —and if the group is not
> "compact," like "the
> consumers," is it then all right?
> "or is the issue plain, selfish
> independence?

Peter. . .did not need to cater to a nebulous "mass
demand." He could, if he wished, write, build,
think, compose or paint for a definite cultivated
group, or for his fellow specialists, or for a few
kindred spirits wherever they could be found.
And plays did have a way of finding their own
special audience, and periodicals and books their
own special readers. (325)

> Are you scared of saying "for
> himself"? Must it be at least "for
> a few," for any few, for
> anything—so long as it's not
> himself?

> Oh God! Don't you see that
> the same principle applies to
> industrial production? What, in
> this sense, is "the consumers"?

Chapter 39

"Isn't this system, even conceding that it is
enormously more productive than any collectivist system, selfish and acquisitive?"
"How?"
"Well, certainly it *rewards* selfishness and
acquisitiveness."

> "Acquisitiveness"—about the
> things one produces oneself?

"Of course it does. And so does any other system." (326)

??!

The point is . . . that self-regarding people under any system will do things that are most rewarded by that system. The real question is—what *are* the actions that are most rewarded by a particular system? (326-327)

Moral communism. What are the non-self-regarding people?

"Doesn't your free market system reward precisely the most selfish and acquisitive actions?"

"No. It might just as well be regarded as rewarding the most altruistic actions. To begin with, under this system our government has sought to *illegalize* every action harmful to others [e.g., fraud, theft, murder]. . . . And by that means we have made it impossible . . . for any enterpriser to succeed except by one thing—by serving the consumers as well or better than his competitors do." (327)

Why evade the issue? Trade is not altruistic. Capitalistic "service" is not unpaid. What altruism demands is the unpaid.

[O]ur specific restrictions on liberty of all kinds can only be justified insofar as they tend to promote the greatest possible safe enjoyment of liberty for everyone. (328)

!!! What's the standard of that?!

[I]f you begin to *demand* altruism legally, there are no logical limits—until everybody has been forced to give away all he has earned. . . . (328)

What about "morally"? Isn't the same true?

Any society worth living in . . . must of course be infused with a spirit of generosity and benevolence. It can't depend solely on negative virtues—on people's merely respecting one another's liberty or their abstaining from deceit or violence. I concede all that to be true. (328)

Oh, must it?

Well, you concede communism.

A society to be worth living in must have a morality. That is, the individuals of which it is made up must adhere to a moral code. (329)

What moral code? That of living for others? How can you have an individualistic society on a collectivistic morality?

We do not want people to succeed by superior chicanery, by more clever deceit, by greater unscrupulousness, by superior ruthlessness. Therefore our laws must do everything possible to close the avenues to success and to create condi-

Can they?

tions under which people can succeed only by
superior zeal and ability in serving their fellows.
. . . It provides them with a system of rewards in
proportion to their success in satisfying the consumer. (329)

> It's not true! It's not done for
> the consumer. It's done by free,
> voluntary, selfish exchange—by
> an even, selfish trade!

Whether a man is seeking to be the richest man
in his community, or the most skillful surgeon, or
the fastest swimmer, or the best pianist, or the
greatest novelist or philosopher or saint, it is his
sense of personal competition that drives him to
wring every ounce of ability or perfection out of
himself. (330)

> Oh, is it? And not the strength
> and clarity of his convictions?

[One function of competition] is to assign each
individual to that place in the social system
where he can perform the greatest service for his
fellows. In a society of status or heredity, everybody is likely to be misplaced—if we judge by
the standard of where he could do the most good.
(330)

> And what about judging by the
> standard of where he would be
> the happiest?

If you do something 'unselfish' in the hope of a
reward, then you are doing something selfish. If
you are doing something 'unselfish' and 'altruistic' under the spur of a material incentive—or
even mainly in the hope of being praised for your
action—then what you do is really selfish and
acquisitive. It is illogical to ask for a reward for
unselfishness. Unselfishness consists precisely in
doing the things for which you are not rewarded.
(331)

> Wonderful paragraph! Unselfish
> consists in doing things which
> bring you no value, no joy
> whatever. And is this, then,
> moral?

I can see, chief, how that promotes wealth and
production, and social co-operation, and mutuality of service. And all that is very fine. But still
the ultimate aim of each of us in this business
relation is self-regarding. Each of us, to put it
bluntly, is trying to make money. (331)

> Of course he is!
> And should be.

A man may earn money to support his family, to
send his son to college, to pursue abstract scientific studies, to contribute to some public cause in
which he deeply believes, to found a new charity.
Now most working people are unselfish in this
sense. Most of them support with their earnings
not simply themselves, but others—a wife, children, aged parents, a sister or brother, and so on.

> !!!

> And if he doesn't support any
> parasite whatever? If he is not a
> sacrificial beast of burden for

A man works for his family—not so that he alone, but that *they* can have more. In brief, he works not merely for himself but for those he loves. (332)

anyone—do you grant him the right to exist—or don't you? Why is it moral for the "sister or brother" to exist on someone else's production—but not for the producer to exist on the proceeds of his own effort?

Of course under a regime of freedom you can persuade or exhort a man to widen voluntarily the circle of his love or at least good will. (332)

Why? What for?

Then your point . . . is that while we may regret that more people are not more charitable than they are, the fault is not that of the free market or of the private enterprise system, but of human nature? (332)

Then if men were communists, that would be virtue? You mean, communism is noble, but human nature isn't good enough for it?

[*At the end of Chapter 39, Ayn Rand wrote the following:*]
Why, in this chapter, since you're so concerned with the "welfare" of people, is there not a single word about the wishes and the personal happiness of individuals? Why—if it's an individualist society that's being discussed—is there not a single word or thought given to the rights of the individual, apart from his "serving" of the "consumers"?

Chapter 40

It is only this system, in short, that makes the fullest use of capital, of the tools of production, and so takes burdens off the back of labor, constantly and enormously increases the worker's productivity and wages and well-being. (337)

Fine! But why is that capitalism's justification? The well-being of those who are raised? Why not the well-being of those who do the raising?

[Capitalism's] secret, perhaps, is that it protects the right of everyone to keep what he has made. He is allowed to have and to hold the product of his labor. . .the amount of value he has contributed to production. (338)

Does this mean society owns his production, but lets him keep its equivalent?

Chapter 41

What had been uncovered so far were the works of only three of the ancient bourgeois authors— a William Shakespeare, a Jane Austen, and a Miguel Cervantes. . . . After ten weeks on the island, Peter was strong enough to sit down to his

These would go together!

piano again. As he played <u>Haydn, Mozart, Bach,</u>
<u>Brahms, Schubert,</u> Edith Robinson sat entranced.
(346)

He himself had always been uncompromisingly
opposed. . .to *coercive* monopoly, to monopoly
built up or sustained by any form of force, fraud
or misrepresentation, duplicity or unfair practice,
and he had already labored to define these coercive practices in the law. He had already illegal-
ized every form <u>of conspiracy or secret agree-</u>
<u>ment to reduce output or fix prices</u>. (369)

> Are there any monopolies <u>not</u>
> made by government?
>
> What's that?
>
> !!!

<u>After all, my new definition of a good society is</u>
<u>simple: it is one in which it is possible for a man</u>
<u>who loves Mozart to devote himself to Mozart</u>.
(373)

> <u>Correct</u>! But what about "saving
> the consumers"?

[*On the last page of the book, Ayn Rand wrote the following:*]
Fundamental mistake of story: the great industrial progress <u>would not</u> happen so long
as freedom was <u>given from above</u>, from a benevolent dictator. Men would neither
invest nor invent. The intelligent men would not function by <u>permission</u>—only by
<u>right</u>. This mistake results from the basic mistake about altruism—and both proceed
from the total disregard of human intelligence, of <u>rationalism</u>.

the majority of people who live under it, because no one is free to make his will known, no one is free to act, without risk of torture or murder. Let me put it this way. An economic or political system is always as good as the people who live under it—as long as they are free to change it."

the *right* to exist – or don't you? Why is it moral for the "sister or brother" to exist on someone else's production – but not for the producer to exist on the proceeds of his own effort?

→ You mean, communism is noble, but human nature isn't good enough for it?

Why, in this chapter, since you're so concerned with "the welfare" of people, is there not a single word about the wishes and the personal happiness of individuals? Why – if it's an individualist society that's being discussed – is there not a single word or thought given to the rights of the individual, apart from his "serving" of the "consumers"?

333

1. The idea that humans act to remove uneasiness is quite prominent in *Human Action*. Ayn Rand remarked negatively upon it nearly twenty times.

2. Ayn Rand remarked upon Mises' view that morality is subjective and that the ends of human action are "ultimate givens" nearly thirty times.

3. Ayn Rand noted the first time Mises contradicts or "breaks" this in the margin on page 29. In general, she commented nearly thirty times on Mises contradicting himself or stealing concepts.

4. On page 13, von Mises wrote (and Ayn Rand underlined): "For to do nothing and to be idle are also action, they too determine the course of events. . . . Action is not only doing but no less omitting to do what possibly could be done." (In the margin beside the paragraph containing these lines, Ayn Rand wrote: "Meaningless.")

5. There are over a dozen marginalia objecting to the idea of "the logical structure of the mind."

6. There are over a dozen critical comments on the a priori and what Mises claims to know a priori.

7. A few of Ayn Rand's marginal comments in *Human Action* were addressed to the economist and student of von Mises, George Reisman. In most cases her comments stand on their own, and the references to Dr. Reisman have been omitted. In this case, however, the comment is not intelligible without it.

Part III

Politics and
Culture

Two of A&P's biggest chain competitors, Kroger and Safeway, were indicted a few years ago on almost the identical Sherman Act charges of monopoly and restraint of trade. They did not fight the charge and so pleaded "nolo contendere" [which is Latin for "I do not choose to fight"]. They paid their fines and got off. But it does not make much sense that *three competitors* could each be charged with having a "monopoly," especially in the food business.

The reason so many of A&P's competitors have come to its defense in the public prints seems to be a rather simple one. They are not concerned over the particular fate of A&P in the Antitrust Division's pending suit for A&P's dissolution. Nor would the public need to be concerned about it, if the suit were merely brought to "get" A&P for some political sin or error. But A&P's competitors are concerned because of the *business methods* that have been outlawed, directly or indirectly, in the recent suit. The housewife should be even more concerned, for if A&P is broken up for using these methods, other firms will have to stop using them and her ten-dollar bill at the grocery store will return her a good deal less change, or a good deal less groceries, or both.

[marginalia, left and bottom margins, handwritten by Ayn Rand:]

!!!?!
!!!.!

this is an example of the author's lack of philosophical integration, of broader, basic principles.

The whole public had jolly well better be concerned when and if a government has the power to "get" somebody for political sins or errors!

Anne Fremantle, *This Little Band of Prophets: The British Fabians* (New York: New American Library, 1960)

This book contains the dedication: "for Virgilia and Victor: their book," under which is handwritten: "For Ayn Rand from Victor Weybright." (Weybright was her editor at New American Library.)

Of the few comments Ayn Rand wrote in the margins of this book, most were on quotes from the Fabian socialists themselves, most notably George Bernard Shaw. (In a letter dated January 13, 1950, Ayn Rand wrote: "A good novelist or dramatist is not necessarily a good thinker. Just take a look at the political ideas of Tolstoy, or Dostoyevsky, or Mark Twain, or Bernard Shaw.")

[Quoting George Bernard Shaw:]

"[W]e had rather face a Civil War than such another century of suffering as the present one [i.e., the 19th century] has been." (33)

!! So he got the XX Century!

[Sidney] Webb noted that as soon as production was sufficiently advanced to furnish more than the barest necessities, a struggle for the surplus began. Whatever individuals or classes were in power used it to get hold of that surplus product, leaving the rest of society practically nothing. . . . (87)

There's the soul of mediocrities, who have no idea of where production comes from!

[Quoting Shaw:]

[The Fabian aim was] to persuade the English people to make their political constitution thoroughly democratic and so to socialize their industries as to make the livelihood of the people entirely independent of private Capitalism. . . . [I]t has no distinctive opinions on the Marriage Question, Religion, Art, abstract Economics, historic Evolution, Currency, or any other subject than its own special business of practical Democracy and Socialism. (90)

He just wants "livelihood" somehow!

One of the aspects of Fabian philosophy too often ignored is its realistic concern for the individual. In this same Fabian tract [written by Shaw], Rubric VIII is headed, "Fabian Individualism." This rubric makes it abundantly clear that "the state should not monopolize industry as against private enterprise or individual initiative further than may be necessary to make the livelihood of the people and their access to the sources of production completely independent of both." It goes on,

Neatest little trick! How?

The freedom of individuals to test the social values of new inventions, to initiate improved methods of production; to anticipate and lead public enterprise in catering for new social wants; to practice all arts, crafts and professions independently; in short to complete the social organisation by adding the resources of private activity and judgment to those of public routine, is as highly valued by the Fabian Society as freedom of Speech, freedom of the Press, or any other article in the charter of popular liberties. (90-91)

The individual must initiate, so that the state may nationalize!

Edward Hunter, *Brainwashing in Red China: The Calculated Destruction of Men's Mind* (Tokyo: Charles E. Tuttle, Co., 1952)

Hunter sent Ayn Rand a review of his book from the Singapore Standard, July 18, 1954, with the inscription: "To Mr. and Mrs. Frank O'Connor, With fondest regards, Edward Hunter—Singapore, Aug. 27, 1954." (It is unknown whether she was prompted to read the book because of this or had already read it.)

In a Communist society, the dissenter remains silent, living in a splendid mental isolation in which his feelings, possibly held even by the majority, seem to him to be held only by himself —abnormal, lonely ideas that are uncomfortable and too heavy a burden to carry. (124)

> This is a moral necessity for any man anywhere! (But not in silence.)

[*Here, and in much of what follows, the author is discussing the Communist play, "The Question of Thought":*] [In this play] the Communists. . . arouse one of the main motivations of young men and women anywhere in the world—the strong appeal that the sacrificial has for idealistic youth. (128)

> The sacrificial? or the moral?

[*A principle of the Communists:*] Today, whether we are in our country or in the rest of the world, there is no third road, no middle of the way. On one side are the imperialists and their lackeys, and on the other side are the Communist Party and the people. (138)

> !!! The enemies knew it, but what about the free people?

The play teaches that people should live in glass houses and they should throw stones, and that each man and woman is his neighbor's and his parent's keeper. (138-139)

> Don't the free people teach just that?!!

In one of the early dramatic scenes the youthful Wang informs the group that he had been snooping on Miss Yuan in the bathroom, where he saw her using cosmetics. Wang, who is presented as a commendable character, then produces Miss Yuan's diary, which he has filched, and reads several romantic sentences. That such teachings, so contrary to the whole basis of both Eastern and Western civilizations, can be seriously put forward and so accepted, seems inconceivable. (139)

> Why? If "public good" is the standard, then this is moral!

There can be no privacy, no secrets, in such an environment. The students room together, and their responsibility is to watch each other. A pillow placed in an unusual position, a bed moved to the side, all these are noticed, arouse suspicions, and their significance is discussed. The students refer to anything out of the ordinary in the speech or action of any of their comrades. (139-140)

> If we preach collectivism, then this is logical and proper!

Even to desire something that is contrary to Party wishes is considered an act against the wishes of the people, a sin. Only in religion can anything comparable be found. (140)

> To the author: Think over the full implications of this!

[The author is speaking of a Communist rally:] How could anyone, even if he had come because he knew that he had to, and not because he wanted to, have failed to be impressed by the curious sense of being caught, of participation in a momentous event? (159)

> If they couldn't, that's the root of their damnation. They got what they deserved.

Fulton J. Sheen, *Communism and the Conscience of the West* (New York: Bobbs-Merrill, 1948)

> Leonard Peikoff reports that although Ayn Rand enjoyed watching Bishop Sheen's widely seen television program, her opinion of him was mixed: She thought he was the best a Catholic could be—she approved of his attempts to attack communism and to disentangle faith and reason—but she knew that qua Catholic he would ultimately be unsuccessful. In a letter to Isabel Patterson (April 11, 1948), Ayn Rand writes: "What shocked me about Fulton J. Sheen's book is a blatant hatred for capitalism. It seems to underlie the whole tone of the book. To tell you the truth, it reminded me of the tone which struck me and which I hated in Soviet books on dialectics and economics, when I read them for the first time in college."

Chapter 1: The Decline of Historical Liberalism and the Rise of the Antireligious Spirit

The third idea being liquidated today is rationalism understood in the sense that the supreme purpose of life is not the discovery of the meaning and the goal of life, but solely to devise new technical advances to make this world a city of man to displace the City of God. Rationalism properly understood is reason concerned with ends and means to an end; modern rationalism is reason concerned with means to the exclusion of ends. This was justified on the grounds that progress made ends impossible. The result was that man, instead of working toward an ideal, changed the ideal and called it progress. (18)

?

(Sounds like fancy fudging.)

Liberalism is a dangerous term to use simply because the modern mind never makes a distinction. If liberalism means a system which believes in progress toward freedom as the *right* to do whatever man <u>ought</u>, then liberalism is to be encouraged. If liberalism means a progressive repudiation of law and truth in the sense that freedom means the *right* to do whatever man *pleases*, then it is to be condemned. (18-19)

Who decides <u>that</u>?

?!

The French liberals who protested against the authority of king and altar in the name of liberty were reactionaries, for they did not believe in extending that liberty to the proletariat. (19)

?

(Marxism)

<u>The individual liberties which historical liberalism emphasizes are secure only when the community is religious and can give an ethical foun-</u>

Did they have liberties in the Middle Ages?

dation to these liberties. (21)

From now on the struggle will be not for the
colonies and national rights, but for the souls of   **True!**
men. (22)

[*Quoting C.S. Lewis:*]
This Devil has not sprung from a series of more
or less authentic or ancient texts. For he is a permanent agent of human reality as we live it when
we really live, in our state of free creatures, that
is to say, constantly placed before choices, in
contradiction and perplexity, paradox, tragedy.
All this assumes and poses the existence of a
good and of something other than the good. Oth-
erwise where would choice, tragedy, liberty lie?   In your use of <u>reason</u>, you fool!
(28)

Chapter 2: Is Communism the Enemy of the Western World?

[O]ur bourgeois, capitalistic civilization teaches   Well, isn't it? Or should we
that religion is an individual affair. . . . (51)   have the Inquisition?

Every single idea of communism is Western   What about Plato?
bourgeois in its origin. (52)

[U]nless there is a moral revival in our Western
world, a fulfillment of the pledges of the Atlan-   ?!
tic Charter, a rebirth of family life, communism
may be the instrument for the liquidation of a   Does that <u>please</u> him?
bourgeois civilization that has forgotten God.
(54-55)

The barbarian invasion broke the crust of that   Is <u>that</u> what he wants?
[i.e., Roman] paganism and allowed Christianity
to become a vital influence in the souls of men.
(55)

Chapter 3: The Philosophy of Communism

[Communism] seeks not only to dominate the
periphery of life but to control man's inner life as   And don't <u>you</u>?
well. (58)

Underneath Communist ethics is the principle   <u>Who</u> originated that slogan?
"the end justifies the means." (66)

Chapter 4: The Basic Defects of Communism

The Church says both [capitalism and communism] are wrong, for though the right to property is personal, the use is social. (79)

How?!

The Christian concept denies there is an absolutely owned private property exclusive of limits set by the common good of the community and responsibility to the community. (80)

And these are the people who boast of belief in absolutes!

Conservatism is . . . often nothing else than a pseudo philosophy for the prosperous. The Church, however, knows that the disorganization of the world is largely due to the fact that it is not organized by any conscious acceptance of purpose other than the immediate interest of a capitalist class on the one hand, or a Communist class on the other hand. (81)

Marxism

Organized by whom? What purpose?

Marx was baptized a Christian not for religious but for political reasons. It was only natural for a man who himself used religion as an opium to think that everyone else should use it the same way. (86)

What? At the age of six?

The great difference between Communist and Christian violence is that Communist violence is directed against the neighbor, and Christian violence is directed against oneself. The Communist sword points outward to fellow man, the Christian sword points inward to egotism, to selfishness and to acquisitiveness, to lust and the thousand and one things which would make for antisocial elements in society. (91)

Good God!

And maybe he's right. In this definition, Christianity does make a man do violence to himself.

Christianity agrees with Communists when they point out the need of a revolution, but Christianity places the blame not on institutions but on men; not on legislation but on legislators; not on politics but on politicians; not on property but on man. (92-93)

This is plain gibberish!

Something had to be done to counteract individual selfishness and economic inequalities and the flouting of standards; some way had to be discovered to lift men out of their individual egotisms and make them look for the good of all.

!!!

Here it is!

but how make man realize that he is his brother's keeper? Religion could have done it by restoring a sense of morality and justice from the *inside*, but since religion was rejected as a solution, partly because minds had lost the love of truth, there was only one way left, and that was to *force them to live for the general welfare;* that is, seize wealth and use power to equalize the inequalities. (100-101)

!!!!!

Pretty, ain't it?

If the sheep will not of themselves run together in the unity of the sheepfold, then dogs must be sent barking at their heels. If individuals will not be responsive to their God-given consciences prompting them to recognize their social responsibilities, then dictators will force them to do so. (101)

"You'd better be communists voluntarily, or else—"? Is that the idea?

Communism supplied one defect of the liberal theory of freedom, by offering a purpose which is social, but it made this purpose so absolute as to destroy completely freedom of choice. (102)

He envies that, doesn't he?

From the Christian point of view both historical liberalism and totalitarianism are half right and half wrong. Half right because they take a part of freedom; half wrong because they ignore the other part. They separate that which never should have been separated, namely, free choice as a means to an end which is self-perfection. (106)

???!

Look out for that one! That's their pet catch!

The freedom man ultimately craves is neither in the indefinite choice of indifferent goals nor in the surrender of choice to the kingdom of earth. Man seeks to make a choice which will dispense him from the necessity of choosing again. (106)

Not really! Now is that dehumanizing man, and a mechanistic human, or isn't it? So man must seek to stop being man?

Barry Goldwater, *The Conscience of a Conservative* (Victor Publishing Co., 1960)

In a letter to Senator Goldwater dated June 4, 1960, Ayn Rand thanked him for the autographed copy of The Conscience of a Conservative he had sent her, and then wrote: "I regard you as the only hope of the anti-collectivist side on today's political scene, and I have defended your position at every opportunity. Therefore, I am profoundly disturbed by some dangerous contradictions in your stand. . . ." She went on to discuss the book at great length.

Ayn Rand also discussed Goldwater in: "A Suggestion," The Objectivist Newsletter, vol. 2, no. 10 (October 1963); "How to Judge a Political Candidate," The Objectivist Newsletter, vol. 3, no. 3 (March 1964); "The Argument from Intimidation," The Objectivist Newsletter, vol. 3, no. 7 (July 1964) (reprinted in The Virtue of Selfishness); "'Extremism' or the Art of Smearing," The Objectivist Newsletter, vol. 3, no. 9 (September 1964); "It Is Earlier Than You Think," The Objectivist Newsletter, vol. 3, no. 12 (December 1964); and, "The New Fascism: Rule by Consensus," The Objectivist Newsletter, vol. 4, nos. 5 and 6 (May-June 1965) (reprinted in Capitalism: The Unknown Ideal).

In 1963, Ayn Rand wrote that Goldwater "is not an advocate of laissez-faire capitalism—this is one of the contradictions in his stand. Like all of today's political figures, he is the advocate of a mixed economy. But the difference between him and the others is this: they believe that some (undefined) element of freedom is compatible with government controls; he believes that some (undefined) government controls are compatible with freedom. Freedom is his major premise" ("How to Judge a Political Candidate"). A year later she wrote: "In former campaigns, Republican candidates had been guilty of compromise, evasion, cowardice, 'me-too'ism.' Barry Goldwater was not; he had courage, frankness, integrity—and nothing to say. . . . Barry Goldwater did not lack moral courage: what he lacked was intellectual courage—a quality one cannot acquire except from a set of firm philosophical convictions" ("It Is Earlier Than You Think").

Ayn Rand also wrote three pages of notes on The Conscience of a Conservative, some of which are included here.

Chapter 1: The Conscience of a Conservative

In some countries, freedom is altogether down and order holds absolute sway. (14)

False dichotomy of "freedom vs order," and implication that dictatorships represent "order."

Chapter 6: Freedom for Labor

As time went on, we found that the working man's right to bargain through a collective agent needed legal protection; accordingly Congress

???! He has lost the whole case!

enacted laws—notably certain provisions of the Clayton Act, the Norris LaGuardia Act and the Wagner Act—to make sure that employees would be able to bargain collectively. (47)

Right-to-work laws derive from the natural law: they are simply an attempt to give freedom of association the added protection of civil law. (49)

(That's why people object to it. "Added" protection is a nice euphemism for statist power.)

It is one thing to say that a man *should* contribute to an association that is purportedly acting in his interest; it is quite another thing to say that he *must* do so. (49-50)

Why doesn't he apply this same principle to an employer's right not to bargain with any union?

As long as union leaders can *force* workers to join their organization, they have no incentive to act responsibly. (50-51)

(Dreadfully improper use of this concept.)

Why should they—so long as political power is allowed to enter economics?

Unions should therefore be forbidden to engage in any kind of political activity. . . . I see no reason for labor unions—or corporations—to participate in politics. (54)

By what right, code or principle?

Chapter 7: Taxes and Spending

The size of the government's rightful claim—that is, the total amount it may take in taxes—will be determined by how we define the "legitimate functions of government." With regard to the federal government, the *Constitution* is the proper standard of legitimacy: its "legitimate" powers, as we have seen are those the Constitution has delegated to it. (60-61)

This is a deadly definition: since the people have an unlimited right to amend the Constitution, the people have an unlimited right to confiscate one's property.

Chapter 9: Some Notes on Education

Nobody should be surprised that aid has led to controls. It could, and *should not* be otherwise. Congress cannot be expected to appropriate the people's money and make no provision for how it will be spent. (81-82)

Good

We have forgotten that the proper function of the school is to transmit the cultural heritage of one generation to the next generation, and to so train the minds of the new generation as to make them

Total nonsense! This is the traditionalist conservatism.

capable of absorbing ancient learning and applying it to the problem of its own day. (84)

[W]e cannot develop such leaders unless <u>our
standards of education are geared to excellence
instead of mediocrity. We must give full rein to
individual talents</u>, and we must encourage our
schools to enforce the academic disciplines. . . .
<u>We should look upon our schools</u>—not <u>as a place</u>
to train the "whole character" of the child —a
responsibility that properly belongs to his family
and church—but <u>to train his *mind*</u>. (84)

These are good statements, but
they are contradictory and
impossible on the above here
[i.e., the previous passage]

<u>Our country's past progress has been the result,
not of the mass mind applying average intelligence to the problems of the day, but of the bril-
liance and dedication of wise individuals</u> who
applied their wisdom to advance the freedom and
the material well-being of all of our people. (84-
85)

Here's the deadly contradiction
within <u>one</u> sentence: the first
part of the sentence is true—
but the second part is the
morality of altruism. Brilliant
and dedicated individuals do <u>not</u>
work for the "material well-
being" of <u>all</u> the people. (The
"package-deal" confusion here
is on the issue of <u>freedom</u>:
since freedom is a political and
moral issue, an individualist has
to fight for the freedom of <u>all</u>
the people when he fights for
<u>his own</u> freedom; but the
purpose here is <u>not</u> altruistic.
"Material well-being" is
different; a productive individual
contributes <u>only</u> to the well-
being of other productive
individuals, and only as a
secondary consequence, <u>not</u> as
a primary goal.)

Chapter 10: The Soviet Menace

The American people are being told that, however valuable their freedom may be, it is even
more important to live. A craven fear of death is
entering the American consciousness; so much so
that many recently felt that honoring the chief
despot himself was the price we had to pay to
avoid nuclear destruction. (88)

<u>This</u> is the most disastrously
dangerous argument ever
advanced (again, this is the
influence of the <u>mystics</u> of
Conservatism): do not tell the
people that it is "noble" to die;
tell them that it is necessary to
<u>defend their lives</u>.

The real cause of the deterioration can be simply stated. Our enemies have understood the nature of the conflict, and we have not. They are determined to win the conflict, and we are not. (88-89)

> Excellent!

It is equally clear, however, that our leaders have not made *victory* the goal of American policy. And the reason that they have not done so, I am saying, is that they have never believed deeply that the Communists are in earnest. (89)

> This is not the only reason; the reason is that one side has no idea of what to fight for and, therefore, no idea of what to consider a victory.

There are ways which I will suggest later on—not easy ways, to be sure—in which we may save both our freedom *and* our lives; but all such suggestions are meaningless and vain unless we first understand what the objective is. We want to stay alive, of course; but more than that we want to be free. We want to have peace; but before that we want to establish the conditions that will make peace tolerable. (91)

> There again is the acceptance of that false dichotomy: life or freedom—instead of explaining why they are inseparable corollaries. Just as the Conservatives accepted, with disastrous results, the false dichotomy of "freedom or security," so they are now accepting another one: "freedom or life." On these terms, what's the use, meaning or value of freedom?

[Foreign policy] cannot . . . be defended as a charity. The American government does not have the right, much less the obligation, to try to promote the economic and social welfare of foreign peoples. Of course, all of us are interested in combating poverty and disease wherever it exists. (95)

> Good—but the very next sentence undercuts it.
>
> Endorsement of altruism, in connection with foreign aid.

[W]hen the Soviets challenged our rights in West Berlin, we handed them a victory by the mere act of sitting down at the conference table. By agreeing to negotiate on that subject, we agreed that our rights in Berlin were "negotiable". . . Our answer to Khrushchev's ultimatum should have been that the status of West Berlin concerns only West Berliners and the occupying powers, and is therefore not a matter that we are prepared to discuss with the Soviet Union. That would have been the end of the Berlin "crisis." (101)

> Excellent!!!

Are the American people ill-informed as to the nature of Communism and of the Soviet state? True, some Americans fail to grasp how evil the

> Wonderful!

Soviet system really is. But a performance by the Bolshoi Ballet, or a tour of the United States by Nikita Khrushchev, is certainly not calculated to correct *that* deficiency. (104)

As long as the Russian people do not control their government, it makes little difference whether they think well of us or ill. It is high time that our leaders stopped treating the Russian people and the Soviet government as one and the same thing. The Russian people, we may safely assume, are basically on our side (whether or not they have the opportunity to listen to American musicians); but their sympathy will not help us win the Cold War as long as all power is held firmly in the hands of the Communist ruling class. (104-105)

Great!

It is a mistake to measure the success of this Communist operation by the extent to which it converts Americans to Communism. By that test, of course, the operation is almost a complete failure. But the Kremlin's aim is not to make Americans *approve* of Communism, much as they would like that; it is to make us *tolerant* of Communism. (105)

Great!

[*Goldwater presents ten guideposts that he claims will help us avoid straying from the proper course in the attempt to defeat Communism:*]
1. The key guidepost is the Objective, and we must never lose sight of it. It is not to wage a struggle against Communism, but to win it. (118)

Good

5. In all our dealings with foreign nations, we must behave like a great power. Our national posture must reflect strength and confidence and purpose, as well as good will. . . . We must protect American nationals and American property and American honor—everywhere. (119)

Excellent

7. We should declare the world Communist movement an outlaw in the community of civilized nations. (120)

Excellent

8. We should encourage the captive peoples to revolt against their Communist rulers. . . . To this end we should establish close liaison with under-

ground leaders behind the Iron Curtain, furnish-   <u>Good</u>
ing them with printing presses, radios, weapons,
instructors: the paraphernalia of a full-fledged
Resistance. (120)

10. We must—ourselves—be prepared to under-   <u>Great</u>!!!
take military operations against vulnerable Com-
munist regimes. (121)

[*At the end of Chapter 10, Ayn Rand wrote:*]
He is at his best on the question of fighting Communism. But here are the unsolved
issues in his position: if we want victory over Communism, we must define, clearly,
specifically, and unequivocally, what Communism <u>is</u>. Otherwise, how would we be
able to distinguish friend from enemy? And it is here that his whole crusade will
collapse, in a clash with <u>Socialism</u> and <u>Statism</u>. Unless we fight for full <u>Capitalism</u>, we
cannot fight <u>nor win</u>.

[*At the end of her notes on this book, Ayn Rand wrote the following:*]
<u>Main issues</u> (errors):
1. <u>The alliance with religion</u>—its meanings, its consequences (Foreword, pp. 10-11,
    p. 84, p. 99)
2. <u>Altruism</u> (pp. 73-74, p. 95, p. 98)
3. <u>The false dichotomy of "freedom vs life"</u> (p. 88, pp. 91-92, p. 123)
4. <u>Economic errors</u>: "right-to-work laws"—"monopolies"

<u>Over-all philosophical errors</u>: "Freedom" is not a primary (to be a morally powerful
concept, freedom has to be justified <u>morally</u>)—"Constitutionalism" is not a primary
(the <u>moral rightness</u> of the Constitution has to be stated and upheld).

Harold Fleming, *Ten Thousand Commandments: A Story of the Antitrust Laws* (New York: Prentice-Hall, Inc., 1951)

This book was reviewed by Ayn Rand in The Objectivist Newsletter, *vol. 1, no. 4 (April, 1962). In "America's Persecuted Minority: Big Business" (a lecture given at Ford Hall Forum, 1961, published in* Capitalism: The Unknown Ideal)*, Ayn Rand said: "I recommend to you a brilliant little book entitled* Ten Thousand Commandments *by Harold Fleming. It is written for the layman and presents—in clear, simple, logical terms, with a wealth of detailed, documented evidence—such a picture of the antitrust laws that 'nightmare' is too feeble a word to describe it." At the end of her (very favorable) review of the book, she wrote: "In the last two chapters [24 and 25] of his book, attempting to explain and evaluate the monstrous facts he has presented, he resorts to some vague, superficial generalities, such as the suggestion that some sort of 'Freudian' fear is the motive for the persecution of businessmen. But he is too good a reporter to let his theory interfere with the facts he is presenting. And this book is so good that the inadequacy of his explanation can be safely overlooked."*

Tropismatically suspicious, the government lawyers in the FTC and the Antitrust Division feel that businessmen will use such information [i.e., widely publicized information about what everybody else charges] to avoid competing. But by the same reasoning, of course, the common use of the English language, the decimal system, and of the old English nomenclature of ounces, pounds, and tons also contributes to the possibilities of "conscious parallel action" by businessmen. (13)

Excellent!

Thus if a man drives off in his car, there is a reasonable *possibility* that he may have an accident—but (if he is a good driver) no reasonable *probability*. Most people would agree that if there were a reasonable *probability* of his doing damage, his license ought to be revoked. But if drivers' licenses were granted only to drivers who could prove there was no reasonable *possibility* of their hitting anybody, the roads would be empty. (30-31)

Good!

[*Quote from an editorial from* Commerce *(June 1, 1950):*] The Sherman Act was not designed to punish dynamic progress, and to reduce competitors to a common level of mediocrity. . . . (56)

(Yes, it <u>was</u>—whether they knew it or not.)

In April 1938, President Roosevelt sent a mes-

(Perfect example of business as

sage to Congress asking it to look into the concentration of American industry. He intimated that it was getting worse and that it might be the cause of the "quickie" depression that had just come on the country. He mentioned a "concentration of private power without equal in history," which, he said, was "seriously impairing the economic effectiveness of private enterprise as a way of providing employment for labor and capital." (67)

scapegoat)

Thus the people who use what might be called the "Mexican jumping bean" theory of industrial prices are hardly being fair to businessmen. They seem to expect businessmen to produce price "jiggles" in all directions at all times. It is an impatient view. These critics seem to feel that because businessmen do not compete like tennis-players (which they seldom do) but like chess-players (which they usually do) they are not "really" competing. The critics are in a hurry for action. But it takes some time to see the moves in a game of business competition, as in the game of chess. (103)

(Range-of-the-moment Attila-ism)

The reason so many of A&P's competitors have come to its defense in the public prints seems to be a rather simple one. They are not concerned over the particular fate of A&P in the Antitrust Division's pending suit for A&P's dissolution. Nor would the public need to be concerned about it, if the suit were merely brought to "get" A&P for some political sin or error. But A&P's competitors are concerned because of the *business methods* that have been outlawed, directly or indirectly, in the recent suit. (142)

!!!?! This is an example of the author's lack of philosophical integration, of broader, basic principles. The whole public had jolly well better be concerned when and if a government has the power to "get" somebody for political sins or errors!

. . . the proposed action would materially lessen efficiency in any line of commerce. (146)

(There's the catch-word for non-objective law.)

The development of power tools in the eighteenth century brought the industrial revolution, rising from the mill. (157)

(Author's error. Short-range view.)

But for as long as there is written history, the question "How good is bigness?" has been at

!!! (The issue here is: "How good is ability?" asked by an

least a farm problem. The Roman Senate, the British Parliament, and the Soviet government have, in their turns, wrestled with the problem of large, efficient estates versus small family farms. (158)

envious mediocrity armed with a gun.)

The struggle has, then, been over the question of whether the new economies should be abandoned so as to save the old social pattern, or whether new patterns could be worked out. (158)

(Which means: progress or stagnation)

By and large the predominant purpose of large corporate managements, in all their major policies, is to make sure the company will remain indefinitely in business. They don't keep the company in business to make profits, they see that it makes profits so it can stay in business. The aim is to keep the company's fences mended at all times on all fronts: competitive, financial, political, and ethical. (159-160)

Here is the author's basic failure. This is apologetic sophistry and hypocrisy. He is trying to bypass "profits."

Lousy evasion and equivocation!

A long series of corporate policies are far more easily explained this way [i.e., the way described in the previous passage] than in the conventional way. Among these are "administered prices," held down in boom times to protect the company's good name with customers and the public and held steady in bad times to protect the company from bankruptcy. Another is the maintenance of sound, rather than speculative, capital structures. Still others are the diversification of markets and products and the long-range planning and development of new products and heavy investments in research. . . . The recently increased investments in "public relations" on the community and national levels may be included here, too. (160)

This is long-range self-interest.

(This passage is an example of "selfishness" being thought of as Attila-istic.)

Washington economists say big business has power over many people, but big businessmen say they "serve" many people. To sum it up, it is servant to as many people as it "dominates." (162)

Apologies of this kind is what kills them.

The majority in the Columbia Steel case . . . said, "It is not for the courts to determine the course of the Nation's economic development. . . . If businesses are to be forbidden from entering into dif-

And it is not for Congress, either—except on a collectivist premise.

ferent stages of production that order must come
from Congress, not from the courts." (167)

For back of all this legislation and interpretation   No, much more than that.
and economic theory is the fear of big—meaning
powerful—privately owned corporations. (187)

[*Ayn Rand wrote the following at the end of* Chapter 24: The Folklore of Trust-Busting:]
This chapter is very bad: petty, superficial; artificial and illogical. The author seems to
have lost all of his incisive logic. That is the penalty of an amoral approach to a subject
of this kind. He is trying to evade and by-pass morality. The result negates and
undercuts all the facts presented in his book. He talks as if no collectivist trend
existed in the world and as if all of it can be explained by some silly, unexplained
"fears."

[*Ayn Rand wrote the following at the end of* Chapter 25: Conclusion:]
(The conclusions are weak and bad, caused by the same amorality.) But this book is
so good that the last two chapters can be safely ignored.

A.D. Neale, *The Antitrust Laws of the United States of America: A Study of Competition Enforced by Law* (Cambridge University Press, 1960; third edition, with D.C. Goyder, 1980)

In *"America's Persecuted Minority: Big Business," Ayn Rand wrote: "I recommend to your attention an excellent book entitled* The Antitrust Laws *of the U.S.A. by A.D. Neale. It is a scholarly, dispassionate, objective study; the author, a British civil servant, is not a champion of free enterprise; as far as one can tell, he may probably be classified as a 'liberal.' But he does not confuse facts with interpretations, he keeps them severely apart; and the facts he presents are a horror story."*

Ayn Rand's comments (on the first edition) were not written in the margins, but on sixteen separate pages of notes. It is sometimes unclear precisely what passage she was commenting on, but in every case an intelligent guess (at the very least) is possible. The page numbers are from the third edition.

Chapter 4: Monopolization I: The Criteria for Offenses Under Section 2 of the Sherman Act

In effect, Judge Hand's test puts the onus on the defendant to show that he simply cannot help having monopoly power: to any extent that he reaches out to grasp or strives actively to hold his leading place, he is denied the right to claim that he has no unlawful intent. (110)

This is the purest penalizing of ability and success for being ability and success.

Chapter 6: Monopolization III: Section 2 of the Sherman Act and Oligopoly Situations

Mr. Justice Douglas, speaking for the Supreme Court when the [Federal Trade Commission v. Motion Picture Advertising Service Company] case was appealed, made much of the fact that, if M.P.A. were taken together with three other companies which used similar types of contract, the exclusive-dealing arrangements for advertising films covered about 75% of the cinemas that used such films. There was no suggestion that the four big companies were acting in concert. But Mr. Justice Douglas . . . put the issue as follows: "Due to the exclusive contracts, respondent and the three other major companies have foreclosed to competitors 75% of all available outlets for this business throughout the United States. . . ." (161-162)

The Motion Picture Advertising Company Case—pure horror: a company can be made to be a "conspirator" through the actions of other companies, not its own (<u>collective guilt</u>).

[In response to Justice Douglas' remarks in the

United States v. Paramount case, the author writes:]
To 'participate in evolving' a system or to 'acqui-
esce' in a system and so 'further its existence' are
tests that seem to fall short of a 'meeting of the
minds.' By these tests might not Beethoven,
Brahms and Sibelius be held co-conspirators in
the business of writing symphonies? (169)

Good observations on the
"tests" of "conspiracy."

Chapter 7: The Clayton Act I: Introduction; Mergers and Acquisitions

Much was made in the debates of the point that
what was 'unfair' competition on the part of a
powerful firm against small rivals might very
well be 'fair' when used by the small against the
powerful. (182)

Arguments for Clayton Act
openly advocating a double-
standard of "fairness" for the
"powerful" and the "small"
rivals.

Chapter 10: Patents and Antitrust

Just as Judge Hand [in the ALCOA case] drew
the line somewhere between legitimate competition 'by virtue of superior skill, foresight and industry' and the exclusionary activity of 'progressively embracing each new opportunity as it
opened,' so, in cases dealing with patent monopolies, the courts must make fine distinctions
between activities designed to improve a firm's
economic performance and activities aimed at
impeding competitors. (307)

Preposterous contradiction in
their view of business "skill" and
"foresight."

Chapter 12: The Administration of Antitrust

It is sometimes suggested that more could be
done by the Department of Justice by way of informal procedures for enforcing the law: for example, the businessmen and their lawyers should
be able to apply to the Department of Justice for
advice as to whether some proposed practice
would be regarded by the Department as legal or
illegal. Although this type of informal, administrative adjudication has increased, there are of
necessity severe limitations to what can be done
in this way. . . . The Department has a public duty
to prosecute offenses against the laws, and the
individual lawyer on the staff clearly could not
commit himself, and still less the Department, to
saying that a proposed scheme was lawful if he
were in any doubt as to the full facts of the case.
. . . (381)

Incredible horror: the
"informal" consultations with
the Department of Justice
(when even the Department
cannot tell what may turn out
to be "criminal" in the future,
yet the businessman has to act
and take that chance). (If this is
not retroactive law, I do not
know what is.)

The dissent of Mr. Justice Jackson in Federal Trade Commission v. Ruberoid Company (Supreme Court, 1952) explained why the Federal Trade Commission must have a measure of discretion in interpreting the law under the Clayton Act. . . . Statutes like the Robinson-Patman Act, Jackson says, are 'inchoate law'; an administrative body has to be interposed to formulate a complete expression of the law on a particular case. 'By the doctrine that the Federal Trade Commission exercises legislative discretion as to policy in completing and perfecting the legislative process, it has escaped executive domination on the one hand and been exempted in large measure from judicial review on the other.' (387-388)

> Unbelievable horror: the non-objectivity of "inchoate law"— and the arbitrary power of the Federal Trade Commission, not subject to review by anyone.

Chapter 13: Antitrust Remedies

[*Commenting on the penalties imposed in the famous ALCOA case (399-403), Ayn Rand wrote:*]
The "remedies" in <u>the Alcoa case</u>. This is horror and vicious insanity: <u>because</u> Alcoa is needed even for <u>national security</u>, the judge decided it to be his duty to make it as hard for Alcoa to be successful as he could, including the building up of an independent <u>foreign</u> (Canadian) competitor. (The reasoning: Alcoa had to be hamstrung, <u>in case</u> Reynolds and Kaiser failed!!!) This is as crude a case of penalizing ability for being ability and of national suicide via anti-capitalism as one could invent in any fiction.

In the du Pont/ICI case of 1952. . . , Judge Ryan . . . ordered the compulsory licensing of their existing patents in the fields to which their restrictive agreements applied. . . . In this case an auxiliary remedy was awarded which had become common in later years. Both I.C.I. and du Pont were ordered to provide applicants, at a reasonable charge, with technical manuals which would show in detail how the patents were practiced. (410)

> Horror-case, straight out of "Atlas Shrugged": They were ordered to <u>teach</u> their competitors how to use <u>their</u> confiscated patents (!!!)[1]

[*From Judge Forman's decision in the United States v. General Electric Company case:*]
Where the profit margin on the production of lamps is as narrow as it is at the present time any licensing fees may prove an important factor in limiting or inhibiting the growth of competition. In view of the fact that General Electric achieved

> The decision in the General Electric case (1953) shows blatantly that the whole messy vagueness of forced competition has only <u>one</u>

its dominant position in the industry and maintained it in great measure by its extension of patent control, the requirement that it contribute its existing patents to the public is only a justified dilution of that control made necessary in the interest of free competition in the industry. . . . (411)

meaning in practice: <u>the penalizing of ability for success and the granting of the unearned to mediocrities</u>. (Observe that General Electric lost its patent because it had brought the margin of profit so far down that the looting parasites [the competitors] could not have afforded to pay a royalty for the patents. "Public interest," huh?)

The decisions of the courts on remedies naturally set limits to what the Government can obtain in consent decrees. A defendant is unlikely to accept by consent measures which would not be awarded by the courts in litigated cases. Nevertheless, the advantages which defendants may obtain from consent settlements are such that the measures obtained by the Government in consent decrees often press hard against these limits. Sometimes they have even seemed to anticipate rather than follow the edicts of the courts and some of the most remarkable and comprehensive examples of judicial legislation are to be found among negotiated consent decrees. (412)

The indignity of "voluntary agreement" under a gun, or "government by blackmail."

[At the end of Chapter 13, Ayn Rand wrote:]
The ASCAP case shows that the antitrust laws lead, through "consent decrees," to the surrender of a business organization into total government control. The price of such "consent decrees" is the surrender of the freedom of decision-making and term-setting. (Since the antitrust laws <u>are</u> based on a collectivistic principle, they had to lead to collectivization, confiscation and government controls—even though the proponents of these laws were doing it in the name of free enterprise. This is a good example of the power of principles—and how they work out to their ultimate logical conclusions in practice.)

Chapter 14: Treble-Damage Action

The fear of treble-damage actions is one of the most potent influences in securing compliance with antitrust. It is important, however, to understand the limitations of this type of action. The treble-damage action is not a means of enforcing the law by common informers. A member of the public or a businessman who sees what he regards as flagrant breaches of antitrust law going

This <u>is</u> a chance for worse than "common informers": for envious, unsuccessful competitors and vicious mediocrities.

on may complain to the Department of Justice. . . .
(419)

Another area in which treble-damage actions
have been common is that of patent licensing.
Once the Government had shown that many conditions imposed by patent holders on licensees
were a misuse of the patent grant, it became possible for private firms not only to infringe these
patents. . . , but also, if the patentee's sue for in-
fringement, to counterclaim for treble damages
on the ground that restrictive conditions in patent
licenses also constituted illegal restraint of trade.
(419-420)

> As if the above horror wasn't
> obvious enough, note the
> parasites who sue for "treble-
> damages" in patent cases (!!!)

Chapter 15: Antitrust as an American Policy

[There is] a real dilemma that any anti-monopoly
law must needs solve. On the one hand it seems
good sense to judge the monopolist by his works.
If his record as an innovator is good, if his prices
and profits are reasonable and there are no com-
plaints of predatory conduct, if the productivity
and rewards of the labour he employs are high—
are not the various social ends of industry being
achieved? The difficulty with this view is that
there are not—and probably cannot be—satisfactory performance tests to apply. As Chief Justice
Stone put it, any judgement of performance requires 'a complete survey of our economic organization and a choice between rival philoso-
phies.' Even if we can say that a monopolist is
technically advanced or low-cost at the moment,
how do we know that he would not be more so if
he had to compete, and how do we know where
he will stand in five years' time? Economics provides no rules of thumb by which questions of
this kind can be answered in the consistent way
required by a rule of law. (454)

> The dilemma here is the result
> of the fact that any economic
> law is part of a context that
> involves an "economic
> philosophy" and cannot be
> taken out of that context and
> can be judged only by means of
> the basic principles of such
> context. The antitrust laws are
> based on the principle of
> collectivism, yet were created in
> the name of individualism and
> free enterprise—hence their
> grotesquely tragic results.

There is little doubt that in a modern antitrust suit
evidence of price uniformity. . . coupled . . . with
quite slight (though distinct) indications of an
'agreement to agree' would be enough to establish illegal collusion. (458)

> Similarity of prices, which they
> want to regard as "collusion,"
> will usually be simply the
> proper operation of the market,
> that is: of the law of supply and
> demand.

[*Ayn Rand ended her notes with the following:*]
<u>General notes on Neale's book</u>:

The "conscious parallelism" theory[2] would demand that men act without knowledge.

The <u>preventive</u> aspect of "monopolizing" cases is preventive law, and treats businessmen worse (less objectively) than criminals. It is one thing to consider intent <u>after</u> a crime has been committed; it is quite another to guess or "presume" an intent, without having to prove by factual evidence that a crime has been committed. (Censorship or curfew laws could be justified by this same type of reasoning: men should be censored to prevent their uttering a lie, or should stay home at night to prevent their committing a robbery.)

The Government representatives, in most cases, were subtly and gradually working to establish precedents for collectivistic principles, always in the direction of gaining more discretionary powers and of leaving businessmen at the mercy of the Government's arbitrary whim (called "interpretation").

The preposterous thing in the antitrust laws (as shown particularly in the patent-pooling cases) is that the businessman is forced by law to function as an individual—while the workers today are forced to act as a collective. The consequences and implications of this double-standard are enormous and all evil.

Lowell Mason, *The Language of Dissent* (New Canaan, Conn.: The Long House, Inc., 1962). Originally published by The World Publishing Co. (Cleveland, 1959)

This book was reviewed by Ayn Rand in The Objectivist Newsletter, *vol. 2, no. 8 (August 1963), and included in the Recommended Bibliography at the end of* Capitalism: The Unknown Ideal. *In her review, she recommended this book (despite her rejection of Mason's advocacy of a "mixed economy"): "I invite all those who are concerned with tyranny to read this book. It is an important historical document and it offers irrefutable information on the subject of antitrust, which is confronting us with growing frequency—and growing fogginess—in today's news, as the major threat to this country's freedom."*

Chapter 5: The Attack on the Right to Compete

The truth of the matter is that between Russia and ourselves, Russia is on the way up with competition—and we are on the way down. When the Russians compete, they compete for keeps. The rewards for superiority (I use the word in its aggressive, nonmoral sense) in the field of government are cars, caviar, fur coats, and the enforced adulation of the entire population of the communist dominated countries. In Russia the losers in the competitive race get the dubious privilege of confessing their errors prior to the firing squad or, in milder cases, ignominy in Siberia. (115)

Very bad equivocation on the concept of "competition."

Chapter 10: The Morality of Law and the Ethics of Enforcement

These [i.e., "the most fruitful and worthwhile" laws] are the rules of civilization, in which the adjustments of man to man are <u>rooted in the sentiment of the community</u>. (274)

No! In common sense, i.e., in reason.

Government misses the mark when too many laws are passed which rely on enforcement rather than acceptance for their observance. (276)

How can you "accept" or "observe" <u>a non-objective law</u>?

[*Quoting Harry Babcock, the Attorney in Charge of the Federal Trade Commission's Washington Field Office:*]
The businessmen of the country desire something more than that the menace of legal process in these matters be made explicit and intelligible. They desire the advice, the definite <u>guidance and information which can be supplied by an</u>

Good god, how vicious! <u>This</u> is the root of the whole rotten non-objectivity. ("Advice" and "guidance" at the point of a gun?)

administrative body, an interstate trade commission. (280)

I wanted to establish as a public policy that where the state of the law was obscure, we would not sue without first giving the businessman an opportunity to comply with our interpretation of what we thought the law required. This was, of course, just what President Wilson had in mind when he urged the creation of a Federal Trade Commission in a message to Congress in 1914. But President Wilson's attorney general heartily disapproved of any such candor on the part of the government. Nor does the Federal Trade Commission today feel any more kindly about it. Wilson, by sheer force of the obvious justice in his proposal, succeeded at the time in persuading Congress to pass the Federal Trade Commission Act. Its purpose was guidance. In other words, it was to make unnecessary or at least reduce the work of the Department of Justice which punished for violations of business law after they occurred. The Commission was to give direction to the channels of trade, so that businessmen would know in advance what was right and what was wrong. That was the original conception of the Federal Trade Commission. Shortly after the creation of the Commission, the First World War broke out, and in the hurly-burly of preparedness, the ideals of President Wilson were soon lost and never found again. Today, outside of some lip service to the Wilsonian ideas in trade association speeches, few at the Commission look with any favor on what was the original purpose of this body. This is understandable, because the disposition of issues by any other means than litigation could hardly appeal to those whose sole function in bureaucracy is to prosecute. (293)

> This is an excellent example of what happens to the welfare-statists' "good intentions." "Guidance" at the point of a gun—and "law" arbitrarily "interpreted" by a government bureau.

And who cares about due process? It has become so most people think due process (the right to confront your accusers, etc.) only pays off for those charged with a crime. The constant association of due process with alleged communists, thieves, kidnapers, and bank robbers degrades the high regard that this basic concept of liberty and justice once commanded. This denigration occurs simply because these protections to liberty

> (No. Because these principles are never invoked publicly in regard to businessmen. Because anti-trust laws nullified them.)

are seldom dramatized except when called into play by the arrest, indictment, or trial of those charged with crime. (302)

A life insurance policy pays its owner something of value every minute he is alive. The same can be said for the Bill of Rights. Nothing is as valuable as an assurance of your own security, be it in terms of a policy on your life or in terms of a policy on your liberty and your pursuit of happiness. (302)

(Good!)

Appendix: 1947 Minority Recommendations

Commissioner Mason submits individually two minority proposals as follows:

1. That the Commission recommend to Congress legislation which will promote the cooperative elimination upon an industry-wide basis of acts and practices prohibited by the statutes administered by the Commission by giving trade practice conference procedure and rules a clear statutory basis, by facilitating the acquisition of the information necessary to the initiation and conduct of such conferences, by affording an opportunity for cooperation by the Department of Justice and the Department of Commerce in the initiation of trade practice conferences and in the formulation of the rules to be promulgated. . . . (306)

(Here, Mr. Mason follows Mason's Law—involuntarily—and proposes greater power for some ambitious bureaucrat. The fault is in the principle of government controls: they have to grow, since they cannot and do not work, but merely create growing problems.)

Allen Churchill, *The Incredible Ivar Kreuger* **(New York: Rinehart & Co., 1957)**

In her Introduction to Night of January 16th *(New York: New American Library, 1968), Ayn Rand wrote that "The springboard for the story was the collapse of Ivar Kreuger—or, more precisely, the public reaction to that collapse. On March 12, 1932, Ivar Kreuger, the Swedish 'Match King,' committed suicide. His death was followed by the crash of the vast financial empire he had created, and by the revelation that that empire was a gigantic fraud. . . . Ivar Kreuger was a man of unusual ability who had, at first, made a fortune by legitimate means; it was his venture into politics—mixed-economy politics—that destroyed him. Seeking a world monopoly for his match industry, he began to give large loans to various European governments in exchange for a monopoly status in their countries—loans which were not repaid, which he could not collect and which led him to a fantastic juggling of his assets and bookkeeping to conceal his losses." Regarding the public reaction to his collapse, she wrote: "It was not a crook that they were denouncing, but greatness as such; it was greatness as such that I wanted to defend."*

Kreuger's conception was a 125-room edifice, complete with board room, executive offices, staff offices and a match museum. For the location of his magnificent new structure he did not choose the business section of Stockholm. Instead, he picked a dignified residential street. . . just off the Royal Gardens. It was lined with mansions of the *ancien régime* and Kreuger's Match Palace. . .did nothing to destroy its atmosphere of old world elegance. (90)	Take note of the <u>material luxury</u> premise. (Or substitute?)
<u>As a man whose mind was capable of a conception of such earth-shaking dimensions, Kreuger stood on the verge of one of the greatest careers his time offered.</u> He was assured of the power he seemed so desperately to crave, and limitless millions as well. . . . All this he could now attain and keep forever. There was only one price he must pay: he must be honest. (121-122)	The author of this book is an abysmal fool! Here is the whole of today's irrationality in a teaspoon. How? With a fundamentally crooked scheme?
<u>There was nothing the least bit fraudulent about most of the monopolies he secured.</u> . . . (138)	(Except the <u>fact</u> of monopoly-by-force)
It is likely that [Kreugar] opened negotiations with Primo de Rivera, and with characteristic impatience immediately had a contract drawn up. Then, if the negotiations proceeded slowly, or broke off, the superior, confident man could not face the fact and began speaking as if the loan were settled. (140)	(Possibly: loss of touch with reality or <u>autism</u>)?

The first three are "obscenity" cases which Ayn Rand discussed in "Censorship: Local and Express," The Ayn Rand Letter, vol. 2, nos. 23-25 (August 13-September 10, 1973), reprinted in Philosophy:Who Needs It. The Roth case was also discussed in greater detail in "Thought Control," The Ayn Rand Letter, vol. 2, no. 26-vol. 3, no. 2 (September 24-October 22, 1973). On the DeFunis case (which concerns "affirmative action"), see "Moral Inflation," Part III, The Ayn Rand Letter, vol. 3, no. 4 (April 8, 1974).

Roth v. United States (June 24, 1957).

[*Justice Brennan delivered the opinion of the court.*] In Alberts, the trial judge applied the test laid down in People v. Wepplo. . . , namely, whether the material has "a substantial tendency to deprave or corrupt its readers by inciting lascivious *thoughts* or arousing lustful desires."

This is an expression of the view that sex is evil.[3]

The fundamental freedoms of speech and press have contributed greatly to the development and well-being of our free society and are indispensible to its continued growth.

Bad justification: on social or historical grounds—not on grounds of rights.

In Public Clearing House v. Coyne. . . , this court said: "The constitutional principles underlying the administration of the Post Office Department were discussed in the opinion of the court in Ex parte Jackson. . . , in which we held that the power vested in Congress to establish post offices and post roads embraced the regulation of the entire postal system of the country; that Congress might designate what might be carried in the mails and what excluded. It may refuse to include in its mails such printed matter or merchandise as may seem objectionable to it upon the ground of public policy. . . . The constitutionality of this law we believe has never been attacked.

Good Lord! (Same issue as interstate commerce—creating an out-of-context absolute. Same argument was used to justify the draft [power to "raise an army"].)

Miller v. California (June 21, 1973).

[*Justice Burger delivered the opinion of the court.*] The mere fact juries may reach different conclusions as to the same material does not mean that constitutional rights are abridged. As the Court

True—but the definition of

observed in Roth v. United States. . . , "[I]t is common experience that different juries may reach different results under any criminal statute. That is one of the consequences we accept under our jury system. . . . "

Under a National Constitution, fundamental First Amendment limitations on the powers of the States do not vary from community to community, but this does not mean that there are, or should or can be, fixed, uniform national standards of precisely what appeals to the "prurient interest" or is "patently offensive." These are essentially questions of fact, and our nation is simply too big and too diverse for this Court to reasonably expect that such standards could be articulated for all 50 States in a single formulation, even assuming the prerequisite consensus exists.

> crimes are more exact.[4]

> Here goes objectivity!

"The protection given speech and press was fashioned to assure unfettered interchange of *ideas* for the bringing about of political and social changes desired by the people," Roth v. United States. . . .

> Here's J.S. Mill.
> The answer is: "No! To protect individual rights—i.e., the freedom of the mind." (Besides, this formulation restricts freedom of speech to politics.)

[*Justice Douglas, dissenting.*]
If there are to be restraints on what is obscene, then a constitutional amendment should be the way of achieving the end. There are societies where religion and mathematics are the only free segments. It would be a dark day for America if that were our destiny. But the people can make it such if they choose to write obscenity into the Constitution and define it.

> (That's what's wrong.)

If [obscenity] is to be defined, let the people debate and decide by a constitutional amendment what they want to ban as obscene and what standards they want the legislatures and the courts to apply.

> Disgusting notion!

Paris Adult Theater I v. Slaton (June 21, 1973).

[*Chief Justice Burger delivered the opinion of the court.*]
If we accept the unprovable assumption that a complete education requires certain books. . . ,

and the well nigh universal belief that good books, plays, and art lift the spirit, improve the mind, enrich the human personality and develop character, can we then say that a state legislature may not act on the corollary assumption that commerce in obscene books, or public exhibitions focused on obscene conduct, have a tendency to exert a corrupting and debasing impact leading to antisocial behavior?

No! If you can't define what is obscene!

Our prior decisions recognizing a right to privacy guaranteed by the Fourteenth Amendment included "only those personal rights that can be deemed 'fundamental' or 'implicit in the concept of ordered liberty'. . . . This privacy right encompasses and protects the personal intimacies of the home, the family, marriage, motherhood, procreation, and child rearing.

?

(Only these? What about the mind?)

Where communication of ideas, protected by the First Amendment, is not involved, nor the particular privacy of the home protected by *Stanley*, nor any of the other "areas or zones" of constitutionally protected privacy, the mere fact that, as a consequence, some human "utterances" or "thoughts" may be incidentally affected does not bar the State from acting to protect legitimate state interests.

The by-passing (and shrinking) of the concept of rights.

!!!

The state statute books are replete with constitutionally unchallenged laws against prostitution, suicide, voluntary self-mutilation, brutalizing "bare fist" prize fights, and duels, although these crimes may only directly involve "consenting adults." Statutes making bigamy a crime surely cut into an individual's freedom to associate.

BS!

No! They involve state-granted status of marriage.

[*Justice Brennan, with whom Justice Stewart and Justice Marshall join, dissenting.*]
Although I did not join the opinion of the Court in Stanley v. Georgia. . . (1969), I am now inclined to agree that "the Constitution protects the right to receive information and ideas," and that "this right to receive information and ideas, regardless of their social worth . . . is fundamental to our free society."

What about "to give ideas"?

[Justice Douglas, dissenting.]
But our society—unlike most in the world—pre-supposes that <u>freedom and liberty are in a frame of reference that make the individual, not the government, the keeper of his tastes, beliefs, and ideas</u>. That is the philosophy of the First Amendment; and it is the article of faith that sets us apart from most nations of the world.

Douglas is the best of them, in the sense of <u>moral righteousness</u>—but he makes it a matter of <u>feelings</u> (belief, faith, taste).[5]

DeFunis v. Odegaard (April 23, 1974).

[Justice Douglas, dissenting.]
The key to the problem is the consideration of each application *in a racially neutral way.* Since LSAT reflects questions touching on cultural backgrounds, <u>the admissions committee acted properly in my view in setting minority applications apart for separate processing</u>. These minorities have cultural backgrounds that are vastly different from the dominant Caucasian. Many Eskimos, American Indians, Filipinos, Chicanos, Asian Indians, Burmese, and Africans come from such disparate backgrounds that <u>a test sensitively tuned for most applicants would be wide of the mark for many minorities</u>.

Good God!

!!?!! Is Douglas crazy?

The melting pot as I understand it is a figure of speech that depicts <u>the wide diversities tolerated by the First Amendment under one flag</u>. . . . Minorities in our midst who are to serve actively in our public affairs <u>should be chosen on talent and character alone not on cultural orientation or leanings</u>.

!!!

??! What in hell does <u>this</u> mean?

I do know . . . that many of the young Indians know little about Adam Smith or Karl Marx but are deeply imbued with the spirit and philosophy of Chief Robert B. Jim of the Yakimas, Chief Seattle of the Muckleshoots and Chief Joseph of the Nez Perce which offer competitive attitudes toward life, fellow man, and nature.

What does <u>this</u> mean?

There is . . . no bar to considering an individual's prior achievements in light of the racial discrimination that barred his way, as a factor in attempting to assess his true potential for a successful legal career. <u>Nor is there any bar to considering on an individual basis, rather than according to</u>

Is <u>altruistic collectivism</u> to be enforced by government as a

racial classifications, the likelihood that a particular candidate will more likely employ his legal skills to service communities that are not now adequately represented than will competing candidates.

Constitutional right?

The State . . . may not proceed by racial classification to force strict population equivalencies for every group in every occupation, overriding individual preferences. The Equal Protection Clause commands the elimination of racial barriers, not their creation in order to satisfy our theory as to how society ought to be organized.

True.

How does he reconcile this with the BS about "different cultures"?

A segregated admissions process creates suggestions of stigma and caste no less than a segregated classroom, and in the end it may produce that result despite its contrary intentions.

True.

Among Ayn Rand's papers were four boxes full of dozens of files containing newspaper and magazine clippings. In most cases these files were organized according to topic and/or with a view to an article she was thinking about writing or had already written. Generally these clippings contained no more than underlining, exclamation points, and question marks. But there were some significant exceptions, the best of which follow (in chronological order, with one exception).

Benjamin F. Fairless (President, United States Steel Corporation), "Guilty Before Trial." [*An address at the Boston Jubilee of 1950, Mid-Century Celebration of Progress, Boston, Mass., May 18, 1950. Published as a pamphlet by U.S. Steel.*]

The defining of those boundaries [i.e., the boundaries of good and lawful business practice] should not be left to those who hate business, to those who seek personal or political power over it, nor to theorists who want to experiment with it. . . .

If the realistic and informed men of Government will ever sit down with reasonable and experienced men of business and make up their collective mind as to what monopoly really is, what competition is, what business conduct is ethical and proper, and what business conduct is injurious and wrong, I think we will find fewer monkey wrenches in the machinery, and the Government will be able to get out of the crutch business in short order.

> Here is the root of the businessmen's trouble—the sign of an anti-intellectual attitude. The above is <u>not</u> a job for government officials and businessmen, but for <u>philosophers</u>, specifically <u>political</u> and <u>ethical</u> philosophers.

Elmo Roper, "The Reader is Your Market: Ways to Break the Roadblocks to Bookbuying," *Publisher's Weekly,* **June 16, 1958.**

Now, how does this sort of thing [i.e., the popularity of baseball, as compared to intellectual achievement] come about? I suspect that an important part of the answer is what has been referred to as the *folk status* of baseball in our society. Through the length and breadth of the land, and up and down the social and economic brackets, it is considered a good thing for a father to play catch with his son. It is a good thing for a boy to get outside and play ball with other kids. . . . There is a folk tradition about baseball that touches our whole population, that seeks out talent, that nurtures it toward its potential, that prods and praises and disciplines exceptional

> Do the "intellectuals" offer anything as <u>objectively</u> and <u>rationally</u> suited to its purpose?

ability, that recognizes achievement at various levels between the sand lot and the World Series, and that selects and honors and rewards according to the outcome of uncompromising competition.

There is no widespread folk tradition that seeks out and trains and sponsors and takes pride in exceptional intellectual talent. There are no "little leagues" of the mind. It is good if a child gets high grades on his report card; but beyond that, a love of abstract ideas, a thirst for knowledge, a gnawing intellectual curiosity—these are more likely to be regarded as worrisome symptoms than as promising abilities. . . . We chuckle at the observation regarding college professors that "them that can does and them that can't teaches." And note that we seem to like especially the bad grammar in this canard.

> Do current books provide this?

> What about the "intellectuals'" love of four-letter literature?

Let's face it: Intellectual achievement and the intellectual elite are alien to the main stream of American society. They are off to the side in a sub-section of esoteric isolation labeled "odd ball," "high brow," "egg-headed," "doubledome."

> Isn't this what they want and seek?

The search for wisdom and the love of knowledge for its own sake can no longer be left to a gifted and stubborn few. . . .

> So long as this continues, you'll never get the people's interest!

Bookshelves are a symbol of the inquiring mind.

> But the "intellectuals" sr⸍ their effort on prov⸵ there is no mind!

The second inhibition I mentioned is that book buying is economically risky. The central question is this: How are you going to get on speaking terms with the general public? How are you going to gain their attention?

> Look at the non-sequitur! The question of "risk" is not "how are you going to gain attention?" but "Do you deserve attention?" This is an example of trying to by-pass the issue of values. And so is the whole article.

I come now to the third inhibition, namely that book owning is socially deviant. Too few people know the pleasures and rewards available only to book owners: their beauty as decoration, the satisfaction of book plates, the additional meaning

> ?!!!

that comes with underlining and making marginal notes, the stimulation of looking things up when the questions arise instead of planning to do so *sometime*, the comfortable sureness of rereading a treasured passage, the companionship of introducing a child to just the right book at just the right time, . . .

What about: the <u>mind</u> and its one and only proper purpose: to help you solve the problems of <u>your</u> life?

The point that I am suggesting is that book owning is deviant because so many people can't see why any sensible person would *want* to own books.

I don't either!

Automobile companies advertise the mechanical characteristics of their cars, and clothing stores advertise the quality of their fabrics and the caliber of their tailoring. But you also see a lot of stress on what cars and clothing will *do for you* if you buy them. Could we find a way to sell people on the satisfactions and rewards of owning and reading books?

But would this work if the automobiles could not move and the clothes could not be worn?

There is an urgent need—in fact a national survival need—<u>for invigorating intellectual life, for upgrading the general regard for intellectual excellence, for broadening the base of intellectual interests—for a renaissance that establishes a genuine folk status for things of the mind</u>—respect for the Learned Man. Booksellers can and should play a significant leadership role in this enterprise. But your efforts may have to be only as a catalytic agent—the force that arouses a half hundred other groups into action. It's a job that's bigger than even your great force.

Observe that his solution is <u>group</u> action—with not a word about intellectual values or the individual's responsibility to think and judge—which includes writers, publishers, critics, booksellers. What would happen in the automobile industry if <u>subjectivism</u> was their standard?!

Advertising Age, **February 27, 1961.**
[*This article was sent to Ayn Rand by a fan. Title and author's name were not given.*]

[*The following is a quote from Minnesota Supreme Court Justice Loevinger, who advocates greater government limitations on competition:*]
"It is certainly true that one aspect of competition is selling to divert to one's self the trade of a competitor. It does not follow, however, that this does not <u>constitute injury to a competitor</u>. . . . No proposition is better established in the field of law than that diversion of trade from a competitor is an injury for which the law provides a remedy if the means are improper."

Just <u>how</u> are you going to "<u>compete</u>" if you cannot "<u>injure</u>" a competitor? Just what are "<u>proper</u>" means?

Clarence B. Randall, "For a New Code of Business Ethics," *The New York Times Magazine,* **April 8, 1962.** [*Randall was president and chairman of Inland Steel Co., and served three Administrations in various capacities.*]

Now most of those crude and crass practices have disappeared from American business practice—most, but not all. For example, the large-scale pirating of trade secrets in big industry is no longer resorted to. In steel, at least, technical information is now openly and freely exchanged.

Good God! "The ethical standards of our society have improved: we don't have any burglars any more—we share all our money with them voluntarily!" (!!!)

Gilbert H. Clee, "The Appointment Book of J. Edward Ellis," *Harvard Business Review,* **November-December 1962.**

Ellis was enough of a realist to know that a rationale for a more effective joint effort between government and private enterprise would not spring full-blown from philosophic discourse or academic study. He felt that it would have to evolve, painstakingly, and bit by bit, from continuous research, out of the ferment of discussion and effective communications, and be fused in the crucible of experience.

!! This is the key to their whole god-damn psychology! ("He was enough of a realist to know that a rational idea would not come from thinking.")!

[W]e should do everything we can to call the attention of government people to policies and actions that in our judgment are not in the national interest.

The goddamn fool doesn't know (doesn't care to know) that statists are not motivated by the "national interest."!

Illustrations of subtle relationships are government policies that may affect interest rates, export and import regulations or tariffs, and government aids to special interest groups—i.e., the aged—that may create a favorable or unfavorable environment for the corporation's present activities, or open up new profit opportunities.

Good God! The "realist" uses the word "subtle" to mean: long-range. !!!

We must determine what information we need in these specific areas in order to anticipate government action or, at least, to adapt quickly to changes in government policy.

The fool thinks it's possible!

[*Ayn Rand's comments at the end of the article:*]
This is probably the most revealing piece of horror I have ever read—revealing of the whole psychology of American businessmen and Coolidge-Hoover type of Republican "conservatives." This is the answer to any question about how and why capitalism was destroyed. The main points:

   1. Abysmal Attila-ism—contempt for ideas, theories, thought, abstract knowledge;

the huffy attitude about "realism" and "practicality."

2. Abject Social-Metaphysics—the acceptance of any given status quo as "reality," the willingness to adjust to it, without any questions about who or what has brought it about, the acceptance of guilt for one's failure to "co-operate" or "adjust." (The author thinks that the system can be made to work!)

3. Abject terror—the unwillingness to conceive that the so-called political "reality" is evil, is ruled by and aimed at evil goals; the terror of the altruist-collectivist ("public interest"-advocate caught in a corner).

4. Underlying cynicism—the concrete-bound, short-range "profits" as the only actual "reality"; the abstract and long-range as "subtle"; the invariable addition of "the public interest" or "service to others" to any statement involving self-interest and individual rights. (By what "instinct" does such a mentality know when to add the protective bromides?)

This piece presents the essence of the kind of soul that would have turned young people to socialism. It is not the soul of a businessman, but of a pro-business "intellectual." This is what has destroyed capitalism.

Roger M. Blough, "My Side of the Steel Price Story," *Look*, **January 29, 1963.** [*Blough was the Chairman of the Board of U.S. Steel.*]

Why did I go to see [President Kennedy]? . . . Neither he nor his advisers seemed, at that time, to fully comprehend the complicated problems of manufacturing costs as we have to face them. . . . I went simply to impart information and hopefully to obtain understanding.

> The naive fools!

You will recall that President Kennedy made what was probably the strongest attack on a private industry ever made by a President. . . . I decided on a tempered answer, although it would have relieved a lot of tension and frustration if I had yielded to natural impulses, as others in the industry did later. But that is not my way. I was sure that an angry answer would only deepen the rift between Government and business which was already so apparent. . . . I was acutely aware that never before in the nation's history had so many forces of the Federal Government been marshaled against a single American industry.

> This is how we are being destroyed.

> Yet he wanted to be "tempered"!

Our 72-hour ordeal was over. Or almost over. I will skip some suggestions made on the Senate floor aimed at breaking up "giant" corporations and giving the President price control powers. Of far more importance to me was that on April 17, exactly a week after I had seen President Kennedy to tell him about the price rise, I saw

> The abject coward!

him again in an atmosphere of mutual cordiality.

I think the President and his advisers <u>began to understand more fully the complicated problem of manufacturing costs</u>—something they had not previously appreciated to its fullest extent.

Or: saw that they couldn't get away with the "he'll do something" policy.

"Meet the Press," September 15, 1963, Guest: Nelson A. Rockefeller. [*Ayn Rand possessed a transcript of the program. She wrote, as a summary of the entire interview:*]

Rockefeller wants to discuss "<u>principles and issues</u>"—"<u>basic principles and basic national purposes</u>"—and yet he names, as ideology of "radical right": abolition of income tax—abolition of "social gains" (which "the people won't stand for"), such as "social security"—withdrawing from U.N.—"impeachment of Warren"—the claim that Eisenhower is a "crypto-communist." (All <u>this</u> is organized by some <u>unknown</u> "financial powers.") (The "radical right," he claims, is an insignificant minority in the Republican Party.)

Rockefeller's objection to Kennedy's program is that there has been too much <u>talk</u> and nothing has been <u>done</u>. (In other words, he, Rockefeller, proposes to achieve Kennedy's goals, which Kennedy has failed to achieve.)

Editorial, "The Goldwater Platform," *The New York Times*, July 13, 1964.

The party of Abraham Lincoln is now cautious on civil rights, criticizing <u>the Justice Department for "police state tactics"</u> despite mounting evidence that some states cannot or will not control lawlessness and anarchy.

A plain lie.

In its fundamental rejection of progressive Republicanism, the Goldwater platform is neither forward-looking nor conservative. On the contrary, <u>it gives a new and reactionary look to the G.O.P. It is ominously radical in its willingness to break with all that is good about the past</u>, and it is dangerously reckless in its demand for <u>measures that will exacerbate differences and conflicts at home and abroad</u>.

!!!

Here's Mr. Mowen speaking.

C.L. Sulzenberger, "Foreign Affairs," *New York Times*, July 13, 1964.

By making more A-bombs and, incidentally, more bombers (rather than missiles), Goldwater thinks he can force our adversaries to cave in. Professor Blackett, a Nobel Prize physicist, argues: "Once a nation places its safety on an absolute weapon it becomes emotionally essential to believe in an absolute enemy."

Quite true!

Editorial, "The Goldwater Nomination," *The New York Times*, July 16, 1964.

Among these [i.e., those defeated by Goldwater] Governor Rockefeller certainly stands first. He fought uphill all the way, from New England to the Pacific Coast, a grueling, personally thankless battle. The disgusting treatment he received and the courage he showed at the convention night before last only added to his stature and detracted from that of the now controlling elements of the party.

BS!

The "courage" of a hooligan smearing people who are not there to answer!

James Reston, "Washington Never Had It So Good or Felt So Bad," *New York Times*, July 31, 1964.

Senator Goldwater can easily decry the race riots and make a powerful constitutional argument that the race problem should be left to the states, but does anyone seriously believe that racial tension would be eased if he were free to put his constitutional theories into practice tomorrow?

Yes!

The Republican convention should have chosen a man in step with his own time in history. . . .

Step—leading where?

Tom Wicker, "The Outlook—If Johnson Wins," *The New York Times*, November 1, 1964.

It has been axiomatic with [Johnson] to seek middle ground, to draw the teeth of adversaries, to attract diverse elements by finding their thread of common interest, to recognize, represent and reconcile existing forces rather than to whip up new ones or cling to old ones.

Wesley Mouch! [See Atlas Shrugged]

Malcolm Muggeridge, "I'd Serialize 'Huckleberry Finn' Instead of 'Peyton Place,'" *T.V. Guide*, May 22-28, 1965. [*This article by the well-known British conservative essayist was part of a series entitled "If I had a network. . ."*]

A television network, in my opinion, should be thought of not in terms of a theater or music hall; not, certainly, of a lecture hall or classroom, but of what was known, in the lower middle-class homes I frequented when I was young, as an evening "social." Someone would bring his or her music, along with a fiddle, a banjo, a squeeze-box, or any other cheerful instrument. There would be games, dressing up and probably a charade. . . . The role of television, as I see it,

The cheap bastard!

is to provide on a national scale something like these "socials."

Looking back on half a century of the cinema, one can see that only in the genre of comedy was anything of enduring interest achieved. It is the same with television. Serious films may have a certain antiquarian interest, but artistically none.

Even more of a bastard!

As a former editor of Punch. . . .

This explains it.

What I should hope to get with Mr. [Zero] Mostel's help would be comedy in soap-opera terms; the comedy of daily life, wrung from some misfortunes and discomforts, as well as skimmed off the ebullient surface of joys and delights; so excellently conveyed in, for instance, the stories of Sholem Aleichem. . . .

Nothing could be duller or worse!

Tom Wicker, "The Road to Reconciliation," *The New York Times*, June 11, 1967.

Israeli troops are not likely to be soon withdrawn from the Sinai Desert or Syria, and General Dayan has suggested that Israel will never give up Jerusalem. Nor does the world possess much leverage with which to force withdrawals on a nation that has won such a sweeping victory entirely alone.

??!!!

To achieve [enormous gains] with the true security that can only be found in easier relations with her neighbors, an Israel magnanimous in victory could afford to accept a large responsibility for resettling and improving the lives of the Arab refugees, dispossessed and embittered for 20 years, and a constant source of the seething hostility it is in Israel's highest interest to alleviate.

I.e., give up everything you've won!

[*Ayn Rand's remarks at the end of the article:*]
Here is the key to the psychology of today's compromisers and middle-of-the-roader's: maintain the status-quo, and try to solve problems without morality, without right or wrong, with the wishes or emotions of people as sole criterion. This is why the good, the right and the competent have to lose. Or: the winners have to lose.

Olive Evans, "The Montessori Method—Pro and Con," *The New York Times*, July 7, 1968.

[*Quoting Dr. Littner, a critic of the Montessori method:*] If [the student] already is emotionally

The mind versus social

deprived, what he needs more than anything else is the opportunity to make <u>emotional contacts</u> at school, rather than the reverse.

metaphysics <u>that</u> early! !?!

Harry Schwartz, "Rejection of Science Worries American Scientists," *The New York Times,* **April 15, 1970.**

At one extreme there are those Dr. Weinberg calls the "scientific abolitionists: the very noisy, usually young, critics who consider <u>the whole scientific-technological, if not rationalistic,</u> mode of the past 100 years a catastrophe."

Open mystics

A second group consists of those who are appalled by the unintended, negative effects of science and technology.

Hidden mystics and cowards

Another group of critics feels that pure science is now less and less relevant to the nation's real problems. . . .

Open collectivists

Finally, Dr. Weinberg identifies those he calls the "scientific muckrakers, mostly journalists, who picture the scientific enterprise as being corrupted by political maneuvering among competing claimants for the scientific dollar."

Hidden collectivists

William V. Shannon, "Diversity Endangered," *The New York Times,* **October 1, 1971.**

A truly humane politics, call it liberalism or conservatism, would help a society to protect diversity. But here the power of the law is again used to make life level and uniform.

<u>True.</u>

Every American car of standard size is made lower, wider and more powerful until adults, doubled over, are now entering them almost on their hands and knees. None is so comfortable or as easy to enter as the high square London taxi.

<u>True.</u>

<u>Man is a natural traveler because sameness oppresses and the unknown invites. But technology and economics work together to eradicate the unexpected.</u>

True

False

The worldwide ecological movement is not only a response to life-threatening dangers of pollution but also <u>a belated affirmation of the impor-</u>

!!

Is there any diversity in pre-

tance of diversity.   industrial misery?

Patrick McMahon, "Magruder: Bringing Technology Down to Earth," *National Journal*, October 21, 1971.

William M. Magruder, 48, was appointed a consultant to the President Sept. 8 and assigned the job of searching for ways to apply high technology to solving social and economic problems.

What does it mean—"to solve social and economic problems" by technology? Is it free benefits that they want to give?

[*On a separate page of notes on this article, Ayn Rand proposed the following:*]
If it's "defense of technology" [that is meant by "to solve social and economic problems by technology"]:
     Break up the package deal between "pollution" and "ecology."
     Find scientists who can blast the "ecologist's" panic-claims and get them good p.r.—and place articles.
     Form a Science Defense League.
     Take a look at the Humanities Departments of Technological schools.
     Publicize what science has done for the standard of living.
     Give "humanitarian" prizes for inventors or designers and manufacturers of the best (most time-saving) appliances.
     Finance the production of TV documentaries on the standard of living in non-technological countries.
     Arrange for sponsorship of a book contest or prizes for the best pro-technology, anti-ecology book—i.e., give fellowships for research writing of such books, and publicize them.

Marshall Cohen, "*A Theory of Justice*, by John Rawls," *The New York Times Book Review*, July 16, 1972. [*This review is discussed in "The Untitled Letter," The Ayn Rand Letter, vol. 2, nos. 9-11 (January 29-February 26, 1973), reprinted in* Philosophy: Who Needs It.]

[*Ayn Rand wrote at the top of the first page, presumably referring to Rawls:*]
The most abysmally evil thing I have ever heard of! (Except for Kant.)

William V. Shannon, "Which Way to Social Stability," *The New York Times*, August 20, 1972.

[S]ocial peace in our cities is possible only if the contending groups can share a larger pie rather than pull and haul over a small one. How to make the pie bigger?

The spirit of the egalitarian bastards! What do they think will happen to the higher economic classes, the providers of the "pie"? (Shannon, I think, is primarily an altruist.)

Only an Administration committed to full employment can ease the rivalry for jobs.

On the liberal policies, there will be no jobs for either group, i.e., a smaller pie.

Tom Wicker, "The Trouble with 'One America,'" *The New York Times,* **August 27, 1972.**

In fact, of course, equal treatment and nothing else—no further effort to remedy the effects of past discrimination—cements those effects into society. Those who, figuratively speaking, have been relegated by discrimination to a low place on the seniority list will be fixed in that low place by equal treatment and nothing more.

> This is the vicious BS: the "effects" are taken out on innocent victims of other races.

[F]or the mass of the disadvantaged, in a society ever more intricately technological, in which unskilled labor and individual crafts are becoming little needed, the old social Darwinism concept of individual enterprise has virtually no meaning or utility.

> This is what all those bastards are against!

William V. Shannon, "The Sullen Emperor," *The New York Times,* **October 6, 1972.**

The [Nixon] White House not only has a press secretary now but also a "Director of Communications" with a staff of public relations men much larger than any previous Administration.

> This is self-defense!

This election is the last opportunity anyone will have to remind Mr. Nixon that he is not administering a giant corporation on behalf of a few insiders. He is supposed to be conducting the affairs of a free people.

> Since when are the reporters "the people"? (Remember the story about Comm. Vanderbilt.)

[Ayn Rand's comment at the end of the piece:]
This malicious nonentity shows why Nixon hates them.

James Reston, "Mr. Nixon's Adjustable Principles," *The New York Times,* **October 13, 1972.**

As a working strategy for the campaign, this may very well work, but as a strategy for unifying and governing the nation, it probably will not last. For he may win by appealing to the fears of the comfortable majority against the militant blacks, the liberated women, and the student demonstrators; but come next year, he will be left with the war and the poor, and a frustrated and angry minority he has overwhelmed but not convinced.

> Here's a pragmatist talking—and "unity" is "surrender." (There is no compromise on basic principles.)
>
> What about the frustrated rightists, if he were to please the leftists.

Arthur Miller, "Politics as Theater," *The New York Times,* **November 4, 1972.**

People always respond best to a call for right-

> The bastard!

eousness when it is accompanied by the call to
lunch.

If I am right, then McGovern is trying out for the wrong play. We are not casting the Moses to lead us out of the desert, but the chief officer of a bank in which we are all depositors.	Quite true. There are no "suffering masses."

Editorial, "On Pornography," *Wall Street Journal*, June 27, 1973.

[I]f we are to interpret "liberty" in its broadest historical sense, we must interpret freedom of speech in the same way. Historically and traditionally this is to exclude obscenity. . . .	Not meaning, but "tradition."
[F]rom 1776 to 1931 and beyond our political liberties somehow evolved and flourished despite obscenity laws. Similarly, most of the world's democracies today somehow survive with censorship of sexual materials.	!! (They want an earlier stage of the cancer!) The pragmatists!

"Transcript of Nixon's Speech on Energy Situation," *The New York Times*, January 20, 1974.

With the proud dedication we Americans have always displayed when confronted with great challenges, we can and we will achieve the great goal of Project Independence. Where energy is concerned, we, the American people, shall be the sole masters of our fate.	Under government controls?! He deserves to be impeached!

Editorial, "An Age of Scarcity," *The New York Times*, April 7, 1974.

[*At the top of the article, Ayn Rand wrote:*]
(Here is the Age of Envy.) This is a real picture of the collectivist-"conservationalist"
soul—as openly vicious as it can be in print.

Abundance is a modern idea. For millennia, men had to live with the hard, grinding knowledge that resources of land, water and minerals are scarce and that poverty is the lot of most. That is still true in many parts of Asia, Africa and Latin America.	Before the Industrial Revolution?!
Americans are 6 per cent of the world's population but consume 35 per cent of the world's energy. In moral terms, Americans have no right to pre-empt so large a share of the world's resources; in practical terms, the economic costs	!!!!!

and strategic risks are too great. Nor is this
country's energy consumption static.

The bastards!

Yet the United States has no policy <u>for limiting
economic growth</u> and reducing the regular increase in demand for energy. There are, for example, no national plans . . . <u>to abandon their en-
ergy-wasting private automobiles</u> in favor of
trains and buses.

The bastards!

As it has been throughout human history, scarcity
is a challenge to men's capacity to act together in
civilized ways.

There is only <u>one</u> civilized way:
<u>freedom.</u>

Nina Totenberg, "Discriminating to End Discriminating," *The New York Times Magazine,*
April 14, 1974.

Advocates of affirmative action like to compare
the racial situation in America to two runners,
<u>one of whom has had his legs shackled for 200
years.</u> Suddenly, the shackles are removed, but,
of course, one runner is still much faster than the
other.

Good God!

One brief filed by De Funis's lawyers reads: "The
predominance of whites in the university law
school may well be explained by a lack of incli-
nation or aptitude on the part of blacks for such
studies. <u>Any observant person knows that certain
races have certain bents or inclinations.</u>"

<u>True</u>

<u>False!!</u>

A ruling permitting "benign" discrimination
could eventually come back to haunt the court,
for a survey of the race cases of the past 20 years
would show that many, if not most, acts of discrimination were alleged to be done benignly.

True.

Rex Reed, "Liz Steals the Final Scene at Cannes," *New York Sunday News,* **June 2, 1974.**

[*Ayn Rand's only comment on the article, written at the top, was:*]
(That Cannes Festival seems to be the symbol of what all the controls, dictatorships
and collectivism are for: <u>the posturings of pretentious mediocrity.</u>)

Tom Wicker, "Whose Commitment?" *The New York Times,* **March 28, 1975.**

[I]f anyone really believes that three more years
of any kind of aid, at any level, might make
South Vietnam self-sustaining, he has not been in

All the arguments against
interventionalism abroad apply
as well against altruism at

this world but in some other for the past fifteen years.

home.

Editorial, "Of Men and Liberty," *The New York Times*, July 6, 1975.

The central English ideas were the common law evolved by juries, judges, and parliaments and a belief in limited government. . . . The United States, although it early broke away from British rule, never broke away from these benevolent traditions of law and limited government.

Definition by non-essentials

Steven V. Roberts, "Monuments vs. the Environment," *The New York Times*, March 28, 1976.

The Greek Government recently announced that a large shipyard would be built at Pylos [near the site of the ruins of the Bronze Age Palace of Nestor] and that steel and cement plants would also be constructed in the vicinity. . . . The Pylos project poses a difficult question. Greece clearly wants, and needs, the benefits of economic growth. Just as clearly, the monuments and landscape of the country belong to the whole civilized world, and should be preserved.

!!!

Today the "sacred way" [*i.e., the 10 miles between Athens and Eleusis, the site of the mysteries of Demeter*] is lined with shipyards, oil refineries and other industry. The site of the mysteries is surrounded by factories and choked with smoke.

!!!

The Sanctuary of Demeter cannot be appreciated if there is an oil refinery looming in the background, belching yellowish effluent. The view from Nestor's palace across the Bay of Navarinos is almost as important as the building itself.

How many "mysteries" are to be preserved—and for how long?

!!!

[T]he beach at Marathon, where the Greeks fought the Persians in 490 B.C., is now pocked with tar and littered with refuse.

So what?!

The jobless and the industrialists are not merely money-grubbers, but given a choice, they will take progress over preservation almost every time. As one business man in Pylos put it, "What are we going to eat, beauty?"

"Money-grubbers" because they want to eat?!

Pylos also resents the intellectual elites in Athens

who already have their comforts and chide others
for wanting the same thing. The intellectuals re-
ply that precisely because they do not have a di-   At whose expense?!!
rect economic interest in Pylos, they can, and
should, defend other values.

[The] Greek philosopher, Aristotle, posited the   That is not the answer!
ideal of the golden mean. It is as difficult to find
as ever.

[*Ayn Rand's comment at the end of the article:*]
This is an example of the world being sacrificed to mediocrity—not even to the
"poor," but to the phony make-up jobs of "esthetic" mediocrities.

Rosalind H. Williams, "High Life in the Opal Office," *The New York Times*, **February 25,
1981.**

This reconciliation of incompatible social morali-
ties, although widespread, has always been uneasy. It is now untenable, not because of its im-
morality but because of its unreality. In fact, eco-   How bastards try to adjust
nomic success is far less due to talent and hard   today.
work than to birth and luck. In fact, there are social limits to enjoyment of luxuries (a traffic jam
of Cadillacs is still a traffic jam). In fact, there
are material limits to the resources we consume
so voraciously. And, finally, there is in fact a
world outside America laden with people living
in famine, misery, and ignorance, who are not
going to wait patiently for material comforts to   !!!
trickle down.

Lester C. Thurow, "Holes in Re g n m cs," *The New York Times*, **November 8, 1981.**

What Reaganomics forgets is that government   This is an excellent example of
plays an important role in creating feelings of   inversion and non-hierarchy:
mutual obligation and respect. . . . Public filthi- non-essentials determining
ness lowers our standards of living but, more im-   essentials, etc. "Clean streets"
portantly, it affronts our self-respect. . . . [I]f no as a basic premise!
one gives a damn about a clean environment, the
feeling quickly grows and spreads to other more
important areas of life. People start to be rude to
each other when they meet face-to-face on the
street. From there it is a simple step to even more
hostile actions. Municipal services—clean streets
. . . , effective police and fire protection—make
life easier to live. But they play an even more important role in binding us together and reminding

us that we depend upon each other for survival.
. . . As municipal services decline in quality, citizens feel that they have no stake in the society. . . .
[Thus] voting does not matter. With fewer people
voting, government becomes less representative
and fewer people feel that it is *their* government.
The world becomes a place . . . where we solve
our quarrels by clubbing each other. . . .

Jack Barnes, "What's Your Love Quotient?" *New York Sunday News*, **October 19, 1975.**

1. Do you find it hard to take criticism? (a)   Not if it's rational.
Hardly ever; (b) some times; (c) usually.

2. If someone tried to show you a different
method for doing something you've done for a
long time, would you (a) listen intently, with an
open mind, (b) listen begrudgingly or (c) consider it a waste of time?

3. When you look in the mirror, do you (a) usu-   None of these
ally like what you see, (b) start thinking mostly
about what you could do to look better or (c) feel
instantly displeased with the way you look?

4. Do you think your mate should have (a) the   None of these
qualities you aspire to, (b) the same shortcomings
as you, but different aspirations or (c) different
qualities and aspirations?

5. Do you think it is important to a marriage's
success to have both mates feel romantically toward one another? (a) The two aren't really related; (b) it sometimes helps; (c) it's necessary.

6. Do you regard unrequited love as (a) something that a healthy person can stay away from,
(b) sometimes inevitable but terrible or (c) sometimes inevitable but beautiful?

7. Can one enjoy a normal social life with his
friends while conducting an intensely romantic
love relationship? (a) Most times; (b) some
times; (c) hardly ever.

8. Do you believe in love at first sight? (a) No;
(b) maybe; (c) yes.

9. Does an intense love relationship tend to interfere with your work habits? (a) No; (b) some times; (c) yes.

10. Would you marry someone you didn't plan to have children with? (a) No; (b) maybe; (c) yes.

able circumstances, or backing down. And these are immense advantages.

The future, as I see it, will unfold along one of two paths. Either the Communists will retain the offensive; will lay down one challenge after another; will invite us in local crisis after local crisis to choose between all-out war and limited retreat; and will force us, ultimately, to surrender or accept war under the most disadvantageous circumstances. Or *we* will summon the will and the means for taking the initiative, and wage a war of attrition against them—and hope, thereby, to bring about the internal disintegration of the Communist empire. One course runs the risk of war, and leads, in any case, to probable defeat. The other runs the risk of war, and holds forth the promise of victory. For Americans who cherish their lives, but their freedom more, the choice cannot be difficult.

Do not concede this!

He is at his best on the question of fighting Communism. But here are the unsolved issues in his position: if we want victory over Communism, we must define, clearly, specifically and unequivocally, what Communism is. Otherwise, how would we be able to distinguish friend from enemy? And it is here that his whole crusade will collapse, in a clash with Socialism and Statism. Unless we fight for full Capitalism, we cannot fight nor win.

Ayn Rand's marginalia from Barry Goldwater's *The Conscience of a Conservative*

1. See, "America's Persecuted Minority: Big Business, *Capitalism: The Unknown Ideal* (New York: New American Library, pb. ed.), pp. 56-57.

2. Neale writes: "The Federal Trade Commission got as far as enunciating the principle that 'where a number of enterprises follow a parallel course of action in the knowledge and contemplation of the fact that all are acting alike, they have in effect formed an agreement'; and the Supreme Court at least did not dissent from the proposition in the *Triangle Conduit* case that 'conscious parallelism of action' on the part of the individual firm could be an unfair method of competition." (458)

3. See the first page of "Thought Control," Part II, *The Ayn Rand Letter*, vol. 3, no. 1 (October 8, 1973).

4. See "Censorship: Local and Express," *Philosophy: Who Needs It* (Bobbs-Merrill,1982), p. 217.

5. See "Censorship: Local and Express," p. 225.

INDEX